About *The Way Into...*

The Way Into... is a major series that provides an accessible and highly usable "guided tour" of the Jewish faith and people, its history and beliefs—in total, a basic introduction to Judaism for adults that will enable them to understand and interact with sacred texts.

The Authors

Each book in the series is written by a leading contemporary teacher and thinker. While each of the authors brings his or her own individual style of teaching to the series, every volume's approach is the same: to help you to learn, in a life-affecting way, about important concepts in Judaism.

The Concepts

Each volume in *The Way Into...* series explores one important concept in Judaism, including its history, its basic vocabulary, and what it means to Judaism and to us. In the Jewish tradition of study, the reader is helped to interact directly with sacred texts.

The topics to be covered in *The Way Into...* series:

Torah
Jewish Prayer
Encountering God in Judaism
Jewish Mystical Tradition
Tikkun Olam (Repairing the World)
Judaism and the Environment
The Varieties of Jewishness
Covenant and Commandment
Holiness and Chosenness (*Kedushah*)
Time
Zion
Money and Ownership
Women and Men
The Relationship between Jews and Non-Jews

The Way Into

Tikkun Olam
(Repairing
the World)

Elliot N. Dorff

דרך למוד דרך למוד   דרך למוד   דרך למוד
דרך למוד

JEWISH LIGHTS Publishing

The Way Into Tikkun Olam *(Repairing the World)*

2007 First Quality Paperback Printing
2005 First Hardcover Printing
© 2005 by Elliot N. Dorff

For information regarding permission to reprint material from this book,
please write or fax your request to Jewish Lights Publishing, Permissions
Department, at the address / fax number listed below, or e-mail your request
to permissions@jewishlights.com.

Grateful acknowledgment is given for permission to use material from the
following source: "Bubbie—*Tzedakah,* Discipline, and Arms Raised for
Hugs," in Leo Lieberman, *Memories of Laughter and Garlic* (Margate, N.J.: ComteQ
Publishing, 1999), pp. 28–30.

Library of Congress Cataloging-in-Publication Data
Dorff, Elliot N.
The way into tikkun olam (repairing the world) / Elliot N. Dorff.
p. cm. — (The way into—)
Includes bibliographical references and index.
ISBN-13: 978-1-68336-447-4 (hc.)
1. Jewish ethics. 2. Jewish way of life. 3. Jewish families—Conduct of life. I. Title:
Tikkun olam (repairing the world). II. Title. III. Series.
BJ1285.2.D67 2005
296.3'6—dc22
2005024824
ISBN-13: 978-1-58023-328-6 (quality pbk.)

The publisher gratefully acknowledges the contribution of Rabbi
Sheldon Zimmerman to the creation of this series. In his lifelong
work of bringing a greater appreciation of Judaism to all people, he
saw the need for *The Way Into...* and inspired us to act on it.

Manufactured in the United States of America
Cover Design: Glenn Suokko & Jenny Buono
Text Design: Glenn Suokko

Published by Jewish Lights Publishing
www.jewishlights.com

In honor of Jewish Family Service of Los Angeles, which has provided social services for Jews and non-Jews in the greater Los Angeles area since 1854.
I am currently honored to serve as its president, and I am thrilled to complete during my tenure a volume devoted to the Jewish roots of the many forms of *tikkun olam* that JFS does. That includes more than sixty programs of loving-kindness *(gemilut chasadim)*, through which JFS–LA fixes the world each day.

"These are the deeds that yield immediate fruit and continue to yield fruit in time to come: honoring parents; doing deeds of loving-kindness; and making peace between one person and another. Study of Torah is basic to them all."

—Mishnah, *Peah* 1:1

1000 B.C.E.   1 C.E.

////

c. 2700–2200 B.C.E.   c. 500 B.C.E.–476 C.E. **Roman Republic/Empire**
**Egypt's Old
Kingdom;**   c. 330 B.C.E.–1453 C.E. **Byzantine Empire**   >
**construction of
the pyramids**   c. 323–30 B.C.E. **Greece's Hellenistic Period**

                                                                           • 622 C.E.
                                                                             **Muhammad,
                                                                             founder of
                                                                             Islam, flees
                                                                             to Medina
c. 2000–   c. 1050–450 B.C.E. **Age of the Prophets**   (hegira)**
1700 B.C.E.
Age of the   c. 167 B.C.E.–500 C.E. **Rabbinic Period**
**matriarchs
and patriarchs**   • 167 B.C.E.–70 C.E. **Period of the Pharisees**
                                      • 70–200 C.E. **Period of the Tannaim**
                                          • 200–550 C.E. **Period of the Amoraim**
                                                                           • 750–
                                                                             1038 C.E.
                                                                             Period of
                                   c. 146 B.C.E.–400 C.E. **Rule of Rome**   **the Geonim**

Events   • c. 1250 B.C.E. **Exodus from Egypt and settlement in Land of Israel**
                • c. 1007 B.C.E. **Saul, first king of Israel, killed in battle against Philistines**
                • c. 1000 B.C.E. **David becomes king of Israel**
                    • c. 950 B.C.E. **Solomon begins building the Temple**
                      • c. 925 B.C.E. **Israel divided into Northern Kingdom of Israel and
                        Southern Kingdom of Judah**
                          • 722 B.C.E. **Northern Kingdom destroyed by Assyria**
                            • 586 B.C.E. **Southern Kingdom destroyed by Babylonia**
                            • 538 B.C.E. **Return from Babylonian exile; Jerusalem
                              ("Second") Temple rebuilt**
                              • c. 500–400 B.C.E. **The Torah, Five Books of Moses,
                                is compiled/edited, according to biblical scholarship**
                                    • c. 250 B.C.E. **"Septuagint" translation of Torah
                                      into Greek**
                                        • 167 B.C.E. **Hasmonean (Maccabean) Revolt**
                                          • 70 C.E. **Rome destroys Second Temple**
                                            • c. 200 **The Mishnah compiled/
                                              edited by Rabbi Judah ha-Nasi**
                                                • c. 300–600 **The Babylonian
                                                  and Palestinian Talmuds are
                                                  compiled/edited**

1000 C.E.   2000 C.E.

>

• c. 1040–1105 Rashi, French Bible and Talmud scholar and creator of line-by-line commentary on the Torah
    • 1178 Maimonides (1135–1204) completes his code of Jewish law, the *Mishneh Torah*
      • c. 1295 *The Zohar,* Kabbalistic work of mystical teaching, composed
        • 1492 Jews expelled from Spain
          • 1565 Joseph Caro publishes *Shulchan Arukh*, the standard code of Jewish law and practice
           • 1654 First Jewish settlement in North America at New Amsterdam
          • 1700–1760 Israel Baal Shem Tov, founder of Hasidism
          • 1729–1786 Moses Mendelssohn, "Father of the Jewish Enlightenment"
           • 1801–1888 Samson Raphael Hirsch, founder of "modern Orthodoxy"
            • 1836 Yeshiva University founded
           • 1873; 1875 Reform Judaism in U.S. establishes
            Union of American Hebrew Congregations and Hebrew Union College
             • 1887 Conservative Judaism's Jewish Theological Seminary founded
             • 1897 Theodor Herzl convenes first Zionist Congress
             • 1933–1945 The Holocaust (Shoah)
             • 1935 Mordecai Kaplan establishes the Jewish Reconstructionist Foundation
            • 1948 Birth of the State of Israel

Contents

Preface

Tikkun olam—to fix the world. Quite a task! Yet that is precisely the goal that the Jewish tradition sets for our lives. It gives us a mission, and thereby lends meaning to our lives. It also imposes a heavy burden on each and every one of us every day of our lives. We may certainly take time to enjoy ourselves now and then, and we not only may, but should, spend time with our families and at our place of employment. But beyond all these activities, and throughout our lives, we must dedicate at least part of our time, energy, and resources to improving the lot of others.

Jews understand this almost instinctively. Surveys show that even Jews who doubt the existence or significance of God, who are not involved much in Judaism's prayers, rituals, or holiday celebrations, who do not observe Judaism's restrictions on diet and work on holy days, and/or who do not know much about their heritage or devote any time as adults to studying it nevertheless feel in their bones that they have a duty as Jews to make this a better world, that this is the essence of what it means to be a Jew. As a religious Jew, I would say that it is sad that so many people, by their own description, are "not very religious," for such people are missing out on a virtual treasure trove of meaning, joy, intellectual ferment, and communal connections that the Jewish tradition offers us. Still, such Jews are not wrong in identifying "social action" as a key component of what it means to be Jewish, for much of the tradition is devoted to it.

This book describes the roots in Jewish beliefs and laws of the Jewish commitment to improve the world. It explores the many reasons *why* Judaism would have us engage in such activities, reasons that include, but go far beyond, a general humanitarian feeling that we might have or the hope that if you help others, others will be there to help you when you need assistance. It also describes *how* the Jewish tradition would have us seek to fix the world, rooted ultimately in its vision of the ideal world, the goal for which we should strive.

The book is divided into three parts. Part 1 addresses the underlying theory of *tikkun olam*. Chapter 1 describes how the term has developed over time into the meaning it has today. This chapter also indicates other related terms and concepts that Judaism has used for thousands of years to describe the duties we now identify and name as acts of *tikkun olam,* and it cites sources to demonstrate the great significance that classical Judaism ascribes to such activities. Chapter 2 explores why any person, and why any Jew in particular, should care about the lot of someone else. Finally, chapter 3 delves into the complicated but critical issue of the relationship between religion and ethics, exploring what Judaism has to add to our general feeling that it is a nice thing to help someone in need.

Part 2 explores both the theory and the practice of Jewish *tikkun olam* in our social interactions. Thus, chapter 4 deals with language—how we should speak to others and what we should avoid saying. Chapter 5 deals with poverty, including reasons we should be wary of helping the poor, reasons we should nevertheless offer aid, the proper limits of such support, the duties of the poor, and the modes of assistance we should offer. Chapter 6 describes Jewish thought and law on redeeming captives, a problem the Jewish community has unfortunately had to confront from earliest times to our own. Chapter 7 addresses our duties to provide health care to the sick, including the emotional support we must provide the ill by visiting them. Just as the sick need communal support, so too do couples celebrating their weddings and families mourning the loss of a loved one, and so attending to the emotional needs of people in those situations also constitutes a form of *tikkun olam.*

Part 3 addresses *tikkun olam* within families. Thus, chapter 8 considers the duties of spouses to each other, chapter 9 describes Judaism's specification of filial duties, and chapter 10 delineates Judaism's understanding of parental duties. In each case, the chapter cites traditional sources, but it also takes into account the places where modern conditions are really very different from ancient or medieval ones and explores how that might affect our use of traditional materials in approaching a given issue in our day.

Finally, the last section, which would normally be called the conclusion, is instead called the forward, because it pushes us to envision the goals of our specific efforts of *tikkun olam* and hopefully also motivates us all the more to engage in such efforts. The forward describes Judaism's understanding of the components of an ideal world. Here Jewish sources articulate our highest hopes so that we can have a clear sense of what we should be striving for on a daily basis. I hope that this book helps people understand the elements of such a world and the specific directives that Judaism gives us to achieve it through what we do each and every day in many parts of our lives, so that we are all motivated and informed to do what we can to make the Jewish vision real.

A Note on the Translation

The Bible translation I have used in this book is almost entirely from the Jewish Publication Society translation of the *Tanakh* (1985). This translation uses what we today recognize as "masculine God language." This is in contrast to the language that I have used in my text throughout the book, but I leave the masculine God language intact to preserve the authenticity of the citations.

Acknowledgments

There are many people I would like to thank for helping me make this book possible. It was Stuart M. Matlins, the publisher of Jewish Lights, who first suggested that I write such a book and convinced me to do it. It has been a true work of love and hopefully useful besides, and so I want to thank him for developing *The Way Into...* series, an idea created by Rabbi Sheldon Zimmerman, for this book within it, and for asking me to contribute in this way. Alys R. Yablon applied her considerable editorial talents to my manuscript, making it better than the one I created, and I want to thank her sincerely for that. I teach at the University of Judaism, and Steven Edelman-Blank, a rabbinical student in the Ziegler School of Rabbinic Studies there, kindly offered to read the manuscript, suggest editorial changes, and make it conform to the formatting requirements for publication. I want to thank him for taking on this task so willingly and so skillfully. I would also like to thank all the good people at Jewish Lights for their help in publishing and marketing this book. Finally, I want to thank the love of my life, my wife, Marlynn, for her support in joining me in our many acts of *tikkun olam* and for her patience in allowing me to spend the time necessary to write about it. I also want to thank her and, indeed, God, for the incredible blessings of our children and grandchildren—Tammy and her son Zachary Ethan; Michael and Tanya, and their daughter Zoe Elliana; Havi and Adam, and their daughters Noa Yarden and Ayden Chaya; and Jonathan and Mara, and their son Amiel Shalom. As I mention in this book, and as my children have heard me say ad nauseam, children are one of the greatest blessings of life, an integral part of God's promise to Abraham long ago, and so I hope that many more grandchildren are on the way!

I have dedicated this book to Jewish Family Service of Los Angeles. JFS was founded in 1854, seven years before Los Angeles was incorporated as a city. Ever since then, it has engaged in a wide variety of acts of *tikkun olam*. With more than sixty programs, it now serves people through activities including, but not limited to, counseling, drug and alcohol abuse aversion programs, teenage Jewish enrichment and counseling, senior services of all sorts, support groups for the bereaved and for cancer patients and their families, free burial for those who cannot afford to bury their deceased kin in the Jewish way, shelters for battered women and children, food pantries for the hungry, meals on wheels from our kosher kitchen for thousands of people who are not ambulatory, and housing for the homeless. This is truly an agency that does acts of *tikkun olam* and *gemilut hasadim* in the purest sense of those terms. I have been proud to be on its board of directors since 1985, and I currently serve as its president, a post my father also held with Jewish Family and Children's Services in Milwaukee, where I grew up. I had the good fortune to have absolutely wonderful parents, who not only exuded warmth and support but also modeled in their own lives what it means to carry out the Jewish duties inherent in our mission to fix the world. It thrills me no end that I have written this book during my tenure as president, thus exquisitely combining my familial, intellectual, religious, emotional, and practical commitments to *tikkun olam*. Jewish Family Service is a true model of what it means to fix this world, a model from which I hope people who read this book will learn how to make acts of *tikkun olam* part of their own lives.

Introduction

Modern Jews often think of *tikkun olam,* "fixing the world," as a core commitment of Judaism. In fact, in a national poll of American Jews conducted in 1988 by the *Los Angeles Times,*[1] 50 percent listed a commitment to social equality as the most important factor in their Jewish identity, while only 17 percent cited religious observance and another 17 percent cited support for Israel. A 2000 study conducted by Steven M. Cohen and Leonard Fein similarly found that social equality topped the list by far: 47 percent said that "a commitment to social equality" was the most important factor in their Jewish identity, 24 percent said "religious observance," 13 percent said "support for Israel," and 16 percent said "other."[2] Finally, a poll conducted by the American Jewish Committee in 2003 asked 1,008 Jews to choose the quality most important to their Jewish identity; 41 percent said "being part of the Jewish people," 21 percent said "commitment to social justice," and only 13 percent chose "religious observance."[3]

Those deeply committed to Judaism may find these results disturbing, for they indicate that Jews are mistaking the fruit for the tree. After all, in classical Jewish sources, Judaism's commitment to social equality stems from its more fundamental convictions regarding God, covenant, and mitzvot (commandments). Thus, Jews should not only include those elements in their Jewish identity, but also see them as central.

This pattern, though, is apparently not as new as some might suppose. Hundreds of years ago, the Rabbis of the Midrash described their own Jewish community in very similar terms:

> "I sleep, but my heart wakes" (Song of Songs 5:2). The congregation of Israel said to the Holy One: "I sleep" in neglect of ritual precepts, but "my heart wakes" for the practice of loving-kindness (*Shir Hashirim Rabbah* 5:2, par. 1).

That should provide at least some comfort to contemporary Jewish religious leaders!

Moreover, the large percentages who singled out social equality as the most critical factor in their Jewish commitment were not wrong in identifying concern for helping others as an important Jewish conviction. The Torah includes a number of laws and theological tenets that articulate this duty, and later Jewish law and thought expand upon that base. Classical Jewish sources depict our duties as a series of concentric circles, with primary duties to ourselves, our family, our local community, the wider Jewish community, and then the world at large. While this principle continues to define Jewish duties to others, as Jews were accepted more fully into general society in post-Enlightenment times, they became all the more interested in making society as a whole not only fair and equitable, but also supportive and, as much as possible, ideal.

This book will present some of the most important aspects of the social component of the Jewish tradition. After examining the grounds for Judaism's fundamental conviction that we should indeed care for others and the relationships between Judaism and ethics, it will turn to areas of life in which this concern takes concrete expression. Specifically, it will first explore the ways in which fixing the world applies to the social arena, and then will turn to the family. The former section includes chapters on how we should speak with and about others, ameliorate poverty, ransom captives, heal the sick, bury the dead, and comfort mourners. The latter section addresses duties of spouses to each other, as well as obligations of parents to children and of children to parents.

Several important topics that might also reasonably fit within a book on *tikkun olam* will not be treated here. We might fix the world literally by taking care of the environment and by repairing what we have polluted. That is the topic of another book in this series, however, so this book will be limited to discussing how we might fix the world in terms of our relationships with other human beings. Two important components of this arena are our relationships with people of other faiths and our business dealings, but those are also the topics of other books in this series. Although each of those books may be understood on its own, this book's theoretical section will lay the groundwork for the latter two in articulating why we should care about other human beings at all. This book's discussion of social and family life will also prepare readers for the application of Judaism's teachings to the areas treated by those other books. Since Judaism's social message is a significant part of Judaism, and since, as the surveys cited above indicate, this aspect of Judaism is a (if not *the*) fundamental mainstay of the Jewish identity of a large percentage of North America's Jews, this book will hopefully help many Jews understand their Jewish identities and the foundations and directions of their Jewish social commitments.

Part One

Tikkun Olam in Theory

1

The Meaning and Significance of *Tikkun Olam*

The Meaning of *Tikkun Olam*

Jews today speak of *tikkun olam* as a central Jewish precept, and concern for literally "fixing the world" by making it a better place through activities often called "social action" is certainly at the heart of a Jewish perspective on life. That meaning of the term *tikkun olam,* however, is itself very new in Jewish history.

The first occurrences of the phrase *tikkun olam* in the Jewish tradition appear in the literature of the classical Rabbis. They are the people whose work first appears in the Mishnah, *Midrash Halakhah,* and Tosefta (the earliest compilations of the oral tradition, all edited around 200 C.E.) and then in the Talmud (edited around 500 C.E.) and the various books of *Midrash Aggadah,* which were edited from the fifth to the twelfth centuries C.E.

The Mishnah records that the Rabbis instituted a number of changes in Jewish law "for the sake of *tikkun olam.*"[1] In these first usages, the term probably means, as the Reuben Alcalay and Even-Shoshan dictionaries suggest as their first definitions, guarding the established order in the physical or social world (with derivatives *t'kinah* meaning "standardization" and *t'kinut* meaning "normalcy, regularity, orderliness, propriety").[2] In the twelfth century, Maimonides expanded on this idea considerably, claiming that the

Rabbis created *all* of their rulings, customs, and decrees—that is, the entire rabbinic legal tradition—in order "to strengthen the religion and order (fix) the world."[3] In this first meaning of the term, then, rabbis order the world by making Jewish law apply fairly and effectively to their contemporary circumstances. They thus structure the world with proper proportion and balance.

The next time the phrase is used with a different meaning occurs in the second paragraph of the *Alenu* prayer, which was first used in Jewish liturgy in the fourteenth century. That paragraph is much less often sung than the first and therefore is much less well known, even though it is the core of the prayer's meaning. The first paragraph says that we have a duty to praise God for making us Jews a distinct nation and for creating and ruling the world. The second paragraph then states:

> Therefore we hope in You, Adonai, our God, soon to see the glory of Your might, sweeping idolatry away so that false gods will be utterly destroyed, to fix [perfect] the world by [to be] the Kingdom of the Almighty *(letakken olam b'malkhut shaddai)* so that all human beings will pray [call out] in Your Name, bringing all the earth's wicked back to You, repentant. Then all who dwell on Earth will acknowledge and know that to You every knee must bend and every tongue pledge loyalty. Before You, Adonai, our God, they will bow and prostrate themselves, and they will give honor to Your Name. All of them will accept the yoke of Your Sovereignty, and You will rule over them soon and forever; for sovereignty is Yours, and You will rule with honor always and forever, as it is written in Your Torah [Exodus 15:18], "Adonai will rule for ever and ever." Furthermore, it is said [in the Prophets, specifically, Zechariah 14:9], "And Adonai will be acknowledged Sovereign over the whole Earth, on that day Adonai will be one and His Name one."

Notice several things about the concept as it appears in this paragraph. First, because God chose us, created the whole world, and rules it alone (that is, without the aid of any other god), we hope and pray that *God* will fix the world. This is definitely not the modern notion that *we human beings* are called to do that.

Second, the fixing about which the prayer speaks is *not* what moderns call "social action." It is rather theological—that Adonai will be recognized by all human beings (literally, "all creatures of flesh") as the one and sole God. God's rule and therefore God's moral standards will become absolute and universal, forcing "all the evil [people] of the earth" to turn to God and, presumably, change their ways. A fixed world will thus involve universal recognition and acceptance of a clear and exclusive standard of behavior, with everyone fixing his or her attitudes and behavior to conform to that standard. But while this prayer envisions a moral renaissance as a corollary to universal recognition of one and only one God, it does not speak of a world rid of war, poverty, dissension, and disrespect—except, perhaps, implicitly. That is, everyone following God's rules and aspiring to God's ideals for human beings may well produce a world in which those limitations no longer exist. However, that kind of moral ideal is not the explicit message of the prayer. It is, rather, an expression of hope for a theological ideal, that of monotheism.

The third time the phrase appears in Jewish history, in Lurianic Kabbalah, it has yet another meaning. Isaac Luria (1534–1572) created his own, distinctive form of Kabbalah. From the thirteenth century, when the *Zohar* was written, until the time of Luria, Kabbalists had depicted a God consisting of ten spheres *(sefirot)* with multiple interactions among the spheres. Human beings were to try to become one with God through study of the esoteric meanings of the Torah and through obeying God's commandments, which were also given new, mystical meanings. Luria, however, claimed that in creating the world, God used too much energy and benevolence, thus shattering the finite vessels that God had created. (Those "vessels" included all finite beings, inanimate and animate, vegetable, animal, and, especially, human.) When Jews study the Torah, especially its esoteric meanings, and when Jews fulfill their obligations under God's commandments, Luria maintained, they literally help fix the shattered world. Jews thus have immense power—a comforting message to Jews battered by pogroms and massacres—for even if they are often helpless victims in their lives on earth, in the celestial realm, they can do nothing less than fix God and the world God created.

For Luria and his followers, obeying the commandments certainly included what we would call the social and moral imperatives of our tradition, but those social ideals were not their primary emphasis. They focused instead, as did all Kabbalists, on fixing one's own life by making one's will and being one with God. For Luria, Jews observing the commandments would also, quite audaciously, fix God. In a world physically, economically, culturally, politically, socially, and religiously hostile to Jews, one can readily understand how Jews needed to find meaning and hope by turning away from that world and focusing instead on one's own inner life—and, for Luria, on God's as well.

The Maharal of Prague (Judah Loew ben Bezalel, 1525–1609) uses the phrase *tikkun olam* in yet two other senses. First, he maintains that the whole purpose of the Torah is to teach us how to fix the world, ridding it especially of our penchant to do evil. Thus, we—that is, all Jews—fix the world when we obey the dictates of the Torah because we thereby purge the world of evil.[4] This is not our modern concept of social action because the Maharal means both more and less than what moderns have in mind. More, because he clearly thinks that a Jew must obey not only the moral dictates of Judaism but also the ritual commandments to free the world from evil, while moderns usually do not have rituals in mind as part of what they mean by *tikkun olam*. Less, because freeing the world from the desire to do evil is not the equivalent of the much broader agenda that most moderns intend by the phrase, including the need to feed the hungry, house the homeless, and so on.

In another place, the Maharal uses the phrase in yet a different sense—namely, to assert that sometimes common manners, based on our desire to fix the world (make the world work efficiently), contradict the Torah's laws and do so unjustly, whether the desire to fix the world in this sense would lead to stringency or leniency:

> In chapter 2 of *Bava Metzia* (21b) the Rabbis said that a person does not have to return a lost object to its owner once the latter has given up looking for it. But this seems far-fetched to people that a person should take something that is not his and for which he did not work or toil and covet the property of another. This is not according to common manners *(dat ha-nimusit),* for common manners requires that one return an object even after the owner gave up on finding it. The reason why that is so is because common manners requires us to do that which is suited to fix the world, even if reason does not require such an act [as a matter of justice] but rather that is simply the way of fixing the world. Thus sometimes common manners are stringent with regard to a given issue, even if reason and the plain law do not require something.
>
> But sometimes common manners are the more lenient in a given matter even though reason does not approve—namely, when the act is not necessary to fix the world. Thus according to common manners, one must return a lost object after the owners have given up on finding it, and that is a stringency. On the other hand, if he found a silver or gold vessel and announced once or twice that he had found it, and nobody sought after it for a year or

two, he may take possession of it and use it, for there is no fixing of the world [in not doing so] after he announced it several times and waited for a year or two or more, for the owner will no longer come for it [after that]. But that is not according to the Torah, for if he found a silver or gold vessel and announced it many times [and still nobody claimed it], he may never use it. It must just sit there forever until [the Prophet] Elijah comes [to announce the Messianic era], which is a great stringency.

—*Maharal of Prague* (Be'er Ha-Golah #2, pp. 30–32)

The Maharal then claims that in both instances the Torah, which is fully rational and wise, is actually right, and common manners are wrong. Property merely belongs to a person; it is not his or her flesh and blood. Therefore, if a person gives up finding something, the despair of never retrieving it *(ya'ush)* is enough to sever it from him or her. As a result, it becomes ownerless *(hefker)*, and any finder may keep it. On the other hand, if it is clear (from the value of the property, for example) that the owner would not give up the search to find it, then the owner has never done anything to release ownership, and so the finder must just keep it without using it until Elijah comes. Thus, the Maharal is using the term *tikkun olam* to indicate common sense or accepted, utilitarian norms, which are intended to make the world work efficiently, and he is claiming that sometimes Jews must *not* fix the world in that way but rather obey Jewish law.

It is only in the mid-twentieth century that the term *tikkun olam* comes to mean that we human beings (not just rabbis) fix the world of concrete objects, animals, and persons by engaging in both environmental and social care and repair. Possibly a creation of the civil rights era of the 1960s, the term with that meaning first gained its most widespread use in the Reform Movement, which was heavily invested in civil rights work. In the 1960s, the phrase was not well defined, but *tikkun olam* was intended to be a Jewish term to denote any humanitarian action. Conservative and even some Orthodox Jews who gradually began to use the term with that meaning were interested in identifying *tikkun olam* with specific, traditional commandments to work toward social ends, as well as in the legal discussion of those commandments. Now it is used by Jews of all sorts to denote the broad Jewish mandate to care for others.

Older, Related Terms and Concepts

I once was on a panel with a very learned Jew who claimed that the term *tikkun olam* as it is used now is not a Jewish concept, but rather one used by those who want to abandon traditional Judaism and remake Judaism into a religion of social action. He was clearly right about the historical roots of the term; as explained in the previous section, its meaning as socal action appears only very late in Jewish history, and its first meanings were significantly different from what we mean by the phrase today. That meaning is very new, spanning only five or six decades—like yesterday in Jewish time— and *tikkun olam* certainly cannot replace all the rest of Judaism.

At the same time, as I pointed out to him, there are other terms in classical Jewish sources that denote some of the same things that we now mean by the phrase *tikkun olam*. Because these other terms have an ancient pedigree, one that continues throughout Jewish literature to our own day, one certainly cannot maintain, as he did, that social concern is a new form of Judaism unrelated to the Jewish past. He was right, of course, in asserting that social concern is not the whole of Judaism, but it is a central feature of it, as moderns claim, even though it is expressed in different words.

The closest of those classical words for what we mean today by *tikkun olam* are, on the personal level, *chesed,* and, on the social level, *tzedek* and *mishpat*. *Chesed* originally meant loyalty—to God and to one's neighbor. It therefore came to mean what one does in faithfulness to God and one's neighbor, namely, acts of love, kindness, and care.

Tzedek means justice, as in the famous verse, "Justice, justice shall you pursue" (Deuteronomy 16:20). The Torah's vision of justice includes both procedural and substantive elements. That is, it demands that in court we ensure fairness by following specific procedures in judging people ("procedural justice"), and in society generally we must guarantee that there is a substantial safety net so that the poor, orphans, and widows get what they need to live, receive an education, and find a mate ("substantive justice").[5]

Mishpat comes from the root meaning *shofet*, "judge," and thus *mishpat* originally meant the decision of a judge, or a precedent. It has that meaning, for example, in the very first verse of Exodus 21, the opening of the weekly portion called *Mishpatim*, for as biblical scholars have pointed out, the norms contained in that section of the Bible probably originated as judicial precedents.[6] From this origin, the word *mishpat* expanded to mean law generally, especially in the plural form, and so the new American translation of the Bible published by the Jewish Publication Society translates *mishpatim* as "rules." For example, "See, I [Moses] have imparted to you laws *(hukkim)* and rules *(mishpatim)*, as the Lord my God has commanded me ... " (Deuteronomy 4:5).[7] Finally, already in the Bible the word *mishpat* expands yet further to mean justice. For example, "The Rock!—His deeds are perfect, Yea, all His ways are just *(mishpat)*" (Deuteronomy 32:4).

In both the Bible and rabbinic literature, the values of justice and kindness are often spoken of together to indicate that they balance and reinforce each other. So, for example, in a verse Jews recite three times each day, the Psalmist asserts, "Adonai is righteous *(tzadik)* in all His ways and kind *(chasid)* in all His actions" (Psalms 145:17).[8] More expansively, using many of the Hebrew words we have encountered as parts of the way *tikkun olam* was expressed in the past, the Psalmist declares (in the JPS translation):

O Lord, Your faithfulness *(chasdikha)* reaches to heaven;
Your steadfastness *(emunatkha)* to the sky;
Your beneficence *(tzidkatkha)* is like the high mountains;
Your justice *(mishpatkha)* like the great deep;
Man and beast You deliver, O Lord.
How precious is Your faithful care *(chasdikha)*, O God!
Mankind shelters in the shadow of Your wings.

—*Psalms 36:6–8*

This intermixing of terms continues in rabbinic literature, as, for example, in this passage:

Rabbi Elazar quoted this verse, "He has told you, O man, what is good, and what the Lord requires of you: Only to do justice (literally, "to do *mishpat*"), to love goodness *(chesed)*, and to walk modestly with your God" (Micah 6:8). What does this verse imply? "To do justice" means to act in accordance with the principles of justice. "To love goodness" means to let your actions be guided by principles of loving-kindness. "To walk modestly with your God" means to assist needy families at their funerals and weddings [by giving humbly, in private]....

Rabbi Elazar said: Whoever does deeds of charity *(tzedakah)* and justice *(mishpat)* is considered as having filled the entire world, all of it, with loving-kindness *(chesed)*, as it is written, "He [God] loves what is right *(tzedakah)* and just *(mishpat)*; the earth is filled with the loving-kindness of the Lord" (Psalms 33:5). Should you suppose that one may achieve this easily, Scripture says, "How rare is Your loving-kindness, O God" (Psalms 36:8).[9] Should you suppose that difficulty in executing charity and justice also affects those who fear Heaven, Scripture says, "But the Lord's steadfast love *(chesed)* is for all eternity toward those who fear Him, and His beneficence *(tzidkatkha)* is for children's children for those who keep His covenant" (Psalms 103:17).

—*Babylonian Talmud,* Sukkah *49b*

Clearly, then, from the Jewish perspective, doing justice is *not* restricted to abiding or judging according to the rules; it certainly does demand that,[10] but it also requires that one balance justice with kindness.

The rabbinic tradition goes further than that. It values acts of kindness for the objective good they accomplish, regardless of the motive that prompted the person to do them. Thus, it prefers acts of kindness to charity, for kindness can fix the world in more ways than charity can:

Our Rabbis taught: Deeds of loving-kindness are superior to charity in three respects: Charity can be accomplished only with money, while deeds of loving-kindness can be accomplished through personal involvement as well as with money. Charity can be given only to the poor, while deeds of loving-kindness can be done for both rich and poor. Charity applies only to the living, while deeds of loving-kindness apply to both the living and the dead....

—*Babylonian Talmud,* Sukkah *49b*

At the same time, the Rabbis were not blind to the importance of motive. Thus, while they value all acts of kindness for the good they achieve regardless of the reasons people do them, the Rabbis judge the moral worth of such acts according to the degree to which they are done with selfless, benign motives:

> Rabbi Elazar said: The reward for acts of justice ("charity,"
> *tzedakah*) depends upon the degree of loving-kindness
> *(chesed)* in them, as it is written, "Sow righteousness (jus-
> tice, charity, *tzedakah*) for yourselves, reap according to
> (your) goodness *(chesed)*" (Hosea 10:12).
>
> —*Babylonian Talmud*, Sukkah *49b*

Thus, our acts of kindness must, if possible, affect our inner being as well as the world at large.

Here, though, one must remember the fundamental principle of rabbinic educational psychology—namely, that while it is best to do good things for the right motives, one should do the right thing even for the wrong reason if one must, for "from doing the right thing not for its sake one will come to do it for its sake" (Babylonian Talmud, *Pesachim* 50a). For three reasons we should do the right thing now rather than wait for the proper motive: first, the right motive may never come. Second, even if one does the right thing for an improper motive (e.g., to get a good reputation or a favor from someone else), the good act hopefully accomplishes an objective good in society. Third, as the Rabbis say in what was just cited, the way we learn good motives is by doing good acts.

The Importance of *Tikkun Olam* and Its Related Values

The values we are discussing are among the most important of the Torah's values. *Chesed* (acts of kindness) runs through the Torah from beginning to end:

> Rabbi Simlai taught: The Torah begins with deeds of loving-
> kindness and ends with deeds of loving-kindness. It begins
> with deeds of loving-kindness, as it is written, "And the Lord
> God made garments of skins for Adam and for his wife and

clothed them" (Genesis 3:21). It ends with deeds of loving-kindness, as it is written, "And He buried him [Moses] in the valley in the land of Moab" (Deuteronomy 34:6).

—*Babylonian Talmud,* Sotah *14a*

It is also the way we atone for our sins:

Once, as Rabbi Yochanan was walking out of Jerusalem, Rabbi Joshua followed him, and upon seeing the Temple in ruins, he said: "Woe unto us that this place is in ruins, the place where atonement was made for Israel's iniquities!" Rabbi Yochanan responded: "My son, do not grieve, for we have another means of atonement that is as effective. What is it? It is deeds of loving-kindness, concerning which Scripture says, 'I [God] desire goodness *(chesed),* not sacrifice'" (Hosea 6:6).

—Avot de-Rabbi Natan *4:5*

Further, to refuse to care for others is to deny God Himself: "Rabbi Judah said: When a man denies the duty of loving-kindness, it is as though he had denied the Root [i.e., God]" (*Ecclesiastes Rabbah* 7:1, par. 4). Conversely, engaging in acts of *chesed* is nothing less than modeling yourself after God:

"To walk in all His ways" (Deuteronomy 11:22). These are the ways of the Holy One: "compassionate and gracious, slow to anger, abounding in kindness *(chesed)* and faithfulness, extending kindness to the thousandth generation, forgiving iniquity, transgression, and sin … " (Exodus 34:6). This means that just as God is compassionate and gracious, you too must be compassionate and gracious … Just as God is kind, you too must be kind … "The Lord is righteous in all His ways and kind in all His actions" (Psalms 145:17):

Just as the Holy One is righteous, so you too must be righteous; just as the Holy One is kind (loving, *chasid*), so too
you must be kind (loving).

—Sifrei Deuteronomy, Ekev

Finally, it is one of the three values on which the very existence
of the world depends, as we learn in this famous passage from the
Mishnah's tractate, *Ethics of the Fathers (Pirkei Avot)*, famous
both because it comes at the very beginning of the tractate and also
because in modern times it is often sung: "The world depends on
three things: on Torah, on worship, and on acts of loving-
kindness" (1:2).

As indicated earlier, in many ways *chesed* denotes the personal, individual aspects of *tikkun olam,* while *tzedek* and *mishpat*
denote its social elements. Furthermore, similar to *chesed, tzedek*
and *mishpat* are core values of the Jewish tradition. Thus, at the
end of the first chapter of *Ethics of the Fathers* (1:18), we read an
alternative list of values on which the world depends: "Rabbi
Simeon ben Gamliel says: The world depends on three things: on
justice *(ha-din),* truth, and peace, as the Bible says, 'Judge in your
gates truth and justice *(u'mishpat)* and peace'" (Zechariah 8:16).

Like *chesed,* the justice aspects of *tikkun olam* are also part of
God's very essence: "Righteousness and justice *(tzedek u'mishpat)*
are the base of Your throne; steadfast love and faithfulness *(chesed
ve'emet)* stand before You" (Psalms 89:15; see also 97:2). The
Book of Proverbs asserts that if a person pays attention to wisdom,
"Then you will understand the fear of the Lord and attain knowledge of God ... He reserves ability for the upright and is a shield
for those who live blamelessly, guarding the paths of justice *(mishpat),* protecting the way of those loyal to Him. You will then understand what is right, just and equitable *(tzedek u'mishpat
u'meisharim)*—every good course" (Proverbs 2:5, 7–9). Consequently, to seek God is to seek justice: "Listen to Me, you who

pursue justice, you who seek the Lord … For teaching *(torah)* will go forth from Me, My way *(mishpati,* "my justice") for the light of peoples … Listen to Me, you who care for the right *(tzedek),* O people who lay My instruction to heart!" (Isaiah 51:1, 4, 7).

From the Bible's point of view, then, the tasks of discerning the just and the good and then acting on that knowledge are not just central to our Jewish identity; they are what God demands of us: "Do what is right and good in the sight of the Lord..." (Deuteronomy 6:18). Many philosophical questions immediately arise from that verse and the other passages we have been considering. What do we mean by the terms *kind, just, right,* and *good* in the first place, and how are they different from each other? How shall we determine the courses of action that are right or good in morally ambiguous situations? And how is God related to our moral discernment and action? We will consider such questions in chapter 3, but for now, suffice it to say that *tikkun olam* and its component values have deep roots in the Jewish tradition, identifying core values in the identity of both Jews and God.

2

Why Should I Care?

The very idea of *tikkun olam* assumes that we should try to fix the world in both its natural and social aspects. But *why* should we? The reasons we should endeavor to preserve and repair the *natural* world will be discussed in another volume in this series. In this volume, in which we focus on the *human* world, our question boils down to this: why should I care about the plight of other people?

Philosophers differ in their understanding of this question, and politicians do as well. On one end of the spectrum, libertarians such as Robert Nozick maintain that in a just society everyone gets his or her due—that is, what people have is what they have earned. Government should take from me in taxes only enough to accomplish what is necessary to do as a group, including especially public safety (and therefore police, fire, and military agencies), but also services that we all need and must work together to create, such as schools, roads, and bridges. The government has no justification, according to libertarians, to take from me anything more than that, for I should have the right to determine whether I want to spend my hard-earned money on cultural development, on helping people who cannot support themselves, or simply on something that I want for myself or my family. The basis for the libertarian view is seeing oneself as an individual first and foremost, with only limited and voluntary ties to the community to perform tasks that I cannot do on my own and therefore cannot be expected to do individually. All tasks that individuals can do for themselves they have the duty to do, without burdening anyone else.

On the other end of the spectrum, Karl Marx asserted that everyone in a just society has an equal share in society's goods, no matter what he or she contributes to that wealth. "From each according to his means, and to each according to his needs" is his formula for determining who should give to the public purse and who should receive from it, and, in each case, how much. Such a view is grounded in a very strong sense of community. In Communist countries such as the former Soviet Union and contemporary China, this sense is so strong that the government has the right to regulate speech, assembly, and even childbearing in the name of the public good.

Most philosophers and most Western societies have opted for some position in between these two extremes. Some countries, such as Sweden, have adopted a predominantly socialist approach, with emphasis on social equality but with some room for variations in wealth as a result of individual initiative. Others, including the United States, have instead focused on rewarding individuals for their particular skills and efforts while at the same time providing a safety net for those who lose in the capitalist game.

The Jewish tradition has taken an even more moderate approach than either the modified socialism of Sweden or the modified capitalism of the United States. Its legal texts assume a regulated form of capitalism, but its thick sense of community, described below, and its theological base lead it to advocate a much stronger safety net than the United States has ever provided, except, perhaps, during the Depression of the 1930s. At the same time, the Jewish tradition delineates *limits* to what I can be expected to do for others, for it also asserts a strong sense of free will and individual responsibility. In this chapter, we shall examine the first part of that balance, the reasons I should care about others, and then we will see how, in each area of life, Jewish sources strive to determine the limits of one's duties to others.

God's Sovereignty

Many contemporary Jews who are skittish about belief in God but strongly committed to helping others may be disturbed by the centrality of the belief in God in motivating Judaism's commitment to others. Jewish sources provide a series of rationales for caring for others, and some of them, as we shall see, invoke God much less than others do. As a result, atheistic or agnostic Jews can find ample grounds in the Jewish tradition for the duty to help others, and even those who affirm a belief in God will at times be motivated more by Judaism's nontheistic reasons than by its theistic ones. At the same time, it would be misleading to pretend that the Jewish concept of (and belief in) God plays only a minor role in Judaism's demand that we care for others. On the contrary, God is very much at the center of that Jewish duty.

The ultimate theological foundation for Judaism's commandment to help others is the belief that God created the world and therefore owns it. The Torah (Genesis 14:19, 22) describes God as *"koneh shamayim va'aretz,"* which in biblical Hebrew means both Creator of heaven and earth and also Owner of heaven and earth. ("Heaven and earth" is a merism, a biblical device that names the ends of a spectrum and means everything in between as well.) The Bible also spells out this idea in verses such as these: "Mark, the heavens to their uttermost reaches belong to the Lord your God, the earth and all that is on it!" (Deuteronomy 10:14) and "The land and all that is on it belongs to God, the earth and those who dwell on it" (Psalms 24:1).[1]

How does creation convey ownership? In modern times, the Industrial Revolution divided the creation of many things into small parts, with a given person repeatedly doing the same task as one small part of the process of making something. This enabled companies to train people to do only one thing rather than everything necessary to make the object, and the resulting assembly line made things faster, cheaper, and with greater quality control. These advantages, though, came at the cost of separating people from the things they were creating. Thus, we are no longer used to thinking of the maker of something as automatically its owner.

At the same time, we moderns still recognize that when individuals create a complete thing, they own it. So, for example, artists own their paintings until and unless they decide to sell them, and authors own their books until they sign over rights to a publisher. In fact, we have developed rather sophisticated patent and copyright laws to protect even our "intellectual property"—that is, our ideas—apart from any particular object embodying them. So even though we are more used to cooperative efforts in which none or all of the makers of an object own it, we do have many examples in our modern lives in which creating something—and even the idea of something—conveys ownership of it.

In the case of the universe, the Jewish doctrine of monotheism makes God's claim to own the earth and everything on it similar to that of the modern-day artist or author. That is, because Jews believe that God is One, and that no other party was involved in the creation of the world, God alone is both the sole Creator and Owner of the earth and all that is on it. That alone would be sufficient to establish God's ownership of everything in the world; after all, creators of a work of art or an idea do not have to do anything else to own what they have created. Jewish liturgy, though, takes this further: the morning prayers describe God as benignly renewing creation each day.[2] God's ownership of the world is justified not only by what God did in the distant past, but also by God's re-creation of the world each and every day.

As Owner of all assets, God has the right to distribute them at will and to make demands about their use. Human beings may, at God's behest, own property, but only vis-à-vis other human beings. All property that humans own, though, ultimately belongs to God, and we have it only as a temporary loan. As the ultimate Owner, God requires us, as the Torah's commandments indicate, to give charity from "our" resources. Those who refuse to provide for the poor and for others in need thus effectively deny God's sovereignty, for such people dispute God's ultimate legal claim to all the earth and the right to redistribute property to those in need. Consequently the Rabbis deemed a refusal to assist the poor as nothing less than idolatry.[3]

Assisting the poor in biblical times took the form not only of direct aid, but also of relief from servitude, and that too was rooted in respect for God's ownership of the world. Although an Israclite could be sold into slavery to pay a debt, the master was required to set the slave free within six years, even if the debt was not totally redeemed by that time. If the slave chose to remain in servitude, he could do so, but only until the Jubilee year, when even the reluctant had to go free. Moreover, the master could not abuse the slave. The Bible clearly specifies that the rationale behind these command- ments is that all Jews are God's servants, and consequently they may not be perpetually the slaves of any human being:

> If your kinsman under you continues in straits and must give himself over to you, do not subject him to the treat- ment of a slave. He shall remain with you as a hired or bound laborer; he shall serve with you only until the Jubilee year. Then he and his children with him shall be free of your authority; he shall go back to his family and return to his ancestral holding. For they are My servants, whom I freed from the land of Egypt; they may not give themselves over into servitude (Leviticus 25:39–42).

Thus care for the poor, including those enslaved to pay off their debts, is required because ultimately God owns us all, together with the world in which we live.

God's Commandment

As Owner of everything, God also has the prerogative to make demands about how the world's property is distributed. Thus the most straightforward reason in the tradition that we must care for others is that God commands us to do so. So, for example, with regard to the poor, the Torah says this:

> If there is a needy person among you, one of your kinsmen in any of your settlements in the land that the Lord your God is giving you, do not harden your heart and shut your hand against your needy kinsman. Rather, you must open your hand and lend him sufficient for whatever he needs ... For there will never cease to be needy ones in your land, which is why I command you: open your hand to the poor and needy kinsman in your land (Deuteronomy 15:7, 8, 11).

But it is not only the poor whom God commands us to help. In what is one of the most famous verses of the Torah, the one that Rabbi Akiva calls the fundamental principle of the Torah,[4] God commands us to "love your neighbor as yourself; I am Adonai" (Leviticus 19:18).

The Rabbis of the Midrash and Talmud, in interpreting this verse, determine that it requires us not really to love everyone, which they knew was impossible, but to have concern for others and, more important, to act out of that sense of commitment and loyalty to others. So, for example, they use this verse to explain a man's duty to marry a woman who is fitting for him, to forbid a man from having sexual intercourse with his wife during the day lest he see something loathsome in her, to permit a child to draw blood from his or her parent in an effort to heal him or her despite the Torah's prohibition of injuring one's parents (Exodus 21:15), and to require that a person who is to be executed be killed in the least offensive way possible.[5]

Maimonides (1135–1204) uses this verse as the basis for yet other laws: that one must tell the praises of others, avoid self-aggrandizement through defaming others, and concern oneself with other people's money as one would take care of one's own.[6] Furthermore, Maimonides maintains that loving one's neighbor as oneself is one of the grounds for the demand that we rescue captives.[7] He asserts that although the commands to visit the sick, bury the dead, comfort mourners, and help a bride and groom celebrate their wedding are of rabbinic rather than biblical status, they are rooted in this biblical command.[8]

The Rabbis then ask an important question: in commanding us to love our neighbor, why must we be reminded that God is Adonai, our Lord? Four verses earlier, the command not to curse the deaf or put a stumbling block before the blind ends with the clause, "and you shall fear your God" (Leviticus 19:14). On that verse and several others, the Rabbis maintain that even though it is often difficult for other human beings to discern a person's real motive in doing something, God infallibly discerns our motives, and so for all commandments involving something that is in our hearts *(masur la'lev)* God will unfailingly know our intentions and judge us accordingly.[9] Based on those rabbinic comments, Rashi (1035–1104, France), undoubtedly the most famous medieval commentator on the Torah, summarizes this tenet thus:

> Because a person cannot know whether he intends to do a good thing or a bad one [in giving advice to someone who is blind about such matters], and he can pretend [to other human beings] that he intended to do a good thing, therefore

the Torah says, "and you shall fear your God," who knows your thoughts. Similarly, with regard to all other matters that are in the doer's heart, and others cannot know [the person's intentions], the Torah says, "and you shall fear your God" (Rashi on Leviticus 19:14).

Two verses later, the Torah forbids us from standing idly by the blood of our neighbor. The Rabbis interpret that to mean that one must come to the aid of a person drowning or attacked by highway robbers. Rashi similarly interprets the end of that verse, "I am Adonai," as meaning "trustworthy to reward and trustworthy to punish" those who could have intervened but chose to pretend that they did not see what was happening. Thus, "I am Adonai" in our verse as well indicates that even if other people cannot tell, God will know whether we love our neighbor as ourselves and will reward or punish us accordingly. The upshot of God's presence in each of these commandments, therefore, is that even if we do not recognize any other reason to help those in need and to avoid hurting them, we must nevertheless do so because God demands it of us and will unfailingly enforce that demand.

The Torah, though, was keenly aware that enforcement by God would not suffice to motivate people to obey God's commandments, including the ones requiring us to help others. After all, a mere forty days after the People Israel stood at the foot of Mount Sinai, with thunder, lightning, and earthquakes—truly an impressive display of God's power if ever there was one—the people were worshiping the golden calf. The threat of God's punishment for disobedience and the promise of God's reward for obedience are thus not adequate grounds to produce conformity to the law. Therefore, it is not surprising that the Torah and other classical Jewish texts describe a number of additional reasons to help those in need.[10]

The Divine Dignity of God's Human Creature

Jewish tradition places strong emphasis on the worth of the individual. Human worth derives first from being created in God's image, a concept that the Torah repeats three times in the opening chapters of Genesis to ensure that we take note of it:

> And God created the human being in His image, in the image of God He created him: male and female He created them (Genesis 1:27).

> This is the record of Adam's line. When God created man, He made him in the likeness of God; male and female He created them. And when they were created, He blessed them and called them Human (Genesis 5: 1-2).

> Whoever sheds the blood of man, by man shall his blood be shed; for in His image did God make man (Genesis 9:6).

As this last verse indicates, the divine image in each of us is not just a philosophical concept; it also justifies and explains specific laws. The most obvious, in Genesis 9, is that murder is to be banned, for human beings have divine worth. Even murderers, though, are created in the divine image, as are others guilty of a capital offense. The divine image in each and every human being does not require that we like each and every person or approve of his or her actions; indeed, the Torah prescribes capital punishment for many offenses, including not only murder but also striking or cursing one's parents or violating Shabbat. We moderns may have principled objections to capital punishment, or to the widespread use of it, and the Rabbis of the Mishnah and Talmud did too, for they introduced evidentiary procedures that made it virtually impossible to execute a person.[11] Still, it is interesting to note that the Torah prescribes that when people are hanged for committing a capital offense, we must honor the divinity of their bodies (and the holiness of the Land of Israel) by burying them quickly (see Deuteronomy 21:22–23).

The Rabbis took this further. That we were created in God's image is a manifestation of God's love for us; our *awareness* of the divine image within us is a mark of yet more divine love:

> Beloved is man, for he was created in the image of God; but it was by a special love that it was made known to him that he was created in the image of God, as the Torah says, "For in the image of God He made man" (Genesis 9:6).
> —*Mishnah*, Pirkei Avot (Ethics of the Fathers) *3:18*

Exactly which feature of the human being reflects this divine image is a matter of debate within the tradition. The Torah seems to tie it to humanity's ability to make moral judgments—that is, to distinguish good from bad and right from wrong, to behave accordingly, and to judge one's own actions and those of others on the basis of this moral knowledge.[12] Another human faculty connected to divinity by the Torah and by the later tradition is the ability to speak.[13] Maimonides claims that the divine image resides in our capacity to think, especially discursively.[14] Locating the divine image within us may also be the Torah's way of acknowledging that we can love, just as God does,[15] or that we are at least partially spiritual and thus share God's spiritual nature.[16]

In the biblical account, humanity was not only created in the divine image; humanity was also created, initially, in the form of one human being: Adam. In an oft-quoted passage in the Mishnah, the Rabbis spell out several implications of God's first creating a single human being. Two of those ramifications add further to the worth of each individual.

First, killing one person is also killing all of his or her potential descendants—indeed "an entire world." Conversely, someone who saves an individual "saves an entire world." That makes murder of any one individual all the more serious and saving a human life all the more praiseworthy. It also ascribes value to each of us as the possible progenitor of future generations.

Second, when people use a mold to create coins, the image on each coin is exactly the same. God, however, made each human being unique. In accordance with the laws of supply and demand, a one-of-a-kind thing demands a far higher price than something that is plentiful on the market. Think, for example, of the comparative value of a Picasso original, of each of a few hundred prints of that work, and, finally, of a photograph of that work: the more unique the product, the greater its value. The fact that each of us is unique imparts to each of us immense value.

Thinking that the world was created for your sake (as this Mishnah in Sanhedrin suggests)[17] can, of course, produce more than a little arrogance. The following lovely Hasidic saying introduces an appropriate balance: "A person should always carry two pieces of paper in his/her pockets. On one should be written, 'For me the world was created,' and on the other, 'I am but dust and ashes' [quoting Genesis 18:27]."[18] We must have humility before God and before other people, then, while still appreciating our own immense worth and that of every other human being by virtue of our creation in the image of God.

The Rabbis, like the Torah before them, invoke the doctrines that God created human beings in the divine image and uniquely not only to *describe* aspects of our nature, but also to *prescribe* behavior. Specifically, the Rabbis maintain that because human beings are created in God's image, we affront God when we insult another person.[19] Conversely, "one who welcomes his friend is as if he welcomes the face of the divine presence."[20] Moreover, when we see someone with a disability, we are to utter this blessing: "Praised are you, Lord our God, *meshaneh ha-briyyot*, who created different creatures," or "who makes us different (from each other)." Precisely when we might recoil from a deformed or an incapacitated person, or thank God for not making us like that, the tradition instead bids us to embrace the divine image in such people—indeed, to bless God for creating some of us so.[21] Finally, the nonutilitarian basis of the Rabbis' assertion of human worth is graphically illustrated in their ruling that no one person can be sacrificed to save even an entire city unless that person is named by the enemy or guilty of a capital crime.[22]

Even when a person is named by the enemy and condemned to capital punishment, the Rabbis were not convinced that the people within the city should hand him or her over to the enemy:

> Ulla, son of Qoseb, was wanted by the [non-Jewish] government. He arose and fled to Rabbi Joshua ben Levi at Lydda. They [the troops] came, surrounded the city, and said: "If you do not hand him over to us, we will destroy the city." Rabbi Joshua ben Levi went up to him, persuaded him to submit and gave him up [to them]. Now Elijah [the prophet], of blessed memory, had been in the habit of visiting him [Rabbi Joshua], but he [now] ceased visiting him. He [Rabbi Joshua] fasted several times and Elijah appeared and said to him: "Shall I reveal myself to informers [betrayers]?" He [Rabbi Joshua] said: "Have I not carried out a *mishnah* [a rabbinic ruling]?" Said he [Elijah]: "Is this a ruling for the pious *(mishnat hasidim)*?" [Another version: "This should have been done through others and not by yourself."]
>
> —*Jerusalem Talmud,* Terumot 47a

The various positions in this ruling are complex, and I discuss them in chapter 6 and elsewhere.[23] The underlying premise of the debate embedded in all of the various positions of this ruling, however, is that every life has a supreme claim on us, and that value is not a function of a person's social position, wealth, or skills; therefore, no life can be sacrificed even for the survival of many others except under specific conditions—and some say not even then.

This demand that we respect each other means, of course, that we must help others to keep them from indignity, but it also has implications for how we do that—namely, that we must do so while preserving the person's dignity as much as possible. The Torah makes this demand: "When you make a loan of any sort to your neighbor, you must not enter his house to seize his pledge. You must remain outside, while the man to whom you made the loan brings the pledge out to you" (Deuteronomy 24:10–11). It is also evident in the Talmud's demand that "even a poor person who lives entirely on charity must also give charity to another poor person."[24]

Community

In another book, I describe in detail the differences among the American, Christian, and Jewish conceptions of community.[25] For our purposes, it is sufficient to note that with the possible exception of some right-wing Orthodox groups, all modern Jews see the world through Enlightenment glasses, where the individual is the fundamental reality. All individuals are independent agents who may or may not choose to associate themselves with others for specific purposes. In the United States, for example, religious congregations of all faiths are voluntary associations to which individuals belong and from which they may dissociate themselves at any time. That is one manifestation of the enduring existence of individuality in the American system of thought, for even when people join groups, they do not lose their primary identity and privileges as individuals. Another corollary of this view is that even if other people happen to belong to a group to which I too belong, what they do is none of my business and their needs are none of my concern, unless all members of the group have specifically undertaken duties to care for each other in some way or unless the other person's actions have a direct effect on me. Even within groups, Americans retain their fundamental identity as individuals.

This perspective stands in stark contrast to the traditional Jewish view, shared by most pre-Enlightenment theories,[26] that the individual is defined by his or her membership in the group. This membership is not voluntary and cannot be terminated at will; it is a metaphysical fact over which people have no control. God speaks to the entire People Israel at Sinai; it is the people as a whole with whom God makes the covenant and who will be punished or rewarded according to their adherence to that covenant; it is the community's leaders who know the theology and legal stipulations of the covenant and who bear the responsibility and have the right to interpret and apply God's word in each generation; and it is the People Israel as a whole who will ultimately be redeemed in messianic times. Thus, contrary to the concept of the group in Christianity or in American secular thought, in Jewish thought, the community has not only practical but also theological status.

Moreover, the Jewish community is not voluntary, but rather organic. As such, it is not voluntary for those who are born Jewish, and it is not possible to dissociate from the Jewish people any more than your foot can dissociate from the rest of your body. Thus, Jews who convert to another religion lose their *privileges* as Jews—for example, they may not be married or buried as a Jew or count as part of a prayer quorum *(minyan)*, etc.—but even as apostates *(meshumadim)* they retain all the *responsibilities* of Jews! The same is true for converts to Judaism: they clearly choose to convert, but once they have completed the conversion process, from the perspective of Judaism they become an organic part of the People Israel and cannot leave the Jewish fold any more than a born Jew can.

Judaism's theological and organic sense of community has some important implications for our purposes. The indissoluble linkage between the individual and the group means that each individual is responsible for every other simply by being part of the Jewish people, without any specific assumption of that duty by the individual Jew and even against his or her will: "All Jews are responsible for each other" (Babylonian Talmud, *Shevu'ot* 39a).[27] Furthermore, virtually everything that one does is, in Judaism's view, everyone else's business. As the Talmud puts it:

> Whoever is able to protest against the wrongdoings of his family and fails to do so is punished for the family's wrongdoings. Whoever is able to protest against the wrongdoings of his fellow citizens and does not do so is punished for the wrongdoings of the people of his city. Whoever is able to protest against the wrongdoings of the world and does not do so is punished for the wrongdoings of the world (Babylonian Talmud, *Shabbat* 54b).[28]

This might well offend our sense of justice, for we think that we should be responsible only for what we do individually. The Torah does indeed demand that law courts hold people responsible only for their own actions—a major advance in legal fairness, for in most other systems, including English law until 1832, authorities punished not only the guilty person but also family members for treason and other "crimes of attaint." Still, in other passages such as the one just quoted, the Bible and the Rabbis recognize that however unfair we think it may be, we are all both the beneficiaries and the victims of what previous generations of our family and community have done and what they are doing now. Thus, God is depicted as "visiting the sins of the parents onto the children to the third and fourth generation of My enemies but who does acts of kindness to the thousandth generation for those who love Me and obey My commandments."[29] We do not live on isolated islands but within and as part of a family and community, and thus our acts and those of our family and community continually influence each other, even if we do not think that desirable or just.

At the same time, the communal view of traditional Judaism does not swallow up the individual's identity; it actually enhances it by linking it to the larger reality of the group. Law professor and legal philosopher Milton Konvitz expresses the resulting viewpoint well:

> The traditional Jew is no detached, rugged individual. Nor is his reality, his essence, completely absorbed in some monstrous collectivity which alone can claim rights and significance. He *is* an individual but one whose essence is determined by the fact that he is a brother, a *fellow Jew.* His prayers are, therefore, communal and not private, integrative and not isolative, holistic and not separative ... This consciousness does not reduce but rather enhances and accentuates the dignity and power of the individual. Although an integral part of an organic whole, from which he cannot be separated, except at the cost of his moral and spiritual life, let each man say, with Hillel, "If I am here, then everyone is here."[30]

These philosophical and legal differences between American democracy and Judaism—viewing one's fundamental identity as an independent individual or as an organic part of a group, the corollary of voluntary association and disassociation with any group in contrast to integral membership within an organic community created by God with no possibility of leaving, and the resultant status of one's duty to care for others in the group— make it difficult for American Jews to integrate these two parts of their identity. This opposition should not be exaggerated, for other aspects of the Jewish and American senses of community reinforce each other.[31] Still, the strong, organic sense of community that Judaism fosters provides a powerful motive for helping others within the community.

It is this sense of a strong community that, according to a recent poll,[32] is the primary meaning that most Jews find in their Jewish identity. The second most important factor (21 percent) is precisely the Jewish community's social action activities to help those in need. As Jacob Neusner has pointed out, in our own day, when Jews differ sharply in beliefs, practices, and customs, and when we live and work among non-Jews to a much greater extent than in the past, the shared work of collecting and distributing charity, and working in other ways to help those in need, are significant mechanisms through which individual Jews *become* a Jewish community.[33]

One's duty to help the local community provide for those in need depends on how deep one's roots are within a given community, as Maimonides specifies in his code of Jewish law, the *Mishneh Torah:*

> One who settles in a community for thirty days becomes obligated to contribute to the charity fund together with the other members of the community. One who settles there for three months becomes obligated to contribute to the soup kitchen. One who settles there for six months becomes obligated to contribute clothing with which the poor of the community can cover themselves. One who settles there for nine months becomes obligated to contribute to the burial fund for burying the community's poor and providing for all of their needs of burial.
>
> —*Maimonides,* Mishneh Torah, Laws of Gifts
> to the Poor *9:12*

Thus, even though Jews are part of a universal community, with duties to all other Jews, their primary duties are to their local communities. In chapter 5, we shall see that a person's right to claim assistance also works in concentric circles, with the greatest claim on one's family, then on one's local community, and then on the larger Jewish community. Thus, even though "all Jews are responsible for each other," a duty that Jews throughout history have risen to fulfill, the tradition understands that our primary bonds and duties are to those closest to us.

Our Covenant with God

We Jews are part of a larger Jewish community, and traditional sources see that as not only—or even primarily—an ethnic identity. That is, it is not like the ties Irish Americans feel toward anyone whose ancestors came from Ireland or Italian Americans have toward those who immigrated from Italy. Jews do not share one place of residence, speak one language, have a specific cuisine, or sing one set of songs. All those ethnic identifiers are lacking for Jews, for Jews literally have lived and still do live in all regions of the world, with attendant differences in language, food, dress, art, music, literature, and dance.

According to Jewish law, to be a Jew one must either be born by a Jewish woman or be reborn to Judaism through the rites of conversion. In that way, Jewish identity is like American citizenship. As long as someone is born in the United States, even if that person knows nothing about American history or government and does not speak English, he or she is a citizen. So, too, one is a Jew if born to a Jewish woman, even if one knows or affirms nothing about Judaism and has no facility with Hebrew, the primary Jewish language. To join either the American or Jewish group through naturalization or conversion requires considerable knowledge about the group as well as actions in accord with its rules, requirements that are not made of born Americans or Jews.

Birth to a Jewish woman, however, only defines who is "a member of the tribe." The substance of what it means to be a Jew is defined in the covenant between God and the Jewish people. Beginning with Abraham and finding its quintessential expression at Mount Sinai, that covenant is, in part, a contract between God and the Jewish people in which both parties promise to fulfill their parts of the bargain. It is, though, more than that: it is a covenant similar to a covenant of marriage, in which the two parties not only agree to do specific things for each other but also enter into a long-term *relationship* in which they each care for the other. The terms of the covenant, then, are obligatory in part as a function of the morality of *promise keeping*—every Jew in every generation was at Sinai and promised there to fulfill the covenant—and, in larger part, a function of the ongoing *relationship* that was consecrated there. As a Jew, then, I need to care for all other Jews because they are part of my people covenanted to each other and to God in all ages and places.

There are two types of covenants in the Bible. The first is a covenant of mutual promises.

> Then he [Moses] took the record of the covenant and read it aloud to the people. And they said, "All that the Lord has spoken we will do and obey" (Exodus 24:7).

> The Lord our God made a covenant with us at Horeb. It was not with our fathers that the Lord made this covenant, but with us, the living, every one of us who is here today (Deuteronomy 5: 2–3).

> You [the People Israel] stand this day, all of you, before the Lord your God—your tribal heads, your elders, and your officials, all the men of Israel, your children, your wives,

even the stranger within your camp, from the woodchopper to waterdrawer—to enter into the covenant of the Lord your God, which the Lord your God is concluding with you this day, with its sanctions; to the end that He may establish you this day as His people and be your God, as He promised you and as He swore to your fathers, Abraham, Isaac, and Jacob. I [Moses] make this covenant, with its sanctions, not with you alone, but with those who are standing here with us this day before the Lord our God and with those who are not with us here this day (Deuteronomy 29:9–14).

In view of all this, we make this pledge and put it in writing; and on the sealed copy [are subscribed] our officials, our Levites, and our priests … And the rest of the people, the priests, the Levites, the gatekeepers, the singers, the temple servants, and all who separated themselves from the peoples of the lands to [follow] the Teaching of God, their wives, sons and daughters, all who know enough to understand, join with their noble brothers and take an oath with sanctions to follow the Teaching of God, given through Moses the servant of God, and to observe carefully all the commandments of the Lord, our Lord, His rules and laws (Nehemiah 10:1, 29–30).

The second prototype is a covenant of love:

Mark, the heavens to their uttermost reaches belong to the Lord your God, the earth and all that is on it! Yet it was to your fathers that the Lord was drawn in His love for them, so that He chose you, their lineal descendants, from among all His peoples—as is now the case. Cut away, therefore, the thickening about your hearts and stiffen your necks no more. For the Lord your God is God supreme and Lord supreme, the great, the mighty, and the awesome God, who shows no favor and takes no bribe, but upholds the cause of the fatherless and the widow, and befriends the stranger, providing him with food and clothing. You too must befriend the stranger, for you were strangers in the land of Egypt (Deuteronomy 10:14–19).

Love, therefore, the Lord your God, and always keep His charge, His laws, His rules, and His commandments (Deuteronomy 11:1).

A covenant of mutual promises binds both parties only as long as they both abide by their agreement, and the intent of the covenant is to accomplish mutually beneficial goals. A covenant of love, on the other hand, is intended to establish a lasting relationship that will survive misdeeds by either party, for the purpose of the covenant is the relationship itself. As indicated above, the Torah describes God's covenant with Israel in both ways. Therefore, sometimes God calls Israel to account by punishing Israel severely for failing to abide by the terms of the covenant (e.g., Leviticus 26:14–43; Deuteronomy 28:15–29), and at other times God asserts that even when Israel strays, God will stick by the covenant in maintaining the loving and lasting relationship God formed with our ancestors, the patriarchs and matriarchs, in some sources on condition that Israel return to God's ways and in some sources even without the act of *teshuvah,* return (e.g., Leviticus 26:44–45; Deuteronomy 7:6–11; 30:1–10).

Compassion

As the passage cited from Deuteronomy 10 indicates, the covenant idea is not nearly as chauvinistic and narrow as it sounds. That is, while God's special love for, and covenant with, the Jewish people would seem to lead to the conclusion that Jews have duties to help only other Jews, that has not been the history of the covenant idea. According to the Talmud's count,[34] thirty-six times the Torah requires Jews to treat the alien within their midst fairly and even to love the stranger. This is rooted not only in a general, humanitarian feeling of sharing but also in the concrete experience of being strangers in Egypt:

> You shall not subvert the rights of the stranger or the fatherless; you shall not take a widow's garment in pawn. Remember that you were a slave in Egypt and that the Lord your God redeemed you from there; therefore do I enjoin you to observe this commandment ... When you gather the grapes of your vineyard, do not pick it over again; that shall go to the stranger, the fatherless, and the widow. Always remember that you were a slave in the land of Egypt; therefore do I enjoin you to observe this commandment (Deuteronomy 24:17–18, 21–22).

> The stranger who dwells with you shall be with you, and you shall love him as yourself. Just as the Torah says with regard to fellow Jews, "Love your neighbor as yourself" (Leviticus 19:18), so the Torah says with regard to aliens, "And you shall love him as yourself, for you were strangers in the Land of Egypt; [I am Adonai your God]" (Leviticus 19:34). [Therefore you must] know of the souls of strangers, for you were strangers in the Land of Egypt (*Sifra, Kedoshim* 8:4).

Aspirations to Holiness

Finally, a very different kind of reason to help those in need appears in Jewish sources: the aspiration to holiness. This is definitely not "do it—or else!" It is also not "do it because you promised" or "do it because you owe it to the members of your local or extended Jewish community." It is not even "do it out of love for God." It is rather "do it because that is the kind of person you should strive to be." This is not, in other words, the morality of owing God, of promise keeping, or of community involvement; it is rather the morality of aspiration, of doing something because that is the person I want to be and the kind of community of which I want to be a part. In theological terms, this translates into aspiring to be like God:

> The Lord spoke to Moses, saying: "Speak to the whole Israelite community and say to them: 'You shall be holy, for I, the Lord your God, am holy ...'" (Leviticus 19:1–2).

> I have made you a light of nations to be [the vehicle of] My salvation to the ends of the earth (Isaiah 49:6).

> Rabbi Hama, son of Rabbi Hanina, said: "What is the meaning of the verse, 'You shall walk behind the Lord your God' (Deuteronomy 13:5)? ... [It means that] a person should imitate the righteous ways of the Holy One, blessed be He. Just as the Lord clothed the naked, ... so too you must supply clothes for the naked [poor]. Just as the Holy One, blessed be He, visited the sick, ... so too you should visit the sick. Just as the Holy One, blessed be He, buried the dead, ... so too you must bury the dead. Just as the Holy One, blessed be He, comforted mourners, ... so too you should comfort mourners" (Babylonian Talmud, *Sotah* 14a).

In sum, then, the Jewish tradition provides multiple reasons to help those in need. In all human acts, we are motivated by many things, some more prominent in our consciousness and more compelling at the moment than others, perhaps, but all playing a role in getting us to do what we do. Furthermore, what goads us into action today may be different tomorrow. Thus, even though one particular ground for helping others may dominate one person's thinking and acting in this way, other motivations may nevertheless play a role and may, in fact, come to the fore at another place or time. So the Jewish tradition was wise in suggesting multiple reasons to help others in need.

3

Religion and Ethics

Many of the motivations to engage in *tikkun olam* delineated in the last chapter are religious: they invoke, for example, what God demands of us, our covenant with God, and striving to be holy like God. As stated earlier, some Jews will object to motivating acts of social justice in religious terms because they are atheistic or agnostic, and for them some of the other grounds mentioned in the previous chapter for doing *tikkun olam* may be more persuasive.

But even for those who affirm a belief in God, the religious foundation for much of Judaism's commitment to *tikkun olam* comes with problems of two sorts, one dealing with God and the other with human beings. God has not always been the moral paradigm we would expect, and so rooting a commitment to *tikkun olam* in God may strike some as building on quicksand. Furthermore, religious people—including religious leaders—have not always been moral models either, and sometimes they have committed immoral acts not just due to their own human failings but also in the name of religion.

God

The Jewish tradition affirms in many places that God is just and demands justice of us. So, for example, in his last address to his people, Moses proclaims: "The Rock, his works are pure, for all His ways are just" (Deuteronomy 32:4). Three times each day we recite this verse as part of the *Ashrei*: "The Lord (Adonai) is righteous in all His ways and faithful (kind) in all His acts" (Psalms 145:17).

Similarly, consider the following verses that we recite as part of *Kabbalat Shabbat* on Friday evenings: "He judges the peoples with equity … He will rule the world justly, and its peoples in faithfulness" (Psalms 96:10, 13); "Righteousness and justice are the base of His throne" (Psalms 97:2); "The heavens proclaim His righteousness" (Psalms 97:6); "He will rule the world justly, and its peoples with equity" (Psalms 98:9); "Mighty king who loves justice, it was You who established equity" (Psalms 99:4). Finally, in the psalm for the Sabbath, we read: "The Lord is upright, my Rock, in whom there is no wrong" (Psalms 92:16).

And then, of course, there are the verses we recite each weekday morning as we wrap the *tefillin* around our fingers:

> And I [God] will betroth you [the People Israel] forever:
> I will betroth you with righteousness *(tzedek)* and justice
>   *(mishpat)*,
> And with goodness *(chesed)* and mercy,
> And I will betroth you with faithfulness;
> Then you shall be devoted to the Lord.
>
> —*Hosea 2:21–22*

And yet there are parts of biblical and rabbinic literature that raise major questions about God's justice. Probably the most discussed biblical example is God's command to Abraham to take his son, Isaac, to be bound on the altar (Genesis 22:1–19), presumably to be killed there as a sacrifice of the firstborn to God, a rite typical of ancient religions. God, of course, stops Abraham from carrying out the murder, and the story may, in fact, be a clarion call *against* such sacrifice; but God's initial command to Abraham raises the hard question of whether we should obey God's command even if it is not moral. The nineteenth-century Protestant theologian Søren Kierkegaard proclaimed that we should; he used this story, in fact, as proof that sometimes there is a "teleological (or, perhaps, theological) suspension of the ethical," when we need to violate the norms that we human beings construe to be moral in obedience to an all-knowing and all-powerful (and good?) God. The Rabbis of the Talmud and Midrash shrank from such a conclusion, opting instead to interpret the story such that God never intended for Abraham to murder Isaac in the first place but only bind him to the altar as a mark of his faith and obedience. Still, one wonders why a good God would test Abraham so severely in the first place.

Retribution

Another famous instance of questionable justice on God's part occurs when God responds to the incidents of the golden calf and the ten spies who recommend against going forward to occupy the land of Canaan. In both places, God reveals that He "visits the iniquity of the parents upon the children and children's children, upon the third and fourth generations."[1] Similarly, the generation of the spies was told that "your children [will] roam the wilderness for forty years, *suffering for your faithlessness,* until the last of your carcasses is down in the wilderness" (Numbers 14:33; emphasis added). Biblical scholars describe this doctrine as "vertical retribution," in that God's punishment is transferred not horizontally in time to the other members of one's generation, but vertically through time to those of generations to come. In its positive form, in which people receive benefits as a result of what their ancestors did, the Rabbis call it *zekhut avot,* "the merit of the ancestors."

This offends our sense of justice, for we think that people should be responsible only for their own deeds. In human legal proceedings, the Torah demands that courts judge exactly that way.[2] Nevertheless, as discussed in the last chapter, this passage from the ten commandments describes correctly what in fact happens in people's lives, where we both benefit and suffer from what our ancestors have done and what our community is now doing; we do not live on isolated islands but are rather significantly affected by what other people do, however unfair that may seem.

What, though, does this say about God's justice? Shouldn't God have created the world so that it follows the same rule of just deserts for each individual that He demands of human courts? Consider the words of what is probably the oldest challenge to God's justice in human history, namely, Abraham's question to God in the case of Sodom:

> Will You sweep away the innocent along with the guilty? ...
> Far be it from You to do such a thing, to bring death upon
> the innocent as well as the guilty, so that innocent and guilty
> fare alike. Far be it from You! Shall the Judge of all the earth
> not act justly? (Genesis 18:23, 25)

The Bible considered this problem. One strand of biblical literature, associated by scholars with the Deuteronomic tradition, sought to resolve it by claiming that God only punishes the children *when they themselves are guilty* because they continue in the transgressions of their parents. Thus the two renditions of the ten commandments in the Torah—one in Exodus, chapter 20, and the other in Deuteronomy, chapter 5—both describe God in the same language quoted above, but they add identical, crucial phrases that modify the theology to preserve God's justice:

> You shall not make for yourself a sculptured image or any
> likeness of what is in the heavens above, or on the earth
> below, or in the waters under the earth. You shall not bow
> down to them or serve them. For I the Lord your God am an

impassioned God, visiting the guilt of the parents upon the children, upon the third and upon the fourth generation *of those who reject Me,* but showing kindness to the thousandth generation *of those who love Me and keep My commandments* (Exodus 20:4–6 and Deuteronomy 5:8–10, emphasis added).

This means of resolving the problem apparently entered into the consciousness of the masses because it is also articulated in the Book of Psalms, which was used in liturgical contexts:

But the Lord's steadfast love is for all eternity toward those who fear Him, and His beneficence is for the children's children *of those who keep His covenant and remember to observe His precepts* (Psalms 103:17–18; emphasis added).

This modification, however, only mitigated the problem; it did not solve it. For according to this revised theory, if the children continue in the path of their parents, they prosper or suffer not only for their own actions, but also for those of their parents. They now suffer in part for their own sins, but they still suffer for their parents' sins as well.

Another biblical tradition understood the doctrine of vertical retribution as an aspect of God's mercy. In some ways this is similar to the mentality that moderns have about credit cards: we consider it a favor not to have to pay now even though we know that the day of reckoning will ultimately come. In some passages, the Bible similarly considers God's willingness to delay punishment as a manifestation of mercy. God does this only if the sinner shows contrition and therefore merits the postponement. Thus, when King David has Uriah, the Hittite, killed in battle so that David can take Bathsheba as his wife, he admits his sin when confronted by the prophet Nathan, and thereby gains a reprieve. Nathan tells David, however, that his son will die for his sin (2 Samuel 12:13–14). King Ahab's punishment is also postponed, and there the wording of the rationale and the consequences is explicit: "Since he [Ahab] has humbled himself before Me, I will not bring disaster in his days; I will bring the disaster down on his house in the days of his son." (1 Kings 21:29).

Speaking in the name of God, the prophet Huldah applies the same theory to Josiah:

> "Because your heart was softened and you humbled your-self before the Lord when you heard what I decreed against this place and its inhabitants—that it will become a desola-tion and a curse—and because you rent your clothes and wept before Me, I, for My part, have listened," declares the Lord. "Assuredly, I will gather you to your fathers, and you will be laid in your tomb in peace. Your eyes shall not see all the disaster that I will bring upon this place" (2 Kings 22:19–20).

Although this theory is understandable on some levels, on others it simply compounds the problem. Parents who have any compassion whatsoever for their children will never want them to suffer, and certainly not for the parents' own sins. In light of these difficulties, one can understand why the prophets look forward to a world in which children will no longer suffer for the sins of their forbears:

> "See, a time is coming"—declares the Lord— ... "In those days, they shall no longer say, 'Fathers have eaten sour grapes and children's teeth are blunted,' but everyone shall die for his own sins: whosoever eats sour grapes, his own teeth shall be blunted (Jeremiah 31:27–30; see also Ezekiel 18:1–20).

Piety and Justice

Other morally troubling biblical stories depict God as hardening Pharaoh's heart, thus making him incapable of doing the right thing (Exodus 10:1, 27); punishing Saul for having mercy on the women and children of Amalek (1 Samuel 15); and killing Uzzah, who merely tried to save the holy ark from falling from a wagon and breaking apart (2 Samuel 6:6–8). The Rabbis added some morally problematic stories of their own, including, especially, the one of God showing Moses that Rabbi Akiva, despite his devotion to God and Torah, would be flayed by the Romans. When Moses protests, God answers, "Be quiet! So I have decided" (Babylonian Talmud, *Menachot* 29b).

Ultimately, the Rabbis admit, in the world God created, *tzadik v'ra lo, rasha v'tov lo,* "the righteous suffer, and the evil prosper" (Babylonian Talmud, *Berakhot* 7a), and the Rabbis therefore believed in a life after death in which a just God would rectify this unjust state of affairs. That is, they believed in a world to come primarily to preserve God's claim to justice.

If we look at this issue historically, we should not be surprised that such ambivalence about God's link to justice occurs in the tradition. After all, the gods of the ancient world were powerful, but generally not just. Greek and Roman myths about the gods are probably the most well known, but what was true of their gods was true of most other ancient people's gods as well. You had better obey them, for they could do you harm; you at least needed to find one god to defend you against some other god who was angry with you. Justice, though, was not the name of the game; it was rather pitting one power against another in order to survive and maybe even flourish. It was the Jews who gave Western civilization the idea that God was not only powerful but also just, as articulated in the passages cited above and in many other places. But the very texts that assert God's justice—the Bible and rabbinic literature—also describe God acting in seemingly immoral ways.

Philosophically, also, the belief in God's justice raises many issues. Plato already articulated the problem of the relationship between belief in God and morality in the *Euthyphro* (9–10), where Socrates asks, "Is the pious or holy beloved by the gods because it is [intrinsically] holy, or holy because it is loved by the gods?" In other words, is morality independent of religion, so that we recognize goodness on nonreligious grounds, and then God (or the gods) may or may not choose to do what is just; or is morality a function of religion, so that the good is defined by what the gods want—or, for us, what God wants? There (11–12) Socrates also asks, "Is, then, all that is just pious? Or, is that which is pious all just, but that which is just only in part, and not all, pious?" That is, do religion and morality cover the same ground, or is religion a subset of morality, such that there can be moral people who are not religious?

The Bible takes the position that morality is independent of God, because it allows for moral critiques of God's actions. Thus, in defending innocent people in Sodom and Gomorrah, Abraham stirringly proclaims, "Shall the Judge of all the earth not do justice?" That argument apparently works, for it convinces God to agree to save the cities if ten righteous people can be found in them.[3] Similarly, Job readily admits God's power, but he indignantly questions God's justice.[4] Neither of these passages would make sense unless one presumes that morality exists independent of God so that God can be morally called to account. Furthermore, descriptions of God as morally good in the passages with which this section began and elsewhere would be tautologies—that is, they would be saying simply that good is good—unless God and morality occupy separate realms. The fact that religion and morality are logically independent makes the tradition's assertion that God is morally good all the more powerful, for God then could possibly be morally bad or simply indifferent to moral claims but instead chooses to be morally good and thus serves as a paradigm for our own moral struggles.

Furthermore, God demands moral goodness of us. As Isaiah (late eighth century B.C.E.) put it, "The Lord of hosts is elevated through justice *(mishpat),* and the holy (powerful, awesome) God is sanctified through righteousness *(tzedakah)."*[5] That is, God, like the other gods of the ancient world, has power—indeed, more power than they have—but unlike them, God is worshiped not only through acts of submission, but also through justice. Thus God commands us in the Torah to live by several general moral principles, such as "love your neighbor as yourself," "do the right and the good in the eyes of God," and "justice, justice shall you pursue,"[6] but does not leave it to individuals to figure out how such general precepts are to be applied to the concrete situations of life. Instead, the Torah and, even more, the later rabbinic tradition spell out in very specific terms the morals God requires of us.

Although this last point is the subject of debate among Jewish thinkers, I am among those who maintain that the inherent morality of God requires rabbis in each generation to apply the law with moral norms in mind. This requires some explanation. Deuteronomy 17:8–13 says that when a Jew has a question about God's law, he or she should go to the judge of the time and obey that person's instructions. That passage establishes the authority of human judges in each generation to interpret and apply God's law. Because the Torah, unlike the American Constitution, specifically forbids amendment in Deuteronomy 4:2 and 13:1, the Rabbis used their judicial power expansively to enable Jewish law to deal with new circumstances and remain relevant through time. In this process, I contend, rabbis from the time of the Mishnah to our own era have been properly and importantly influenced by the understanding of God as morally good, for that requires that they interpret God's law in ways they construe to be moral. That is, Jewish theology has, and should have, a direct effect on Jewish law. The *extent* to which that is true, if it is at all, and *how* moral concerns should enter into legal debates are both matters of considerable debate among contemporary rabbis and Jews generally. I maintain that Jewish belief in a moral God has an important role to play in shaping the law and in motivating us to live by its demands.[7]

People

American presidents Washington, Jefferson, and Eisenhower, among others, believed that people would be moral only if they were religious, or, at least, that the chances of a person being moral were considerably greater if he or she was religious; to this day, most Americans associate religion with morality. At the same time, we are all aware that some self-proclaimed religious people act immorally. That might be attributed to human weakness. Much worse, then, is the fact that history and even contemporary times are replete with immoral and even morally grotesque acts done *in the name of* religion. Conversely, we all know avowed atheists who are nevertheless moral.

There is, then, no one-to-one mapping of morality onto religion; morality and religion are, indeed, different phenomena. Still, there are strong ties between these two realms of our experience. Some aspects of religion actually make morality harder, while other aspects of religion contribute mightily to our understanding of morality and our motivation to be moral. I discuss the relationships between religion and morality at length in the first chapters and the appendices of my three books on Jewish ethics: *Matters of Life and Death* on medical ethics; *To Do the Right and the Good* on social ethics; and, especially, *Love Your Neighbor and Yourself* on personal ethics. Here, it is sufficient to point out that while religious faith and practice do not guarantee morality, many features of Judaism make morality in general, and *tikkun olam* in particular, more likely to happen. Some of these features are discussed below.

Stories

Stories in the Jewish tradition from the Bible to our own time help us understand the obstacles that people face in life, some things that exacerbate those problems, and other things that ameliorate them. This is especially true for the core Jewish story, the Exodus from Egypt, receiving the Torah at Mount Sinai, and the trek to the Promised Land, for that story articulates powerfully the need to redeem people from their various forms of slavery—their Egypt, which, in Hebrew, comes from the root meaning "straits"— so that they can reshape their lives and move toward the Promised Land. But it is also true for many other Jewish stories that bid us to help others. Here is a touching and instructing modern one, Leo Lieberman's "Bubbie—*Tzedakah*, Discipline, and Arms Designed for Hugging":

> When I was five years old, I learned a lesson that has remained with me for my entire life.... It happened that Grandma (of course, we called her [by the Yiddish word for grandmother] "Bubbie") lived with us. She was well advanced in years, and in those days you didn't talk about putting the elderly members of the family in a Senior Citizen's Residence. (Think we even heard the phrase "senior citizen"?)
>
> All that I remember was that Bubbie did not speak English, that she was a wonderful baker and cook (what she could do with an onion, a carrot, a sweet potato, a—my mouth still waters), that her arms were designed for hugs and embraces, that she smelled warm and soft, and that I was the apple of her eye. We loved each other completely, and I knew that as far as my Bubbie was concerned, I could do no wrong. I could never do anything that was not absolutely perfect ... one hundred percent. Never. Until ...

And so the story. Each week, on Friday, Bubbie baked the special Shabbos Challahs ... And also sponge cake, honey cake, and cookies. (There goes the mouth watering again.) And then, hand-in-hand, we walked five blocks to the Hebrew Orphan Asylum on Clay Avenue in the Bronx.... She gave the delicacies to the Rebbe, a man of indeterminate age with a very determinate beard, and then she had a cup (actually, a glass) of tea while I went into the yard and played with the children who lived in the home. This happened every week. Shabbos came every week, and we went to the Hebrew Orphan Asylum each week.

Although I didn't particularly care for the time I spent with *those* children (they really weren't my friends), I somehow knew that this was my obligation, the cross (oops ...) I had to bear. But then came that Friday when I said, "No." I wasn't going to go with Bubbie. I preferred staying at home and playing with the little boy next door. So I said, "No."

For a minute there was silence, a silence like the sound of an angel's voice. Bubbie looked at me, and I looked at her. And then she spoke ... in halting and difficult English, a language that did not come easily, "You come."

I turned to Mama and Papa to enlist possible allies. But Papa had already retreated to the bathroom, newspaper in hand, and locked the door. This could be a long siege. Mama, who never argued with Bubbie—except maybe about whether to put an extra carrot in the chicken soup— started to defend my position. "Just this week ... he's only a child ... next week for sure" ... Bubbie didn't budge. Her eye was fixed on me, and all she did was repeat, "You come." And I knew that I had lost.

I tried one last maneuver, one final effort. I held out a few coins that I had been saving to help defray the cost of some desired toy. "Take this," I offered. "Put it in the *tzedakah* box." And then ... and then there came a flood of words. Bubbie let me have it with all the strength she could muster, a tirade of English that I never knew she possessed, so many English words and a few choice Yiddish expressions thrown in as well. How could I be so selfish ... to try to buy my way out of doing an act of kindness, doing a real *mitzvah,* being thoughtful to others, to offer a few pennies so that I could cut myself off from my own flesh ... When she finished I took her hand, and once again, hand-in-hand, we walked without speaking to Clay Avenue. The only time that this silence was broken was when Bubbie turned to me, and in a soft but firm accent said, "We do not speak of this again."

And we did not. And each week I went with Bubbie. And each week I played with the children when Bubbie had a glass of tea and delivered the Shabbos breads and cakes. Bubbie continued to hug me and tell me little stories about life in the old country and cradle me in her arms until three years later when she died and all the hugs stopped.

But the lesson remained. I know that as long as there is a child in the world who needs someone to play with, a child who is alone, I should wish most fervently that there would be someone who could hold out a hand to a more fortunate youngster and say, "You come."[8]

Why do stories help us see what we need to do to fix the world and move us to do so? Stories speak of concrete situations like the ones we face in life, and so we can immediately identify with them emotionally. They have the ability to play out a variety of possible reactions to life situations so that we can learn the likely implications of acting in one way or another. The biblical story of how Lot saved his male guests from sodomy by giving his daughters to the mob instead,[9] for example, illustrates both his nobility in protecting people and the highly problematic nature of the way he did so. Moreover, because stories describe life as we know it, in all its glory and messiness, we are likely to remember them much more than we do rules or abstract discussions. That is especially true when the stories are part of Jewish liturgy, so that we come across them many times during our lives. For all these reasons, stories can help us discern what we need to do to help others and motivate us to do so.

History

No nation that has gone through the exile and persecution endured by Jews can possibly have an idealistic picture of human beings; the evil that people have foisted on each other must be part of the Jewish perception of reality. This is, of course, all the more true after the Holocaust, which, among other things, makes Jews very much aware of the human penchant to harm others, even to the point of genocide. Jewish history, then, should make us all the more aware of the need to protect people from violence, starvation, and homelessness.

Despite their own poverty, Jewish communities did that historically to a remarkable degree—to the extent that Lancelot Addison, describing the Jews of Barbary in the seventeenth century, felt the need to dispel the belief prevalent at the time that "the Jews have no beggars." He attributes this error to the "regular and commendable" methods by which the Jews supplied the needs of their poor and "much concealed their poverty."[10] Jewish history gives us lessons based on Jewish relations with non-Jews as well. For example, while all too many of the non-Jews in Europe failed to come to the rescue of Jews during the Holocaust, some did, and they did so at the clear risk of their own lives and those of their families. These historical events, and many, many more, can and should help us see the need to help others and act on it.

Family and Community

We first learn what is acceptable behavior and what is not from our parents. They make us aware of the whole realm of moral norms. They also provide the first motivation to act morally as we try to please them. Thus, parents and, after them, siblings and other relatives are critical to the moral development of any human being. In fact, children who lack continual moral guidance from parents or other caring adults from infancy on are in serious danger of never understanding the moral dimension of life or acting morally. Judaism therefore takes care to buttress family life with commands that children honor and respect their parents and that, conversely, parents teach their children Torah as well as a trade.[11] Beyond these legal boundaries, Jewish family rituals are rich and pervasive, thus strengthening the family further, and this emphasis on the family has been translated into Jewish consciousness through such media as popular literature and even Jewish jokes about family relationships.

Many of us learn to be committed to *tikkun olam* from our family and friends. Parents can be an especially potent model for this. Chills ran down my spine when I was asked to become president of Jewish Family Service of Los Angeles because my father had been president of Jewish Family and Children's Service of Milwaukee. This was "from generation to generation" more graphically than either one of us could ever have imagined. His commitment and that of my mother to expend time, energy, and money to help people through that organization and many others, both because Judaism demanded it and because it was simply the right thing to do, had become my own conviction as well.

As children mature, they come into contact with the larger community. American communities are *voluntary*: you choose to affiliate or disaffiliate as you wish. Even American citizenship is voluntary: if you were not born in the United States, it is hard to become an American citizen, but unless you have committed a felony, you can renounce your citizenship at will. In contrast, Jewish sources understand the Jewish community as *organic,* such that one who is Jewish by birth or conversion can never stop being Jewish.

Although such tightly knit communities can have the negative effects of squelching independent moral analysis and action, thus making moral sensitivity and action more difficult, they can also have morally salutary effects. They can lead us to see all others as brothers and sisters whom we must help when they need it. Moreover, throughout life a strong part of our motivation to help others stems from our desire to have friends and to be part of a larger community. We also aspire to moral ideals, in part, because we crave the esteem of other people, especially those near and dear to us.

Leaders and Other Moral Models

Just as children learn morality first from their parents, so too adults learn to discern what is moral and gain the motivation to work for moral goals from their leaders and other moral models. Nobody is perfect, of course, and part of the task in seeking moral leadership is to understand that specific people may be ideal in certain ways and not in others. When some of our political or religious leaders are shown to have moral faults, that sometimes unfairly and unrealistically undermines our appreciation of their real moral leadership on other matters. Thus, the leadership in civil rights shown by presidents Kennedy and Johnson should not be forgotten just because they were each involved in morally questionable behavior in other aspects of their lives.

Similarly, Judaism uses leaders such as the patriarchs and matriarchs, Moses, other biblical characters, and rabbinic figures throughout the ages as models of ideal behavior generally and of doing acts of *tikkun olam* in particular. The Hasidic tradition is especially rich in its stories about such models. Similarly, teachers, counselors, friends, and even our children and students can show us how to behave. Although Rabbi Hanina (or Rabbi Judah Ha-Nasi) was probably referring to the intellectual knowledge of the Jewish tradition, his famous dictum can apply equally to the moral lessons we learn from it and specifically to our motivation to engage in *tikkun olam:* "Much have I learned from my teachers, more from my peers, but most from my students."[12]

General Values, Maxims, and Theories

Jewish sources announce some general moral values that should inform all our actions—values such as formal and substantive justice, saving lives, caring for the needy, respect for parents and elders, honesty in business and in personal relations, truth telling, and education of children and adults. The Torah's laws articulate some of these general moral values, and others find their way into books of moral maxims. The Book of Proverbs and the tractate of the Mishnah (c. 200 C.E.) titled *Ethics of the Fathers (Pirkei Avot)* are two important ancient reservoirs of Jewish moral precepts, and medieval and modern Jewish writers have produced some others, such as Moses Hayyim Luzzato's *Paths of the Righteous (Mesillat Yesharim).* These moral principles are often in the minds of people acting to fix the world.

In addition, some medieval and modern Jewish thinkers have formulated complete theories of morality, depicting a full concept of the good person and the good community, together with justifications for seeing them in that particular way and modes of educating people to follow the right path. Although some are more conducive to *tikkun olam* than others, some lead directly to social action. The modern French Jewish philosopher Emanuel Levinas, for example, maintains that the very presence of another human being immediately imposes on me the duty to work for his or her welfare.[13]

Theology

As in other Western religions, Judaism makes God central not only in defining the good and the right, but also in creating the moral person. God does this in several ways.

First, acting in judicial and executive functions, God helps assure that people will do the right thing. God is the infallible Judge, who knows "the secrets of the world," as the High Holy Days liturgy reminds us. Nothing can be hidden from God, and God cannot be deceived. Moreover, God holds the power of ultimate reward and punishment. To do the right thing just to avoid punishment or to gain reward is clearly not acting out of a high moral motive, but such actions may nevertheless produce good results. Moreover, the Rabbis state many times over that even doing the right thing for the wrong reason has its merit, for eventually correct moral habits may create a moral person who does the right thing for the right reason.[14]

God also contributes to the creation of moral character in serving as a model for us. As discussed in the first part of this chapter, the underlying conviction of the Bible is that God is good, and God's actions are, as such, paradigms for us. We, then, should aspire to be like God: "As God clothed the naked, ... so you should clothe the naked; as God visited the sick, ... so you should visit the sick; as God comforted those who mourned ... so you should comfort those who mourn; as God buried the dead, ... so you should bury the dead."[15]

God's role as covenant partner and as Israel's lover probably has the greatest effect on creating moral character within us and doing acts of *tikkun olam*. Our covenant with God is not only a legal document, with provisions for those who abide by it and those who do not, but the covenant also announces formal recognition of a *relationship* that has existed for a long while and that is intended to last, much as a covenant of marriage does. Relationships, especially intense ones like marriage, create mutual obligations that are fulfilled by the partners sometimes grudgingly but often lovingly, with no thought of a quid pro quo return. For God, as for a human marriage partner,[16] we should do what the norms of morality require, and then we should go "beyond the letter of the law" *(lifnim m'shurat ha-din)* to do favors for our beloved. In moral terms, we then become the kind of people who seek to do both right and good generally, and acts of *tikkun olam* in particular, not out of hope for reward but simply because that is the kind of people we are and the kind of relationships we have.

Prayer

Along with theology comes a life of prayer. Jews are commanded to pray three times each day, with four services on Sabbaths, festivals, and the New Year and five on the Day of Atonement. Aside from the spiritual nourishment, intellectual stimulation, aesthetic experience, and communal contact that Jewish prayer brings, it also serves several significant moral functions.

One of these is moral education. The Rabbis created a liturgical framework for both morning and evening services, with three biblical paragraphs constituting the *Shema,* and two one-line blessings before it and one after it. (In the evening, there are two blessings that follow the *Shema* in Israeli practice and three in the Diaspora.) Then, following the *Shema* and Its Blessings, there are nineteen one-line blessings constituting the *Amidah.* Thus, in three paragraphs and twenty-two (or twenty-three or twenty-four) lines, Jews have an easily memorized formula for learning the essence of Jewish belief, one that they repeat morning and evening every day (with the *Amidah* recited in the afternoon as well). In fact, this outline is as close as Judaism has ever gotten to a creed, an official statement of Jewish beliefs. The liturgy therefore serves as a handbook of Jewish theology for all Jews over time. This outline also serves to announce and rehearse some of Judaism's central moral values, including those of knowledge, forgiveness, health, justice, hope, and peace.

Moreover, the fixed liturgy reorients us to think about things from God's perspective. Even though the English word *prayer* denotes petition ("Do this, I pray"), and even though Jewish liturgy has room for asking God for things, the vast majority of the fixed liturgy praises and thanks God. This immediately tells Jews that they must get out of their egocentric concerns and think of life from God's vantage point. This alone should help them focus on the important things in life, including family and *tikkun olam*, rather than on the partial goods to which they may devote too much energy.

Study

I once heard a Reform rabbi talk about a project he had initiated in his synagogue in which he and a number of members would remodel a house or build one from scratch for a homeless family during one week each year. Because people were engaged in hard labor the entire day, he hesitated to suggest anything specific for the evenings. To his amazement, those who participated requested that they spend each evening in study of Jewish texts because they wanted to see their activities of the week as rooted in their Jewish commitments. Exactly how study can and should affect our moral thinking and action is a matter of some discussion among Jewish educational thinkers,[17] but study is an age-old way in which the Jewish tradition, much more so than most, gets us to think about life in general and our commitments to others in particular.

Law

All the aspects of the Jewish tradition discussed above can play a major role in helping Jews discern why and how they should engage in *tikkun olam*. The Jewish tradition, however, uses law to do that much more than most other traditions, with Islam and Confucianism close behind. Just as religion can generally aid in moral knowledge and action or impede it, depending upon how it is used, so too can law blind people to the need to do *tikkun olam* or enhance a person's understanding and motivation to engage in it. Here are some of the ways Jewish law can aid in morality in general and *tikkun olam* in particular:

- *Establish minimal requirements.* Law articulates what is minimally expected of people in a society. Because Jewish law creates quite a demanding set of moral standards, including many requirements to help the poor and others in need, Jewish law makes it clear that Jews really must engage in *tikkun olam.*
- *Articulate moral ideals and motivate people to work toward their actualization.* Jewish law, though, does not satisfy itself with establishing a floor of expectations; it also pushes us to aspire to become even better, reaching for an ideal. For example, even though the Torah acknowledges that "there never will cease to be needy ones in your land" (Deuteronomy 15:11), it does not allow us to remain complacent, but rather requires us to support the poor in a variety of ways. Similarly, the Torah announces the ideal of justice and also requires us by law to do a number of things in the quest for both procedural and substantive justice.
- *Weigh conflicting moral values.* Jewish law serves as a forum in which Jewish values that come into conflict can be weighed and a determination made as to which should supersede which. For example, Jewish law requires us to violate all of the Torah's commandments save three if that is necessary to save a human life.[18] The law not only makes such decisions, but it also provides a forum in which these conflicts can be discussed.
- *Give moral norms a sense of the immediate and the real.* Issues are often joined more clearly in court than they are in moral discussions or treatises. That is because in court, the details of the specific situation are made clear. Second, in court people have the responsibility to make a decision, and

that requires them to be absolutely serious about the positions they take; after all, people's lives and fortunes may hang in the balance. Making social policies comes close to the level of responsibility assumed by a judge or a jury, but in that process the ways in which a decision will affect actual people may be less obvious than when the parties are standing in front of you in court.

- *Provide a balance of continuity and flexibility.* Unlike moral principles, laws and judgments are open to change, and that gives them the necessary malleability to adjust to changing sensitivities and circumstances. On the other hand, as a social product, laws have a certain staying power, thus providing a sense of continuity in moral norms; they are not subject to change as a result of one person's whim.

- *Serve as an educational tool for morality.* Obeying the law teaches us what society (or, in the case of a religious legal system such as Jewish law, God) expects of us.

- *Provide a way to make amends and repair moral damage.* Nobody is perfect, and so we all have the need to find a way to make amends for what we did wrong. Jewish law gives us such a way in the process of *teshuvah,* return, through which we can repair whatever damage we did as much as possible and return to the good graces of God and human society.

In all these ways, then, Judaism can and does contribute to our moral knowledge and action. There are no guarantees in life—except for death and taxes, as the quip goes—and so religious people may falter and sometimes even misinterpret religion to justify immoral acts. But Judaism provides a multitude of ways to help us know how to act morally and to motivate us to do so. It thus increases the probability that Jews can be the holy people that God expects of us: "Indeed, all the earth is mine, but you shall be to Me a kingdom of priests and a holy nation" (Exodus 19:6).

Part Two

Tikkun Olam for Individuals and Society

4

How We Talk to Each Other

The Power of Words

On Yom Kippur (the Day of Atonement), the holiest day of the Jewish year, at each of the five services of the day, Jews recite a long litany of sins for which we ask God's forgiveness. A large proportion of that list involves sins we commit through speaking. Clearly, then, the Jewish tradition takes the ethics of speaking very seriously. In fact, the Rabbis of the Talmud note that if one embarrasses someone else in public, the victim's face often turns white, and they compare that to the pale face of the dead so as to say that embarrassing a person is akin to killing him or her:

> Someone taught before Rabbi Nahman bar Isaac: "If a man put his neighbor to shame, it is as if he shed blood." Rabbi Nahman said to him: "Well have you spoken, for we see how the red disappears [in the victim's face] and the pallor comes" (Babylonian Talmud, *Bava Metzia* 58b).

In fact, they go further: such a remark also "kills" both the speaker and the listener. The Rabbis therefore call slander "the third tongue" *(lishan telitae)* because "it slays three people: the speaker, the listener, and the one spoken about" (Babylonian

Talmud, *Arakhin* 15b). Not only do speech violations cause death but they also deprive a person of a place in the world to come:

> There are four great sins that correspond to four great virtues [studying Torah, honoring parents, acts of loving-kindness *(gemilut chasadim),* and making peace between one person and another], in that a person is punished for them in this world, and their capital, or stock, remains in the form of punishment dealt out to him or her in the world to come. These four are idolatry, incest, murder, and slander, the last of which is as bad as all the other three put together (Jerusalem Talmud, *Peah* 1:1 [15d]).

As the Book of Proverbs succinctly puts it, "Death and life are in the hands of the tongue" (Proverbs 18:21).

Words obviously are not altogether a bad thing; like all our other faculties, the moral quality of our speech depends on how we use it. The following rabbinic story makes this point eloquently:

> Rabbi Shimon ben Gamliel said to his servant Tabbai: "Go to the market and buy me good food." He went out and brought back a tongue. He told him, "Go out and bring me bad food from the market." He went out and brought him a tongue. He then asked him: "Why is it that when I said 'good food' you brought me a tongue, and when I said 'bad food' you also brought me a tongue?" He replied: "It is the source of good and evil. When it is good, it cannot be surpassed; when it is evil, then there is nothing worse" (*Leviticus Rabbah* 33:1).

The Misuse of Words

We human beings have been quite creative in developing ways to misuse words, and, as the Yom Kippur liturgy reminds us, we therefore have to be especially careful in how we speak about and to others. We have to take such precautions because we must have respect for others and care for them for all the reasons described in chapter 2. Moreover, as people created in the image of God, we must have respect for ourselves as well; when we abuse our power to speak, we besmirch ourselves as well as the people to or about whom we are speaking.

In making those values concrete, the Rabbis warn us against all of the following forms of speech.

Foul Language *(nivvul peh)*

People use swear words to dishonor others and/or to emphasize some point that they are trying to make. Degrading others is prohibited by Jewish tradition for the reasons discussed in chapter 2: we do not have to like everyone, and we certainly do not have to approve of what everyone does, but we must respond to others—even when condemning their behavior—with respect for the image of God within them.

If the point of using foul language is to stress how intensely one feels about a given point, that use of language involves several problems. First, if one does that often—some teenagers and adults use foul language in virtually every sentence—then verbal inflation takes place and the swear words lose their power. Nobody recognizes that your swear words indicate that you feel especially strongly about a given topic if you use them too much; it is like "crying wolf."

Furthermore, people with a good education can express intense feelings without using foul language, and they are well advised to do so. Nobody respects you more because of your use of swear words; at best, good friends will excuse that behavior. Thus, just as much as respect for others demands that one avoid swearing, so too does self-respect.

Another factor reinforces the point that one should desist from using foul language to protect one's own self-respect. An article assigned in my college freshman English course argued that the swear words various societies use bespeak the aspects of life that they find troubling. In the United States, with its Puritan heritage, foul language is primarily sexual. In Germany, with its focus on cleanliness, swear words are based on bathroom functions. Italians swear using various epithets for the Church. For American Jews, this means that when people swear, they are revealing their discomfort with their own sexual functioning.

From a Jewish perspective, this analysis points to yet another reason obscenities are problematic. Our bodies, including their sexual parts, are, according to Jewish sources, made by God no less than our minds, our emotions, our wills, and all other parts of our inner being (our "souls"). Consequently, to use sexual terms to curse or denigrate others is not only to insult the people at whom the remarks are directed but also to slur God.

Finally, obscenities befoul the social atmosphere, making it rough and uncouth rather than respectful and polite. It is, as this source suggests, a form of pollution: "Rabbi Elazar ben Jacob said: 'A person who uses rough language is like a pipe spewing foul odors in a beautiful room'" (*Derekh Eretz Rabbah* 3:3).

The Rabbis undoubtedly had many of these factors in mind when they ascribed many maladies to using foul language:

> Because of the sin of using foul language *(nivvul peh),* problems increase and harsh decrees are instituted, and the youth of Israel die,[1] orphans and widows shout out and there is nobody to answer them, as it says (Isaiah 9:16–17), "That is why my Lord will not spare their youths, nor show compassion to their orphans and widows; for they are ungodly and wicked, and every mouth speaks impiety ... For all this His anger has not turned back, and His arm is outstretched still." What does "His arm is outstretched still" mean? Rabbi Hanan bar Abba said: "Everyone knows why

a bride enters the bridal canopy, but even though it had been decreed in heaven that a person should live seventy good years, if he dirties his mouth [by describing the couple's ensuing sex] with foul language, he causes that decree to be reversed." Rabbah bar Sheilah said in the name of Rabbi Hisda: "Anyone who uses foul language falls deeper into hell, as it says, 'The mouth that speaks perversity [others: of a forbidden woman] is a deep pit'" (Proverbs 22:14). Rabbi Nahman bar Isaac said, "Also for one who hears and is silent [does not protest], for it is said [in the next part of the same verse], 'He who is doomed by the Lord [for not protesting] falls into it'" (Proverbs 22:14).

—*Babylonian Talmud,* Shabbat *33a (see also Babylonian Talmud,* Ketubbot *8b)*

Moses Hayyim Luzzato (1707–1746, Italy), in his book *Mesillat Yesharim* (*The Path of the Just,* [or "Upright" or "Righteous"]), describes swearing and listening to it as prostituting the mouth and ear. He cites the Jerusalem Talmud, which, based on a play on words between *davar* (thing) and *debbur* (words), makes swearing nothing less than a violation of the Torah:

With regard to prostitution of the mouth and the ear, that is, speaking words of prostitution (*z'nut,* obscenities) or listening to them, our Sages "screamed like cranes" (Jerusalem Talmud, *Terumot* 1:4 [6b], that is, emphatically denounced such actions) in saying, "Let God not find anything unseemly among you' (Deuteronomy 23:15), that is, unseemly words," which is befouling one's mouth *(nivvul peh)* ... If one would gain your ear and tell you that the Sages said what they did about obscene speech only to frighten you and to draw you far from sin, and that their words apply only to hot-blooded individuals who, by speaking obscenities, would be aroused to lust, but not to those who air them only in jest, who have nothing whatever to fear—tell him that his words are those of the evil inclination; for the Sages have adduced an explicit verse in support of their statements (Isaiah 9:16): "That is why my Lord will not spare their youths, nor show compassion to their orphans and widows; for they are all flatterers and speakers of evil, and every mouth speaks impiety ... " This verse mentions neither idol worship, nor illicit relations, nor murder, but flattery and slander and obscene utterance, all sins of the mouth in its capacity of speech; and it is because of these sins that the decree went forth ... The truth, then, is as our Rabbis of blessed memory have stated, that uttering obscenities constitutes the very "nakedness" of the faculty of speech and was prohibited as an aspect of fornication along with all other such forms of it. Although outside the realm of illicit relations themselves (as indicated by the fact that [the penalty for] obscene speech is not as harsh as it is for illicit sexual relations, [which is] being cut off from the Jewish People [*karet*] or the death penalty), obscene speech is nonetheless prohibited in itself, apart from its leading to immoral sexual acts, as explained above in the analogy from the law concerning the Nazarite.[2]

Lies *(sheker)*

Telling lies—that is, knowingly and intentionally telling someone something that you know to be false—undermines people's trust in one another. Indeed, at the extreme—that is, if everyone lied so often that one could never assume that the next person was telling the truth—social cooperation, commerce, and even friendships and family relations would become impossible. We would all be living in a fantasy world, and a terrifying one at that. It is not surprising, then, that the Torah specifically prohibits lying: "You must not carry false rumors (*shaima shav,* literally, "worthless words to be heard") … Keep far from falsehood *(sheker)*" (Exodus 23:1, 7) and "You shall not steal; you shall not deal deceitfully nor lie to one another" (Leviticus 19:11).

The Rabbis understood the social consequences of lying: "This is the penalty for the liar: even when he tells the truth, no one believes him" (Babylonian Talmud, *Sanhedrin* 89b). They also condemned it as a form of theft, indeed the worst form of theft: "Stealing a person's thought [*genevat da'at,* i.e., deception] is the worst form of theft" (Tosefta, *Bava Kamma* 7:8).

Why did the Rabbis think of lying as the worst form of theft? Why is it worse than stealing money or property from a person? One answer is that even though people who have been robbed often feel personally violated, in the end it is one's property that the thief has encroached upon, not one's person. Often the thief does not even know the person from whom he or she has stolen. Deception, though, is immediately and directly personal: the liar did not think enough of you to tell you the truth, and so you rightly feel dishonored and molested. We will see below how the Rabbis make the same kind of distinction between one's property and person with regard to slander.

Of course, sometimes one tells a falsehood without knowing and without intending to do so. In such cases, the level of moral culpability is much less; one has simply made a mistake. Nevertheless, the Rabbis warn us against our very human desire to be seen as someone who knows everything, for that may lead us to give people false information: "Teach your tongue to say 'I do not know,' lest you invent something and be trapped" (Babylonian Talmud, *Berakhot* 4a).

"I do not know" is a really important sentence to make part of one's common speech patterns, for then the hearer knows exactly how much you trust what you say if you then venture a guess. Under those circumstances, nobody is deceived. The hearer may just accept the guess or suggest one of his or her own if the matter does not mean very much to either person. On the other hand, if the hearer really needs to know the answer for some practical or personal purpose, the speaker has put him or her on notice that even though the speaker *thinks* that the answer is X, the hearer will have to go elsewhere to find out conclusively. That is, by saying "I do not know," the speaker has transferred responsibility for discovering the answer back to the hearer. Doctors, for example, can sometimes tell patients exactly what is wrong and what needs to be done, and then they should surely do so. Often, however, the diagnosis or prognosis is much less clear, and then patients feel more respected if the doctor acknowledges that fact, sometimes even suggesting that the patient consult another doctor, than if the doctor pretends to know what he or she really does not know.

Does such an admission, though, undermine our own self-respect and the honor that others will give us? Not really, for in our heart of hearts we realize that none of us is all-knowing, as God is believed to be. Therefore, one should not be embarrassed to admit not knowing something. Even if the question is in the hearer's area of expertise, the questioner will appreciate an honest admission of a lack of knowledge—especially if the person asked then goes to the trouble to find the answer, if one is known. Honesty about what one knows and does not know is always the best policy so that one can avoid telling even unintended falsehoods and thus be trusted.

Gossip (rekhilut)

The Hebrew word for gossip comes from the root *rokhel*, which means a peddler. Gossips spread news about people, just as peddlers hawk their wares. Even though gossip, by definition, consists of truths about other people—or, at least, what the speaker thinks is true—and even though the speaker tells of matters that do not in and of themselves degrade the person being described, nevertheless the

Torah forbids spreading gossip: "Do not spread tales *(lo talekh rakhil)* among your people" (Leviticus 19:16).

Unfortunately, the Torah is not clear about what it is prohibiting. What, then, is gossip, and how does it differ from ordinary conversations in which friends sometimes describe what other people are doing?

The Mishnah identifies at least one aspect of gossip that is interdicted, and it quotes a verse from the Torah and another from the Book of Proverbs that uses the same Hebrew phrase *(holekh rakhil)* to make its point:

> How do we know that when one of the judges leaves the court, he may not say [to the litigant who lost the case], "I voted to acquit you, but my fellow judges made you liable. What could I do, given that my colleagues outnumbered me?" On such speech the Torah says, "Do not spread tales among your people," and the Bible says, "One who spreads tales reveals secrets [but a trustworthy soul keeps a confidence]" (Proverbs 11:13).
>
> —*Mishnah*, Sanhedrin *3:7*

Maimonides expands on this example when he offers a more general definition of gossip and describes its consequences:

> One who spreads rumors about someone else violates the negative commandment, "Do not spread tales among your people" (Leviticus 19:16). And even though we do not whip a person who violates this negative commandment [despite the fact that flogging is the usual punishment for violating a negative commandment], nevertheless it is a great sin and causes the killing of many souls of Israel. Therefore, this part of the verse is juxtaposed to the next part, "Do not stand idly by the blood of your brother." Go and learn from

what happened to Do'eg the Adumean [whose disclosure of information to Saul led to the killing of eighty-five innocent men and their wives and children: 1 Samuel 22, 23].

What is "a tale-bearer"? It is someone who claims things and goes from one person to another, saying: "This is what so-and-so said," and "This is what I heard about so-and-so." Even if it is true, such speech destroys the world.
—*Maimonides,* Mishneh Torah, Laws of Ethics (De'ot)
7:1–2

Although Maimonides clarifies some things, he leaves us with two important questions: First, does this verse prohibit ordinary conversation? Second, why do the forms of speech Maimonides is describing "destroy the world"?

Obviously, if this prohibition of tale bearing is interpreted to mean that we cannot speak to each other about the normal things that are going on in our lives, including news about other people, it will set an impossible demand. Moreover, it would do clear harm, because part of the way we satisfy our deep need for companionship is by talking with one another, and some of those conversations naturally center on the people in our lives.

What, then, is true speech about others that is not negative and yet "destroys the world"? Maimonides' own example indicates one type of such speech. Do'eg revealed to Saul that David had been in the city of Nob, a city of priests *(kohanim)* and their families, and that one of the priests there had prayed for David and had given him provisions and the sword of Goliath. This led to the deaths of the entire community, for the priests did not know that King Saul saw David—and therefore also anyone who supported him—as an enemy. Sometimes, then, true speech about people can ultimately harm them if the hearer wants to do that.

Rabbi Joseph Telushkin[3] suggests another kind of true speech that can have bad consequences—namely, great praise. Sometimes, as he points out, great praise for a person can be accompanied by mentioning the one thing that the speaker does not like about the person, and then the only thing that anyone remembers is the negative factor.

The folktale in the first two chapters and the last chapter of the Book of Job combines both of these problems. God heaps praises on Job before Satan, who clearly wants to harm Job. God's praise sets the stage for Satan to challenge Job's piety; Satan gets God to test Job by inflicting all sorts of tragedies on him. Although the story ends with Job triumphing, his life certainly would have been better without incurring the misfortunes in the first place. Because we can never know who likes or dislikes whom, except, perhaps, among our closest friends, the best policy is to share as little as possible about other people, especially in the company of people we do not know well.

The lesson, then, is that one must beware what hearers will make of information about another person, even when it is true and even when the speaker intends no ill. This is especially true when in the company of people one does not know well, where the less said about other people, the better. The more one knows the listener, the more one can share about family and friends, and so normal conversation with such people is fine. Frictions often exist, though, even among family and friends, and so even in that context one must tailor one's remarks to the listener in order to avoid bad consequences for the person described.

Slurs (lashon ha'ra) and Slander (motzi shem ra)

The Jewish tradition is harsher still in its condemnation of negative remarks about another person. While saying false, negative things about a person (slander) is obviously problematic, in most situations Jewish law also prohibits negative comments that are true (slurs). It even prohibits comments that are not themselves defamatory but imply negative things about someone (*avak lashon hara*, "the dust of saying bad things" or "the dust of slurs"). Maimonides defines these prohibitions this way:

> There is a sin much greater than this [that is, greater than telling tales about someone else], and it is included in this negative prohibition, namely, slurs (literally, "talk about the bad," *lashon hara*). That is someone who talks negatively about someone else, even if he speaks the truth. But one who [additionally] tells lies is called "one who spreads a bad name" *(motzi shem ra)* about someone else. One who engages in such slander sits and says: "So-and-so did this," "So-and-so were his ancestors," "I heard such-and-such about him," all of which are [false and] defamatory. For such a person Scripture says, "May the Lord cut off all flattering lips, every tongue that speaks arrogance" (Psalms 12:4).
>
> The Sages said [Jerusalem Talmud, *Peah* 1:1 (15d)]: "For three sins, a person is punished in this world, and he has no place in the world to come: idolatry, incest/adultery, and murder—and slander is like all of them combined."
>
> There are also words that are "the dust of slurs" *(avak lashon hara)*. How so? If A says to B, "Who would have ever thought that C would be as he is now?" Or A says, "Don't ask about C; I don't want to tell you what happened," and similar talk. Also, anyone who compliments a person in front of his enemies speaks the dust of slander, for that [positive talk] will cause his enemies to speak negatively of him. About such speech Solomon said: "He who greets his fellow loudly early in the morning shall have it reckoned to

him as a curse" (Proverbs 27:14), for from his compliment comes defamation. Similarly, one who slurs another through a joke or frivolity, that is to say, he does not speak in hatred [but nevertheless insults a person engages in the dust of slander]. This is what Solomon in his wisdom said: "Like a madman scattering deadly firebrands, arrows, is one who cheats his fellow and says, 'I was only joking'" (Proverbs 26:18–19). Similarly, someone who slurs someone through deceit, as, for example, he speaks innocently as if he did not know that what he was saying was a slur, and when people protest, he says, "I did not know that this is a slur or that So-and-so did that" [when he in fact does know the defamatory character of what he was saying is a person who engages in the dust of slurs].

All these are people who slur others. It is forbidden to live in their neighborhood, and even more to sit with them and listen to them. "The decree against our ancestors in the wilderness [to wander in the wilderness for forty years] was sealed only because of the slur [of the Land of Israel by the ten spies described in Numbers 14]" (Babylonian Talmud, *Arakhin* 15b).

—*Maimonides,* Mishneh Torah,
Laws of Ethics (De'ot) *7:2–4, 6*

Spreading false, negative comments about people—that is, slandering them—clearly attacks their integrity and reputation, and that is, as Maimonides says, akin to murder. But even slurs—that is, true but negative comments about someone *(lashon hara)*—can be nothing less than lethal. Oliver Sipple is a woeful case of this. Sipple, an ex-Marine who saved the life of President Gerald Ford by deflecting the gun directed at him by Sara Jane Moore, became an instant national hero. Despite his request to reporters, "Don't publish anything about me," many noted in their articles that Sipple was active in the gay community. This led to rejection by his parents, who had not known about that aspect of his life—even to the point of his father telling him that he was not welcome at the funeral of his mother—which, in turn, led Sipple to drink heavily and to die alone at age forty-seven. The reporter who first publicized Sipple's homosexuality made this postmortem comment: "If I had to do it over again, I wouldn't."[4]

Note that this case illustrates that what constitutes negative information depends largely on how the hearers will respond to it. After all, being gay is not in and of itself a bad thing; for many people now, it is simply a fact of life, like the fact that some people have blue eyes and some have brown eyes. Sipple knew, though, that his parents would think ill of him if they found out that he was gay, and that was all that mattered.

The prohibition of uttering negative speech applies all the more if everyone knows that what the person is saying is negative, for then there is a clear intention to defame a person. *We may not defame a person, for we are required to respect each and every person as being created in the image of God:*

> Ben Azai said, "This is the record of Adam's line. [When God created man, He made him in the likeness of God; male and female He created them]" (Genesis 5:1–2). This is a great principle in the Torah. Rabbi Akiva said: "Love your neighbor as yourself" (Leviticus 19:18). This is a great principle of the Torah, for one should not say that since I have been shamed, let my fellow person be shamed with me, since I have been disgraced, let my fellow person be disgraced with me. Rabbi Tanhuma said: "If you did so, know whom you are shaming, for 'God made him [the human being] in the likeness of God'" (Genesis 5:1).
>
> —Genesis Rabbah *24:7*

Rabbi Eleazar said: "Cherish your fellow human's honor as your own" (Mishnah, *Avot* 2:15 [2:10 in some editions]).

So great is human dignity that it supersedes a negative commandment of the Torah (Babylonian Talmud, *Berakhot* 19b).

The respect demanded by the Jewish tradition for each and every human being does *not* mean that we must accept everything that anyone does. After all, the Torah is filled with laws that categorize certain forms of human behavior as prohibited and others as required, and if Jews fail to abide by those laws, the Torah demands, "Reprove your kinsman and bear no guilt because of him" (Leviticus 19:17). But that reproof must be given in private so as not to disgrace the person in public, and it must be done constructively and with respect for the ultimate human dignity inherent in each of us. The Torah applies this even to someone who is to be flogged for violating a negative commandment: "He may be given forty lashes, but not more, lest being flogged further, to excess, your brother be degraded before your eyes" (Deuteronomy 25:3). Certainly, then, in everyday speech we must respect the dignity of each person by avoiding defamatory speech, even if the negative information is true, and all the more if it is false.

When, though, *may* one say something negative about someone else? Indeed, when *should* one do so?

One may share negative information with someone else—and one *should* do so—when the hearer will be making practical decisions based on that information. If, for example, A has asked you to write a letter of recommendation for him or her to be sent to B, a potential employer, you have a duty to B to be honest about A's qualifications for the job as you see them. Presumably, A would not ask you unless A thinks that you will be generally positive, but even if that is true, you should share with B whichever of A's weaknesses you anticipate will affect A's performance at that job. (You should also be sure to indicate where you have no grounds for assessment about how A would function in specific aspects of the job so that B will not think that by not mentioning those areas you want to indicate that you evaluate A negatively in those respects.) If you really do not think that A is qualified, you may want to tell A that and refuse to write the letter. The same would apply to letters of recommendation for schools.

Note that here the Jewish tradition demands more honesty than what currently happens under American law, where many employers are reticent to share negative information—and sometimes even positive information—about a former employee lest they be sued. Similarly, teachers will write honestly about a former student—or agree to write at all—only if the student waives his or her rights under the Buckley Amendment to see the letter of recommendation. Jewish law requires people who have been asked about a person applying for a job or for acceptance to a school to be honest and forthcoming about both the positive and the negative things they know, because such information has practical implications for the potential employer or school. To refuse to do that, or to lie in favor of the person, ultimately harms the third party, and that we may not do.

Another kind of situation in which a person should say something negative about someone else is if that person is doing something wrong. That is precisely the case where the Torah demands that we reprove someone. In the extreme, where the person is misleading people into worshiping other gods, the Torah demands that even the closest of relatives shun the person and contribute to the person's death:

> If your brother, your own mother's son, or your son or
> daughter or the wife of your bosom, or your closest friend
> entices you in secret, saying, "Come let us worship other

gods"—whom neither you nor your fathers have experienced—from among the gods of the peoples around you, either near to you or distant, anywhere from one end of the earth to the other, do not assent or give heed to him. Show him no pity or compassion, and do not shield him, but take his life. Let your hand be the first against him to put him to death, and the hand of the rest of the people thereafter. Stone him to death, for he sought to make you stray from the Lord your God, who brought you out of the land of Egypt, out of the house of bondage. Thus all Israel will hear and be afraid, and such evil things will not be done again in your midst (Deuteronomy 13:7–12).

Although Jewish courts no longer have the authority to execute people, presumably if someone is leading Jews astray theologically (e.g., Jews for Jesus) or morally (e.g., to take drugs or to harm someone), then we clearly *must* argue against what they advocate, maybe even to the point of suggesting (or, in the case of family or close friends, urging or even demanding) that one stay away from such people.

Along these lines, some recent research suggests that complaining publicly about slackards or those who threaten a group's identity or success in other ways can have the positive effects of defining group membership and reinforcing group norms. It also alerts people, especially newcomers, to guard against those in the group who are not reliable or trustworthy. These cases involve speaking negatively about others to avoid a clear harm, not just for the sake of feeling superior. The research indicates, though, that sometimes gossip and slurs function in a socially and psychologically healthy way even when all they do is relieve loneliness and self-doubt by confirming that other people are having the same problems you are.[5] Defining the line where such speech becomes prohibited *lashon ha-ra* is not always easy.

Oppressive Speech (ona'at devarim)

Aside from lies and slander, which one might have guessed would be banned in Jewish law, and aside from telling tales, negative truths, and even the "dust" of such language, about which readers might not have thought previously, Jewish law bans another form of speech that it calls "oppressive." The foundation for this prohibition is two verses in the Torah that assert that we must not wrong one another: "When you sell property to your neighbor, or buy any from your neighbor, you shall not wrong one another" (Leviticus 25:14); and "Do not wrong one another, but fear your God; for I, the Lord, am your God" (Leviticus 25:17). The Rabbis, following the interpretive principle that nothing in the Torah is superfluous or redundant, determine that the first verse applies to wronging one another in material goods, as the context suggests, and the second, which actually ends the same section about buying and selling, nevertheless refers to wronging people through words:

> Our Rabbis taught: "'Do not wrong one another' (Leviticus 25:17). Scripture refers to verbal wrongs." "You say verbal wrongs, but perhaps that is not so but rather monetary wrongs is meant?" "When Scripture says, 'You shall not wrong one another' (Leviticus 25:14), monetary wrongs are already dealt with. Then to what can I refer 'Do not wrong one another' (Leviticus 25:17)? To verbal wrongs" (Babylonian Talmud, *Bava Metzia* 58b).

The Mishnah and Talmud then define what is included in this ban on verbal oppression:

> Just as there is wronging others in buying and selling, so too there is wronging others done by words. [So, for example,] one must not ask another, "What is the price of this article?" if he has no intention of buying. If a person

repented [of his sin], one must not say to him, "Remember your former deeds." If a person is a child of converts, one must not say to him, "Remember the deeds of your ancestors," because it is written [in the Torah], "You shall neither wrong a stranger nor oppress him" (Exodus 22:20).

—*Mishnah,* Bava Metzia *4:10 [58b]*

Note several things about this list. First, in the Mishnah, it is not oppressive to ask a merchant the price of an object if one is thinking of buying something like it, even if not for a while. It is also not oppressive speech to ask the price if you know that a friend of yours is in the market for such an object and you will convey to him or her how much it costs at a given store. After all, the merchant's business is to sell the object, and sellers know that buyers have the right to compare prices from one shop to another. The only time asking the price becomes oppressive is if you or anyone you know has no intention of buying such an object now or in the near future. For example, if you have nothing to do on a given day and decide to spend your time looking around stores with no money or intention of buying anything, then asking the price of anything is oppressive. Alternatively, if you just bought something and see the same thing in another store and ask the price to see whether you got a bargain, that is oppressive. In both cases, you are stealing the merchant's time and deceiving him or her into thinking there is a chance for a sale. As the Talmud adds, in the end only those asking prices know whether they are doing so legitimately or not, and so the verse forbidding verbal oppression ends with "and you shall fear your God," who presumably knows what people are thinking when they ask a price.

The Mishnah's second example is really rather remarkable. The Jewish tradition demands quite a lot of someone who has harmed another person by requiring the wrongdoer to complete the process of return *(teshuvah)* described in Jewish sources. That process includes acknowledgment of one's wrongdoing, remorse expressed in words to the harmed party, compensation to the victim to the extent that that is possible, and, ultimately, better behavior when the same kind of situation arises again.[6] In some ways, this is even harder than serving time in prison, for some convicts never acknowledge that they have done anything wrong, let alone try to make amends to the people they have hurt. Once a person has completed the process of *teshuvah,* however, this Mishnah demands that people in society not even mention the person's former troubles with the law, for that would be to engage in oppressive speech. Why? Because one would label the person by his or her former offense, undermine and distrust the process of return, and deny the person the possibility of righting his or her former wrong and taking on a new, better identity—writing a new personal script, as it were. This Mishnah thus starkly contrasts with the practice in many American states, where former convicts have to list their convictions on any job application, are ineligible to apply for any government job, and, in some states, lose the right to vote.

As we saw earlier with regard to negative but true speech, however, there is an exception to this rule. If the person applies for a job that entails dealing with situations similar to the one in which he or she committed the offense and thus would tempt him or her to do the same thing again, people who know of the person's past may describe the offense, and potential employers may refuse to take the chance of exposing the person to the same temptations again. In fact, such people have a duty to take these steps to protect other people and even the applicant, for the Rabbis interpret "do not place a stumbling block before the blind" (Leviticus 19:14) to include not only those who are physically blind but those who are morally blind as well.[7] So, for example, people may tell potential employers at a school, camp, or youth group that they should not hire a given person because he or she has abused children in the past.[8]

Finally, the Mishnah's third example—not to remind converts to Judaism of their former religious affiliation and that of their family—may seem strange to modern Jews. After all, the Jewish community has come to know and welcome many Jews by choice, and it is not particularly embarrassing for such people to acknowledge the religious heritage of their past and that of their family. Still, this passage clearly warns us against doing what some Jews still do—namely, talking to and about Jews by choice as if they were not really Jews. They are fully Jews, and any aspersions cast on their Jewish identity (often by Jews who are less religious than the Jew by choice) are forbidden as oppressive speech, aside from being just plain nasty. Furthermore, any words asserting that Jews by choice behave or think in a particular way that does not follow typical Jewish ethnic patterns and is therefore "goyish" is also interdicted by this Mishnah as oppressive speech.

The Talmud adds two more examples of oppressive speech:

If a person is visited by suffering, afflicted with disease, or has buried his children, one must not speak to him as Job's companions spoke to him, "Is not your piety your confidence, your integrity your hope? Think now, what innocent man ever perished? Where have the upright been destroyed? As I have seen, those who plow evil and sow mischief reap them" (Job 4:6–8). If ass-drivers sought grain from a person, he must not say to them, "Go to so-and-so, who sells grain" when knowing that he has never sold any. Rabbi Judah said: "One must not feign interest in a purchase when he has no money, since this is known to the heart only, and of everything known only to the heart it is written [in the Torah], 'And you shall fear your God'" (Leviticus 25:17).

—*Babylonian Talmud,* Bava Metzia *58b*

The first of the Talmud's examples is telling sick people that their past sins are the reason for their suffering. Even if a person with lung cancer smoked three packs of cigarettes a day or a person who had a stroke is obese, so that there is indeed a probable link between their past behavior and their present illness, one may not mention that when visiting the ill person. However, if the person will recover, the doctor may—and probably should—describe that connection and ways of stopping smoking or avoiding overeating because that may have some practical benefit in avoiding a recurrence of the disease; but even a doctor should refrain from blaming the ill for their disease if they have no hope for recovery. People outside the field of medicine who have no practical reason to mention this linkage are definitely prohibited from saying to the ill that they are responsible for their illness, and the Mishnah compares those who do to Job's "friends" who similarly blamed Job for his troubles and who were ultimately chastised by God for doing so (Job 42:7–9). (Note that in asserting that such language is oppressive speech, the Rabbis of the Mishnah seem to prefer the way the Book of Job addresses human suffering to the theology of Deuteronomy 28:58–61, which does link sickness to sin.)

The Talmud's second example of oppressive speech—telling someone seeking grain to go to someone whom the speaker knows has none—is another instance of warning us against "placing a stumbling block before the blind" (Leviticus 19:14)—this time, before the cognitively blind, people who lack information and can be misled by those who give them false directions. To do that is oppressive speech, because it steals not only the questioner's time, but also his or her trust in other people and even his or her self-respect as someone whom others will not intentionally lead astray. Clearly, this does not apply to games where the whole point is to deceive one another (card games such as poker or I Doubt It come to mind), for then everyone enters into the game with the intention of having fun by seeing how acute one is in identifying false information. It certainly does constitute oppressive speech, though, when children taunt each other in this way. Even in less personally charged situations, when, for example, one is asked for directions, one must prefer to say "I don't know" if one in fact does not know, rather than send someone "on a wild goose chase."

Harming another's money or property is clearly prohibited, as the passage in Leviticus 25 that we have been discussing spells out in detail. Even so, after explaining what is included in the category of oppressive speech, as quoted above, the Talmud poignantly indicates why verbal oppression is even worse than that:

> Rabbi Yochanan said on the authority of Rabbi Shimon bar Yohai: "Verbal wrong is worse than monetary wrong because with regard to the former it is written, 'And you shall fear your God (Leviticus 25:17),' but not of the second" [in Leviticus 25:14, which the Rabbis interpret to prohibit monetary wrongs]. Rabbi Eleazar said: "The former [verbal oppression] affects his [the victim's] person, the other [only] his money." Rabbi Samuel bar Nahmani said: "For the latter [monetary wrongs] restoration is possible, but not for the former [verbal wrongs]."

Rationales for Fudging the Truth or Outright Lying: Tact, Peace, or Hope

The Jewish tradition values truth very highly, not only for the practical reason that social relations depend upon being able to trust what others say, but also because God demands it and is even the paradigm of truth telling: "The seal of God is truth" (Babylonian Talmud, *Shabbat* 55a); "God hates the person who says one thing with his mouth and another with his mind" (Babylonian Talmud, *Pesachim* 113b; cf. *Sotah* 42a, *Bava Metzia* 49a). As a result, the general Jewish maxim is that one should tell the truth: "Rabbi Jose

ben Judah said: 'Let your "yes" be yes and your "no" be no'"
(Babylonian Talmud, *Bava Metzia* 49a).

Rabbinic literature, though, describes some exceptions.

Tact

When there is no practical purpose requiring the truth and
those hearing it will only have their feelings hurt, the Rabbis tell us
to choose tact over truth, especially when the truth is a matter of
judgment in the first place. In the following excerpt, the Rabbis' first
example is what we say about a bride on her wedding day: do we
tell the brutal truth and describe her as she is—beautiful or ugly—or
do we describe her as beautiful no matter what she looks like? What
is gained by calling her ugly? More important, note what is lost by
doing that—her self-esteem, her joy, and the exuberance of those
attending the wedding. Similarly, although somewhat less graphically, it is one thing to advise a person before he or she buys something, but once that has happened people should refrain from
criticizing the item (assuming that it cannot be returned).

> What words must be used when dancing before the bride?
> The School of Hillel said: "Say, 'O bride, beautiful and gra-
> cious.'" The School of Shammai said: "If she is lame or
> blind, is one to say, 'O bride, beautiful and gracious'? Does
> it not say in the Torah, 'Keep far from lying'?" (Exodus 23:7).
> The Hillelites said, "Then, if someone makes a bad purchase
> in the market, is one to commend it or run it down? Surely
> one should commend it." Hence the wise say, "Always
> make your disposition sympathetic to that of your neigh-
> bor" (Babylonian Talmud, *Ketubbot* 17a).

Peace

A second exception to the requirement to tell the truth is when
one is engaged in an effort to bring peace. The Rabbis deduce this

exception from the very words of God, who changed Sarah's words to say that she was worried that she was too old to have children rather than that Abraham was; from the lie Joseph's brothers told Joseph after Jacob's death to try to attain his forgiveness and make peace among the brothers; and from God's advice to Samuel to lie to Saul that he was coming to bring a sacrifice even though his real purpose was to tell him that God had decided to wrest the throne from him and give it to David.[9] The ultimate principle, then, is that "all lies are forbidden unless they are spoken for the sake of making peace *(Baraita Perek Ha-Shalom)*."

Clearly, there are some important limits to this. Lies have a way of being discovered, and so lying even in the interests of making peace may not only fail to work but may also make both parties angry at the peacemaker. Moreover, lies cannot cover up realities; if the parties really hate each other, no false reports will magically make things right. On the contrary, both parties, upon finding out about the false report, may reconfirm their animosity toward each other and also distrust the reporter who was trying to make peace. Peace, if it is to be had, must rest on a stronger foundation than lies. So one has to take this example of how God revised Sarah's words when transmitting them to Abraham with the proverbial grain of salt. One surely can and should omit nasty comments if one is trying to make peace; one can speak of each party's benign, broader intentions; and one can even interpret remarks made by one party about the other more positively than the speaker probably meant them; but actually changing what someone said is asking for trouble, even if it is in the name of making peace.

Hope

Finally, rabbinic literature records some rabbis who condone and even demand that those visiting very sick people lie to them about the seriousness of their disease so as to help them retain hope for recovery. Those who take this position base themselves on the biblical stories of Elisha's lie to the emissary of Benhadad, king of Aram, and the change of fate of King Hezekiah.

> The king said to Hazael: "... Inquire of the Lord through Elisha, saying, 'Shall I recover from this illness?'" So Hazael went to meet him ... and said [in the king's name] ... "Shall I recover from this illness?" Elisha said: "Go say to him, 'You shall surely recover,' even though the Lord has shown me that he shall surely die." ... Then he departed from Elisha and came to his master ... and answered, "He told me that you would surely recover" (2 Kings 8:8–10, 14).

> In those days Hezekiah was sick unto death. Isaiah, the prophet, the son of Amotz, came to him and said to him: "Thus the Lord said: 'Set your house in order, for you shall die and shall not live.'" Then Hezekiah turned his face to the wall and prayed to the Lord ... Then the word of the Lord came to Isaiah, saying: "Go and say to Hezekiah: '... I have heard your prayer, I have seen your tears, and I will add to your days fifteen years'" (Isaiah 38:1–7; also 2 Kings 20:1–7).

> "For through the multitude of dreams and vanities there are also many words; but fear the Lord" (Ecclesiastes 5:6). This was the case when Hezekiah, king of Judah, took sick, and God told Isaiah to tell him, "Put your house in order, for you will die and not live." Hezekiah said to Isaiah: "Normally, when a person visits the sick, he says, 'May God show compassion to you.' And when a physician visits a patient, he tells him, 'Eat this and not that, drink this and not that.' And even if it is obvious that he is about to die, one does not tell the sick to put his house in order, in order that he not experience mental distress. And yet you tell me to put my house

in order, for I am about to die! I will not accept this nor listen to your words. Instead I will rely on my forbear, who said, 'Through the multitude of dreams and vanities, there are also many words.'" ... [Later] Isaiah said to God, "God, first you told me one thing, and now you tell me another. How can I go now and tell him this [that God will add fifteen years to Hezekiah's life]?" God said: "Hezekiah is a humble man and will accept your words; besides, the original decree has not gone forth" (*Ecclesiastes Rabbah* 5:6).

If the close relative of a sick person dies, we do not inform the sick person lest he be emotionally overwhelmed *(titaref da'ato)*.
—*Babylonian Talmud,* Mo'ed Katan *26b*

These sources elevate the value of retaining hope for recovery over truth. They do so for two different reasons. First, the visitor never really knows whether the patient will get better or worse, even if God declares that he or she will die of the illness, for God may change the decree in response to the patient's prayers. In our own day, where people cannot depend on a revelation from God for the prognosis but only on the training and experience of physicians, one surely cannot know for certain whether the patient will live or die.

Furthermore, even if one is convinced that there is little, if any, hope for the patient's recovery, one may not deprive the patient of hope; to do so would be cruel. Despite the sexism in its formulation, the *Shulchan Arukh,* an important sixteenth-century code of Jewish law, clearly has this concern:

When a man is about to die, we tell him to say *Viddui* [the confessional prayer]. We tell him, "Many have uttered the confession and not died, and many have not said the confession and died. The reward for saying the confession is that you will live, for whoever says the confession will acquire a place in the afterlife." If he cannot say the confession, he should verbalize it in his heart. Such things should not be said to him in the presence of the ignorant or women or children lest they cry and thereby break his heart.

—Shulchan Arukh, Yoreh De'ah *338:1*

Moreover, depriving the patient of hope for recovery may actually hasten the patient's death, for he or she may then stop following the regimen prescribed by the doctor to stay alive as long as possible. According to some studies, people from a variety of cultures, and even animals, who are convinced that there is no hope for survival give up trying and die earlier than they would have had they tried to live.[10]

This is the line of reasoning that led Rabbi Immanuel Jakobovits, author of the first book on Jewish medical ethics and chief rabbi of the British Commonwealth, to write to me when I was chair of the Jewish Hospice Commission in Los Angeles. Rabbi Maurice Lamm, an Orthodox rabbi, had been its first chair, and I took over when he moved to the East Coast. Hospice care involves a patient's recognition that he or she has an irreversible, terminal illness. At that point, a Jew may choose to enlist any or all experimental therapies, even if their toxicity may hasten the person's death if they do not bring about a cure; a Jew may also, Rabbi Lamm and I concluded, choose hospice care, where one is still under a physician's care but the goal of that care is to maximize activity and minimize pain ("palliative care") rather than to cure an illness that has been diagnosed as incurable.

Rabbi Jakobovits wanted to know how Rabbi Lamm and I justified hospice care in light of the Jewish sources quoted above that require that we maintain a patient's hope for recovery. I answered him that while the Jewish tradition certainly wants us to reinforce a patient's hope, it cannot be plausibly read to require us to instill unrealistic hope, for the tradition has a keen awareness—from the garden of Eden story on—that we are mortal, which, in fact, is one critical factor that distinguishes us from God. Even if the prognosis is terrible, one can legitimately hope for many things—for as little pain as possible, for seeing family and friends or completing a trip or project before one dies, for reconciliation with estranged family members or friends—but we human beings cannot hope to live forever. It was after that exchange of letters that Rabbi Jakobovits permitted hospice care under Jewish auspices in England.[11]

My involvement with hospice is based, in part, on my own experience that the vast majority of people who are seriously ill do much better if they are told the truth than if it is withheld from them, even for the benign purpose of keeping their spirits up. Patients know from their own bodies that things are not good. If everyone around them pretends that everything is fine when in fact it is not, patients will cease to trust anyone. They may go along with the ruse out of their concern that those around them not suffer, but that is the patient caring for the visitor rather than the healthy caring for the sick. A context of secrets and lies also prevents patients from sharing what they really feel and thus makes it impossible for family and friends to come to their aid. It is downright sad to spend one's last days, weeks, or months not being able to trust or talk truthfully with the most important people in one's life.

If, on the other hand, doctors and families communicate honestly about the prognosis—including what the doctor really does not know—families, friends, doctors, nurses, rabbis, social workers, and anyone else involved in the patient's care can work effectively to make the patient's life as long and as meaningful as possible. Doctors in the past knew less about any patient's chances of recovery than they do now, and so dissembling may have had a justification in that lack of knowledge. Today, though, patients expect doctors to know much more and to communicate that knowledge so that they can make important decisions in their lives. Obviously, the doctor should be supportive and compassionate, and he or she should describe the medical alternatives and the degree to which things are not clear. When that is done, I maintain—contrary to these earlier sources—that to help the patient honesty is the best policy.

Using Words for Good Purposes

The Rabbis were all too aware of the power of the tongue to do bad things, despite the many safeguards that God provided in creating it:

> Rabbi Joseph ben Zimra said: [God said to the tongue:] "All the limbs of the human body are vertical, but I made you horizontal; all of them I put outside the body, but you I put inside; and I have even surrounded you with two walls, one of bone and one of flesh" (Babylonian Talmud, *Arakhin* 15b).

Not surprisingly, then, the tradition includes, as we have seen, many prohibitions and cautions about our use of words, to the point that some would prefer that we not talk at all!

> Shimon, his [Rabban Gamliel's] son, says: "All my life I have grown up among the wise, and I have not found anything better for the body than silence" (Mishnah, *Pirkei Avot* 1:17).

> Rabbi Akiva says: ... "A hedge around wisdom is silence" (Mishnah, *Pirkei Avot* 3:13).

Jews, though, have never had trouble speaking up. Just consider the immense body of literature Jews have produced, the intense debates on almost every page of the Talmud, and even the standard joke that where there are two Jews there are at least three opinions. (Someone recently asked me whether you really need two Jews for three opinions!) Although this verbosity and feistiness may seem to Jews like a universal human trait—Jews tend to think that the whole world acts the way we do—the fact is that many cultures encourage much more passive and silent behavior. Jews are anything but reticent to talk, and in this they have been shaped by their tradition.

Although normal conversation about what is going on in one's life, pragmatic matters, and talk related to work or play are clearly sanctioned forms of speech, Judaism especially appreciates three kinds of speech: words of Torah, gratitude, and support and comfort.

Words of Torah

Many, many rabbinic texts encourage us to speak words of Torah—so many, in fact, that one might think that every tradition encourages its adherents to study its texts. That, however, is not true: many traditions presume that only the elite will know the texts, and some (such as the Mormons) even bar anyone but the elite from knowing the secrets of the religion. The Torah already makes it clear that this is not going to be the Jewish way when God tells Moses twenty-seven times in the Torah to "speak to the children of Israel" rather than to the elders alone, and when it requires that the Torah be read every seven years to everyone assembled, "men, women, and children and the stranger within your midst."[12] The rabbinic tradition takes that much further, putting at least a bit of its own text into the early morning service, inserting many biblical passages into the daily liturgy and even more for Sabbaths and holidays, and claiming that Jewish learning should not be restricted to the house of study but should instead pervade our daily activities.

> Rabbi Shimon says: "Three who ate at the same table and did not speak words of Torah are as if they ate sacrifices to the dead ... but three who ate at the same table and spoke words of Torah are as if they ate from the table of the Holy Blessed One ... " (Mishnah, *Pirkei Avot* 3:3).

Words of Gratitude

It is only right and proper to acknowledge when someone has done you a favor. After all, we do not enter this world entitled to everything we need, let alone everything we want. Consequently, when someone provides for our needs or desires, we minimally owe that party an expression of our gratitude.

Jewish prayer is replete with thanksgiving to God. Three examples will suffice:

> It is good to give thanks to the Lord, to tell of your faithfulness in the morning and your trustworthiness at night (Psalms 92:1).

> We thank You, for You are Adonai, our God and God of our ancestors throughout all time, Rock of our lives, the Shield of our salvation in every generation. We thank You and praise You morning, noon, and night for Your miracles that daily attend us and for Your wondrous kindnesses ... Praised are You, Adonai, whose reputation is for goodness and to whom it is fitting to give thanks.
> —*The daily* Amidah, *said three times daily and four times on Sabbaths and festivals*

Could song fill our mouths as water fills the sea
And could joy flood our tongue like countless waves,
Could our lips utter praise as limitless as the sky
And could our eyes sparkle like the sun and the moon,
Could we soar with arms like eagle's wings
And run with gentle grace, as the swiftest deer,
Never could we fully state our gratitude to You,
Adonai, our God and God of our ancestors,
Or praise Your Name sufficiently
For one thousandth or ten-thousandth of the good things
That You have granted to our ancestors and to us.
   —*Babylonian Talmud,* Berakhot *59b, used as part of the*
Nishmat kol hai *on Saturday mornings toward the end of*
pesukei de-zimra

Given that something like 80 percent of the traditional Jewish prayer book (the *siddur*) consists of prayers that either praise God or thank God, one might aptly ask whether that is just too much, whether we are making ourselves far too humble and acting like sycophants. Why should God need our praise and thanksgiving in the first place?

This goes to the heart of the meaning of Jewish prayer. The English word *prayer* misleads us into thinking that the essence of prayer is asking God for things, as in the expression, "Do this, I pray." The Hebrew word for prayer, though, does not mean that. The root *hitpalel* instead means to submit yourself to judgment, to abandon your status of a privileged person to whom everything is owed and instead to recognize that you depend on much that you have done nothing to deserve—good health, family, friends, food, liquids, air, and so on. That is extremely hard for us human beings to do; we tend to be egocentric, thinking only from our own perspective and about our own needs and desires. It is precisely because of that prevalent human trait that Jewish liturgy spends so much time on getting us out of ourselves so that we can gain a proper, humble assessment of who we are, what we have, and what we deserve.

But it is not only God whom we should thank; we also need to express our gratitude to people who do good things for us. That seems obvious to us, and it probably did to the Rabbis as well. Saying thank you or expressing our gratitude in other ways seems like elementary manners, a function of a necessary humility about ourselves and an appropriate respect for others, and Jews probably always saw it as that. Interestingly, though—and, I would say, unfortunately—Jewish sources requiring that we express gratitude to other people who benefit us are remarkably sparse. This is probably an area where we modern Jews need to add to the tradition by articulating what was only implicit in it.

The tradition certainly does encourage gratitude toward other human beings; it just does not demand that we express it. For example, in the following talmudic passage, Ben Zoma combines thankfulness to the many people who enable him to live his life with ease with thankfulness to God for creating such people:

Ben Zoma once saw a large crowd on the steps of the Temple Mount. He exclaimed: "Blessed is the One who has created all these people to serve God." Ben Zoma also customarily said: "What labors did Adam have to carry out before he obtained bread to eat? He plowed. He sowed. He reaped. He bound the sheaves, threshed the grain, winnowed the chaff, selected the ears, ground them, sifted the flour, kneaded the dough, and baked it. Only then was he able to eat. I, on the other hand, get up and find that all these things have already been done for me. Similarly, how many labors did Adam have to carry out before he obtained a garment to wear? He had to shear the sheep, wash the

wool, comb it, spin it, and weave it. Then did he have a garment to wear. All I have to do is get up and find that these
things too have been done for me. All kinds of artisans have
come to my home so that when I awake in the morning, I
find these things ready for me" (Babylonian Talmud,
Berakhot 58a).

Similarly, the Jerusalem Talmud understands the command to
"honor your father and mother" (Exodus 20:12) as "paying a
debt" to them for bringing you into the world and raising you
(Jerusalem Talmud, *Peah* 1:1 [3b]).

Another talmudic passage asserts that those who name the
person who first said something significant or wise "brings salvation to the world": "One who quotes something in the name of the
one who [first] said it brings salvation to the world" (Babylonian
Talmud, *Megillah* 15a; *Hullin* 104b; *Niddah* 19b). The codes, however, never make this a legal requirement, while in modern times we
would say that failure to do that is plagiarism. The one thing that
we can say in defense of the tradition's silence on this score is that
it clearly demands that we thank God multiple times each day;
aside from psalms and prose expressions of such gratitude to God,
the Talmud requires that we utter one hundred blessings of God
each day.[13] Because God serves as our model, expressing our gratitude to God may serve as training for us to express our gratitude
to human benefactors as well. In any case, using words to do that
is certainly a good use of language.

Words of Support and Comfort

Another genre of words that the Jewish tradition especially
lauds are those used to support and comfort others:

Rabbi Isaac said: "Whoever gives a small coin to a poor
man has six blessings bestowed on him [citing Isaiah

58:7–9], but the one who speaks a kind word to him obtains eleven blessings" [citing Isaiah 58:10–12].

—*Babylonian Talmud,* Bava Batra *9b*

Better is one who shows a smiling countenance than the one who offers milk to drink (Babylonian Talmud, *Ketubbot* 111b).

In using words and body language to support others, such as the sick and mourners, we are modeling ourselves after God:

Rabbi Hama, son of Rabbi Hanina, said: "What is the meaning of the verse, 'You shall walk behind the Lord your God' (Deuteronomy 13:5)? [It means that] a person should imitate the righteous ways of the Holy One, blessed be God. Just as the Lord clothed the naked, ... so too you must supply clothes for the naked [poor]. Just as the Holy One, blessed be God, visited the sick, ... so too you should visit the sick. Just as the Holy One, blessed be God, buried the dead, ... so too you must bury the dead. Just as the Holy One, blessed be God, comforted mourners, ... so too you should comfort mourners" (Babylonian Talmud, *Sotah* 14a).

In Sum

The way we speak to one another, then, is a critical part of how we can destroy worlds if we use language badly or build and support them if we use it well. Although we often think of "fixing the world" in more concrete actions taken to aid others, the way we speak to people is at the forefront of our tradition's concerns for how to build a better world. Like every other capacity that we have, the ability to speak is morally neutral; it gains moral character according to the way we use it. The tradition's warnings about how easily we can use speech badly should make us aware of the power and pitfalls of speech, and the tradition's encouragement to use speech to fix the world should encourage us to talk in those ways. The following two passages from the Midrash summarize a number of the lessons in this chapter.

Rabbi Levi said: "There are six things that serve man; three are in his control, and three are not. Eye, nose, and ear are not. He must see, smell, and hear what he may not want to see, smell, and hear. A man may be passing through a street when they are burning incense to an idol, and he has no wish to smell the incense, but his nose forces him to do so. So, too, his eye brings him sinful sights, and his ear blasphemous words, against his will, for they too are not under his control. But mouth, hand, and foot are in his power. He need not desire to labor in Torah [study] with his mouth. He need not wish to slander or curse or blaspheme. He need not wish to fulfill the commandments with his hand. He need not wish to steal or murder. With his foot he can visit the theaters or circuses, or he can go to the synagogues and houses of study" (*Genesis Rabbah, Toledot* 67:3; *Midrash Tanhuma (Buber), Toledot* 70b–71a).

"This is the law of the leper" (Leviticus 14:2). This is what the Bible means when it says, "Death and life are in the power of the tongue" (Proverbs 18:21). Everything depends on the tongue. A person who uses it well merits life; a person who misuses it is culpable for death. A person who uses his tongue to engage in Torah study merits life, for the Bible calls the Torah life, as it says, "It is a tree of life to those who hold fast to it" (Proverbs 3:18); and it [the Torah] is his cure for slurring others *(lashon hara)*, as the Bible says, "A healing tongue is a tree of life" [but the author of the Midrash is probably flipping this verse's meaning to say, "The Tree of Life (i.e., the Torah) is the cure of the tongue"] (Proverbs 15:4). But anyone who engages in slurring others is culpable for death, for slurring others is worse than murder, for a murder kills only one person, but one who slurs others kills three—the one who speaks, the one who listens, and the one spoken about. Thus Do'eg slurred Ahimelekh and was killed ... Moreover, he was uprooted not only from this world but also from the world to come ...

Who is worse—the one who kills with a sword or the one who kills with an arrow? I would say the one who kills with an arrow because one who kills another with a sword must come near to that person to do that, but one who kills with an arrow can shoot the arrow and strike the victim from anywhere that he is visible. Therefore the Bible analogizes slurring others to shooting arrows, as it says, "Their tongue is a sharpened arrow, they use their mouths to deceive" (Jeremiah 9:7) ...

Another interpretation: "Death and life are in the power of the tongue" (Proverbs 18:21). Do not say that since I was given permission (or the power, *reshut*) to speak, I will say anything I want, for the Bible already warned you, "Guard your tongue from speaking evil and your lips from speaking guile" (Psalms 34:14).

—Midrash Tanhuma (Buber), Metzorah, *ch. 4*

5

Helping the Poor

The first thing that comes to mind when many people think about *tikkun olam* is our duty to help the poor. That may be because the poor are so obviously in need of help. It may also be because we feel guilty about having what we need when other people do not, especially if we do nothing to provide what they need. And it may be because our Jewish tradition puts so much emphasis on helping the poor that we seem to imbibe the demand to do so with our mother's milk.

English is a Christian language: it was created by Christians, and still to this day about 90 percent of those who speak it as their native language are Christian. It should not be surprising, then, that English words describe things from a Christian perspective, especially in religious matters—words such as "salvation," "sin," and, as we saw in the last chapter, "prayer." English describes our topic in this chapter as "charity," coming from the Latin word meaning "love" or "caring." That makes you believe that someone who provides money for charitable causes or engages in acts of charity is an unusually good person, going beyond the call of duty. Hebrew, on the other hand, speaks of *tzedakah,* which comes from a root word meaning "justice" and implies that caring for the poor is not an unusually good (a "supererogatory") act, but rather simply what is expected of you. This establishes a Jewish tone and attitude about helping the poor completely different from that of Christianity: it is plain justice to help the poor, not an unusual (and often self-congratulatory) display of love.

To make it clear that the duty to help the poor is not as obvious as it may seem, in this chapter we will first examine reasons why we should *not* help the poor. Then we will explore some of the grounds for which the Jewish tradition nevertheless commands us to come to their aid. Jewish law, though, asserts that the poor also have duties. Finally, we will take a brief look at some of the methods Jews have historically used to help the poor and compare those methods to what we do today.

Before looking at the reasons listed below to abstain from helping the poor and then some of the reasons the Jewish tradition provides to come to their aid, you may find it helpful to create your own lists. Do not feel guilty in suggesting rationales to avoid helping the poor; there are indeed some good reasons to do that, reasons that are not only selfish or stingy, but actually moral and even benign. Those factors make it all the more important to gain clarity about why the Jewish tradition nevertheless bids us to come to their aid. So either individually or in a group, make your own lists first and compare them to what follows.

Reasons Not to Help the Poor

Why, then, should we avoid helping the poor? Some of the following ten reasons apply only to beggars on the street, and some also apply to giving money to, or providing services for, established charities; but it will be good to get all these justifications out in the open.

> 1. *Justice: I earned this money, they did not.* The poor often do not work for a living and therefore do not deserve our help. This is substantive justice in its libertarian meaning.

2. *Dignity: Taking help is demeaning.* Begging—or even getting help from a social service agency—is inherently humili-
ating. Therefore, as individuals and as a society, we should
not encourage behavior that cheapens our collective sense
of the dignity of human beings.

3. *Benevolence: I may be reinforcing physically harmful
forms of behavior if I help the poor.* Sometimes giving
money to the poor contributes to their harmful habits and
thus actually injures them. Stories of poor people who
turn down offers of food or coupons that can only be
exchanged for food reinforce the impression that many
poor people use money they gain from begging for alcohol
or drugs.

4. *Self-sufficiency: By giving the poor aid, I am encouraging
them to stay poor.* To offer aid to the poor may ultimately
be detrimental to them not only physically but also psychologically and economically, for they may come to depend
on it and never take the initiative to extricate themselves
from poverty.

5. *Deception: The people who seem poor may not be.* When
people on the streets ask me for a handout, I never know
whether they really need it. The possibility of falling prey
to deception is great, and nobody likes to be duped. If I am
already going to give some of my money away, I at least
want to know that it is going to needy people.

6. *Danger: I may be subjecting myself to injury or theft if I
open my wallet to give to the poor.* Beggars on the streets
might even pose a danger to you, for if they do not get
what they want, they may attack you or steal from you—
especially if they are on drugs.

7. *Discomfort: Beggars make me feel guilty and invade my
space.* Even if beggars do not pose a physical threat to
pedestrians or to drivers stopped at a light, they are surely

bothersome. The quality of life of society as a whole deteriorates if people cannot walk the streets without being accosted by beggars.

8. *Guilt: Beggars make me feel that I am somehow immoral for being able to support myself and have some luxuries.* Beggars and other manifestations of poverty instill a sense of guilt in us. Even if I earned each penny of my own resources legitimately, how is it that I have enough (and maybe even more than enough) and these people do not? On the other hand, is it right for me to feel guilty when I did not cause their situation and cannot possibly make it so that there are no poor people in the world?

9. *Bad for business: Beggars lead to a deterioration of the business environment.* People will not come to your store if they have to go through a series of beggars to get there.

10. *Hard to decide: There are simply too many individuals and institutions that deserve my help for me to decide whom to help and how much to give.* My duty to help others, coupled with sheer compassion for the plight of the truly unfortunate, makes me want to give money to each and every person I pass. Pandering thus makes it hard to make good decisions about how to spend the part of my own private resources that I can devote to helping the poor.

Rationales for Caring for the Poor

The issues listed above are not trivial or inherently selfish or mean. On the contrary, each is a strong argument suggesting that we should not—or, at least, need not—help the poor. Some of those considerations may lead us to give money only to institutions we know, trust, and care about, but other arguments may lead us not to give any money or service to the poor altogether.

What, then, are the reasons that classical Jewish sources are so insistent that we come to the aid of the poor? Here are some of the considerations that justify that stance, reasons that parallel the motives Jewish sources describe for caring for anyone in need, as discussed in chapter 2, but that are especially relevant to the destitute.

God's Commandment

While the Torah and the later Jewish tradition provide a number of rationales for helping the poor, the ultimate one is that God commands us to do so. This becomes clear, for example, in the following passage. Here the Torah tells us clearly that we should not expect to accomplish the utilitarian purpose of ridding the world of poverty, which might be one of the aims we have in mind in giving charity, "for the poor will never disappear from the earth." Nevertheless, we must help the poor in response to God's command:

> If there is a needy person among you, one of your kinsmen in any of your settlements in the land that the Lord your God is giving you, do not harden your heart and shut your hand against your needy kinsman. Rather, you must open your hand and lend him sufficient resources for whatever he needs ... For the poor will never disappear from the earth, which is why I command you: open your hand to the poor and needy kinsman in your land (Deuteronomy 15:7–8, 11).

God's Sovereignty

God owns the earth. As Owner, God can, like all human owners, decide how to apportion God's property. We human beings own property only vis-à-vis other human beings but not vis-à-vis God. Therefore, when God determines that some of the earth's goods that happen to be in our hands must be transferred to the poor, God has full moral and legal authority to make that demand (to say nothing of the power to enforce it), and we must obey.

In the passages below, the Torah speaks of someone who has to sell himself into slavery to pay off debts. The verses from Exodus make it clear that normally there is a six-year limit on such slavery, however large the debt is. Furthermore, if the slave voluntarily chooses to remain a slave after that time to stay with his wife and children, he undergoes what must have been a demeaning ritual of having his ear bored with an awl, indicating that one is not really supposed to choose to enslave oneself to other human beings, even for that understandable reason. In the verses from Leviticus, the Torah makes clear that the creditor may not treat the debtor as a slave but rather as an indentured servant. Furthermore, although Exodus imagines slavery for life, however unsavory that may be, Leviticus puts a definite limit on it—namely, the Jubilee year—and demands that in the Jubilee year he is not only to be freed but also to regain the ancestral land he had to sell to pay off some of his debts.

> When you acquire a Hebrew slave, he shall serve six years; in the seventh year he shall go free, without payment. If he came single, he shall leave single; if he had a wife, his wife shall leave with him. If his master gave him a wife, and she has borne him children, the wife and her children shall belong to the master, and he shall leave alone. But if the slave declares, "I love my master, and my wife and children: I do not wish to go free," his master shall take him before God [or to the judges]. He shall be brought to the door or the doorpost, and his master shall pierce his ear with an awl; and he shall then remain his slave for life (Exodus 21:2–6).

> If your kinsman under you continues in straits and must give himself over to you, do not subject him to the treat-

ment of a slave. He shall remain with you as a hired or bound laborer; he shall serve with you only until the Jubilee year. Then he and his children with him shall be free of your authority; he shall go back to his family and return to his ancestral holding. For they are My servants, whom I freed from the land of Egypt; they may not give themselves over into servitude (Leviticus 25:39–42).

We no longer permit people to sell themselves into slavery. Nevertheless, these verses should ring true to us, especially if we have gained and lost property over time, for they assert that we should understand that everything we possess is ours only temporarily. Furthermore, because ultimately God owns everything, God morally can and does demand that we reapportion some of our own property to others in need.

Our Covenant with God

The first sentence of the passage quoted below restates God's ultimate ownership of "the heavens to their uttermost reaches ... the earth and all that is on it." The rest of the passage, however, articulates another reason to give to the poor, namely, that it is one of our covenantal duties to God. The covenant between God and the People Israel includes mutual promises, and so part of its authority to demand that we aid the poor comes from the promise that our ancestors—and therefore we—made at Mount Sinai to abide by the terms of the covenant. But the authority of the covenant to require us to act in specific ways is not only rooted in the morality of promise keeping. The covenantal relationship between God and the People Israel also results in a love relationship between them, similar to a covenant of marriage. Therefore, we must give to the poor because our Lover wants us to do that, just as we do many things for our human spouse not because we promised, but out of love.

Mark, the heavens to their uttermost reaches belong to the Lord your God, the earth and all that is on it! Yet it was to your fathers that the Lord was drawn in His love for them, so that He chose you, their lineal descendants, from among all His peoples—as is now the case. Cut away, therefore, the thickening about your hearts and stiffen your necks no more. For the Lord your God is God supreme and Lord supreme, the great, the mighty, and the awesome God, who shows no favor and takes no bribe, but upholds the cause of the fatherless and the widow, and befriends the stranger, providing him with food and clothing. You too must befriend the stranger, for you were strangers in the land of Egypt (Deuteronomy 10:14–19).

The Dignity of God's Human Creatures

Because every human being was created in the image of God (Genesis 1:27; 5:1), each person has an inherent dignity that must not be compromised by poverty. This requires that we aid the poor and that the process of collecting the principal on a loan after it has expired must be a dignified one.

When you make a loan of any sort to your neighbor, you must not enter his house to seize his pledge. You must remain outside, while the man to whom you made the loan brings the pledge out to you (Deuteronomy 24:10–11).

The dignity of the poor person is also the governing value of the famous hierarchy of modes of charity that Maimonides created, culling together and organizing previous sources in his characteristically thoughtful, ordered, and sweeping way.

7. There are eight gradations in the giving of charity, each higher than the other. The highest of these, which has no

superior, is to take the hand of a fellow Jew and offer him a gift, or a loan, or enter into a business partnership with him, or find him a job, so that he may become economically strong and no longer need to ask others for help. Concerning this Scripture says, "You shall strengthen him … so that he may live with you … " that is, you shall assist him so that he does not fall into poverty and need charity … 8. Less praiseworthy than this is giving charity to the poor so that the donor does not know to whom he gave and the recipient does not know who gave it. In this way the act of giving charity is done for its own sake. This is like the Chamber of the Discreet in the Jerusalem Temple. The righteous would secretly deposit funds, and the poor, just as secretly, would enter and be sustained by what they took (Mishnah, *Shekalim* 5:6). Another way of giving charity in this fashion is to give to the community charity fund … 9. Less praiseworthy than this is the charity in which the donor knows the recipient, but the recipient does not know the donor. This is like the practice of our sages who would go about discreetly leaving money in the doorways of the needy … 10. Less praiseworthy than this is the situation when the needy knows the donor, but the donor does not know the recipient. This is like the practice of the greatest of our sages, who would tie coins in their shawls that would trail behind them, so that the needy could come and take without any embarrassment (Babylonian Talmud, *Ketubbot* 67b). 11. Less praiseworthy than this is personally giving a gift to someone before being asked. 12. Less praiseworthy than this is giving after being asked. 13. Less praiseworthy than this is giving less than is appropriate, but doing so graciously. 14. Less praiseworthy than this is giving, but resenting having to do so (Maimonides, *Mishneh Torah, Laws of Gifts to the Poor* 10:7–4).

Furthermore, the dignity of the poor person requires that anyone who receives money from others must also have the honor of giving aid to some other poor person: "Even a poor person who lives entirely on charity must also give charity to another poor person" (Babylonian Talmud, *Bava Kamma* 119a).

Compassion

Undoubtedly the first reason we think of helping the poor is sheer compassion for someone in need. Although each of us can feel compassion for others simply as a function of empathy, a sense that we could easily be in the same position, the Torah finds a special reason that Jews must have compassion for those in need—namely, that we Jews were in Egypt and should know how it feels to be completely without resources. We should therefore treat others as we would want to be treated if we were in such a destitute position.

> You shall not subvert the rights of the stranger or the fatherless; you shall not take a widow's garment in pawn. Remember that you were a slave in Egypt and that the Lord your God redeemed you from there; therefore do I enjoin you to observe this commandment ... When you gather the grapes of your vineyard, do not pick it over again; that shall go to the stranger, the fatherless, and the widow. Always remember that you were a slave in the land of Egypt; therefore do I enjoin you to observe this commandment (Deuteronomy 24:17–18, 21–22).

Community

Another motive that influences many to give charity is their feeling that they have a duty to support their community and give back to it. Jewish law does not leave that to communal feelings alone; it specifies exactly who has the duty to contribute to social causes based on the length of time that the person has lived in a given place.

> One who settles in a community for thirty days becomes obligated to contribute to the charity fund together with the other members of the community. One who settles there for three months becomes obligated to contribute to the soup kitchen. One who settles there for six months becomes obligated to contribute clothing with which the poor of the community can cover themselves. One who settles there for nine months becomes obligated to contribute to the burial fund for burying the community's poor and providing for all of their needs of burial (Maimonides, *Mishneh Torah, Laws of Gifts to the Poor* 9:12).

Aspirations to Holiness

Finally, Jewish tradition provides a rationale for helping the poor that speaks to our own character: we should want to be the kind of people who aid those in need. Whereas non-Jews might help others for similar reasons of self-image and self-respect, the Torah puts these considerations in theological terms: we should aspire to be not only decent and even noble human beings, but also Godlike. We should strive to be holy like God, and part of the way to do that is to provide for the poor, as the following selections make clear.

> The Lord spoke to Moses, saying: Speak to the whole Israelite community and say to them: "You shall be holy, for I, the Lord your God, am holy ... When you reap the harvest of your land, you shall not reap all the way to the edges of your field, or gather the gleanings of your harvest. You shall not pick your vineyard bare, or gather the fallen fruit of your

vineyard; you shall leave them for the poor and the stranger: I the Lord am your God'" (Leviticus 19:1–2, 9–10).

Rabbi Hama, son of Rabbi Hanina, said: "What is the meaning of the verse, 'You shall walk behind the Lord your God' (Deuteronomy 13:5)? ... [It means that] a person should imitate the righteous ways of the Holy One, blessed be He. Just as the Lord clothed the naked, ... so too you must supply clothes for the naked [poor]. Just as the Holy One, blessed be He, visited the sick, ... so too you should visit the sick. Just as the Holy One, blessed be He, buried the dead, ... so too you must bury the dead. Just as the Holy One, blessed be He, comforted mourners, ... so too you should comfort mourners" (Babylonian Talmud, *Sotah* 14a).

Limits on Giving

Some people have no difficulty understanding why they should give to the poor; in fact, they are so convinced by one or more of the rationales described above that they give up all or most of their assets to help others. The Talmud knows of such people.

When the charity collectors saw Elazar Ish Biratha, they would hide from him, for otherwise he would give them everything he had. One day he went to the market to provide a dowry for his daughter. The charity collectors saw Elazar and hid from him. He, however, ran after them and said to them: "I adjure you, tell me what you are collecting for?" They said to him, "We are collecting for an orphan boy and an orphan girl [so that they may marry]." He said to them: "By the Temple Service [the form of making an oath]! The orphans take precedence over my daughter." He took all that he had and gave it to them. He kept, though, one *zuz* [a small denomination of money], and with it he bought wheat, which he brought home and placed in his storehouse. His daughter asked him, "Father, what did you get?" He said to her, "All that I bought I placed in the storehouse." When she went to open the door to the storehouse, she saw that the storehouse was filled with wheat so that it was bursting out of the door lock, so much so that the door would not open [because its openings on the top and bottom were stuffed with wheat]. Elazar's daughter went to the house of study and said to him, "Come and see what your Beloved [God] did for you!" He said to her, "By the Temple Service! This wheat is consecrated [and hereby given to the Temple], and you must only draw from it along with the other poor of Israel" (Babylonian Talmud, *Ta'anit* 24a).

There are some voices in rabbinic literature that express appreciation for such extravagant levels of giving, even though such generosity inevitably produces an ascetic way of living: "One who says, 'Mine is yours and yours is yours is a pious person *(chasid)'*" (Mishnah, *Pirkei Avot* 5:12).

The general thrust of the rabbinic tradition, though, is that divesting oneself of all or most of one's assets to help the poor is *not* the proper path for either oneself or for one's family. The German pietists *(Chasedei Ashkenaz)* of the thirteenth and fourteenth centuries did practice modes of asceticism, for they thought that God had allowed the Crusaders to maim and kill many of their numbers because of their own sins. Influenced by the Christian pietists among whom they lived, they thought that a proper response on their part would be self-denial as a form of penitence. That was very much an exception to the rule, though, for the predominant theme that emerges from the Jewish tradition is that asceticism is not the proper form of piety, that one should not divest oneself of one's property as an act of piety, taking a vow of poverty in the manner of Catholic monks, priests, and nuns. Instead, one has a duty to care for one's own life and health first and then for the needs of one's family. One should therefore seek gainful employment and use one's assets first and foremost to support oneself and one's family. Only after one has taken care of those duties should one begin to give from one's excess to the poor.

Even if one attains wealth, piety (that is, reverence for God in contrast to total self-absorption) is perfectly possible—a very different perception of wealth than is common in Christianity, where "money is [inherently and inevitably] the source of all evil." If one does become wealthy, one can and should remain pious and thankful to God for one's bounty, and one should give to the poor and to other social needs (education, health care, etc.) generously in accord with one's wealth. But to fail to earn a living or to divest oneself of all one's property is an irresponsible neglect of one's duty to support one's family and an ungrateful denial of God's bounty to boot.

> Decreasing one's wealth is not an act of piety if such wealth has been gained in a lawful way and its further acquisition does not prevent one from occupying himself with study of Torah and good deeds, especially for one who has a family and dependents and whose desire is to spend his money for the sake of God ... For you are, as it were, enjoying the Lord's hospitality, being invited to God's table, and should thank God for God's bounty, both inwardly and outwardly (Judah Halevi [before 1075–1141], *The Kuzari* 11:50).

Furthermore, the Rabbis were worried that those who gave too much to the poor would themselves become poor and dependent on society for their sustenance. Consequently, the Rabbis of the Talmud specify that giving 5 percent or less of one's income each year to charity is "mean" and that 10 percent is "middling," and they impose a limit of 20 percent: "In Usha the Rabbis enacted that one should not give more than a fifth of one's income lest he become impoverished himself and dependent on charity" (Babylonian Talmud, *Ketubbot 50a;* Maimonides, *Mishneh Torah, Laws of Gifts to the Poor* 7:5).

These limits affect yearly contributions. What about estate planning, though? One might argue that the wealthiest among us can and should give more than a fifth of their assets to charity when they plan their estates. After death, they obviously no longer need to sustain themselves. While people clearly need to provide for a surviving spouse, if there is one, leaving too much to one's children can diminish their own drive to be productive. Thus for the welfare of one's own children as well as of society, the wealthy among us should probably give more than a fifth of their estates to the poor and other social causes (such as education and health care).

Most of the wealthy—and, for that matter, the well-off, the near-wealthy, and even people with fewer assets—do not give what they should. About fifteen years ago, when American estates over $600,000 were taxed at 50 percent, my estate attorney told me that he made it crystal clear to his wealthiest clients that even with employing all of the legal tax shelters available, estate taxes would take close to half of their estates and that the only way to avoid giving that money to the government was to give it to charities. Furthermore, he showed them that they could arrange to do that in their lifetime in a way that did not prevent them from doing anything they wanted to do for the remainder of their lives; that way they could enjoy and even be honored for the good they did for the causes that mattered to them. Even with all that information, he told me, most wealthy people failed to be generous; they just could not think about parting with their money, even after they died. So the most important part of the Jewish tradition for the vast majority of us to learn is not so much the limits on what we should give, but the imperative to give in the first place.

Responsibilities of the Poor

The well-off have duties to the downtrodden for the reasons described above, but Jewish law imposes duties on the poor as well. Aside from the duty of giving to other poor people, the poor must strive to find work to support themselves. Nobody may avoid work on the presumption that God and compassionate human beings will provide for his or her needs.

> A person should not say, "I will eat and drink and see prosperity without troubling myself since heaven will have compassion upon me." To teach this Scripture says, "You have blessed the work of his hands" (Job 1:10), demonstrating that a man should toil with both his hands and then the Holy One, blessed be He, will grant His blessing (*Tanhuma Vayetze,* sec. 13).

This has direct implications in our own day, primarily in the ultra-Orthodox community, where people devote themselves to study alone. It is fine to do that for a year or two, as many do immediately after high school, or during or after college, or on a sabbatical later in life. Some pursue Jewish study further and become rabbis, earning their living through the many activities that rabbis are called upon to do, including teaching, counseling, consecrating, life-cycle events, and social service; others may like the life of the mind so much that they become professors, earning a living by teaching and doing research in a university or seminary setting. But one may *not* study throughout one's life, contribute nothing to the life of others on the basis of that study, and depend on others for support.

> [On one hand,] One should not say: "I will first accumulate wealth and then devote time to the study of the Torah, or I

will delay study until I acquire what I need and retire from my work," for if you think in that way, you will never merit the crown of Torah study. Rather, make your study of Torah a set part of your calendar and your work temporary, and do not say, "When I have time, I will study," lest you never have time (Mishnah, *Pirkei Avot* 4:10) ... [On the other hand,] anyone who decides to study Torah, not do work, and sustain himself through charity has desecrated God's Name [reputation] and disgraced the Torah ... Sacred study that is not accompanied by gainful employment is itself null and void and leads to sin, for in the end such a person will rob others (Maimonides, *Mishneh Torah, Laws of Studying Torah* 3:7, 10).

Similarly, one can and should remain pious and thankful to God even if one attains wealth.

One who trusts God is not hampered in his trust by great wealth because he does not rely on it. He sees it as a reserve he has been commanded to make use of under certain specific and temporary circumstances. He does not become arrogant if he remains wealthy; he never reminds anyone that he gave money to what he did, and he never asks for compliments for his generosity. Instead he thanks his Creator for having made him an agent of God's kindness (Bahya ben Joseph Ibn Paquda [second half of the eleventh century], *Duties of the Heart, Introduction to the Fourth Gate*).

Those who try to find work but cannot must nevertheless engage in some useful activity, because that will at least contribute to the society that is supporting them and because "a man only dies through idleness":

If one is unemployed, what should he do? If he has a court-yard or a field in a state of decay, let him busy himself with it; as it says, "Six days shall you labor and do all your work" (Exodus 20:9). [Since it seems that the second clause only repeats the command in the first clause,] for what purpose were the words "and do all your work" added? It is to include an [unemployed] person who has a courtyard or a field in a state of decay, that he should go and busy himself with them. A person only dies through idleness (*Avot de-Rabbi Natan*, 11).

Some people, of course, cannot work, and they are exempted from this requirement. What happens, though, if a poor person is simply lazy and does not seek work? The tradition did not con-template such a possibility. That was probably for a combination of factors. First, the work ethic was strongly ingrained in Jews, and so refusing to work when one could would be seen as shameful. Second, Jews by and large lived in small communities, and so one could not be anonymous. Thus, one could not deceive people as to the reality of one's needs as readily as one can in a large commu-nity. Furthermore, the degradation of begging is all the greater if the ones from whom you beg know you. Finally, until the last cen-tury, Jewish communities were seldom wealthy, and so while one could subsist on the support provided by the community, one could not live comfortably on that aid. That made depending on the com-munity unattractive for economic reasons as well as for moral, psy-chological, and social ones.

Principles and Methods for Distributing Aid to Those in Need

In some ways, the distribution of relief to those in need was radi-cally different in times past from what we do today. Most important, governments did not provide such relief; it was totally a matter of generous individuals and religious and social agencies. Nowadays, part of our tax dollars are used to provide a safety net for the poor and needy, and one might legitimately ask whether one can count that percentage of one's taxes toward what one is required by Jewish law to give to those in need. (That percentage would decrease, of course, if the government reduces its support for the poor and others in need, as the American government has done in recent years.) Furthermore, as indicated above, we now live in much larger communities than we did earlier, and so the need for contributing and the sense that one should support one's community may well be weaker. On the other hand, modern media bring news of the destitute around the world into our living rooms, and so we are more aware of the extent of poverty not only in our local community but also around the world. Therefore, when we consider Jewish sources on how to collect and distribute funds, we must take into consideration the differences between contemporary conditions and those of times past.

Still, even during presidential administrations that provided generously for social programs, there has been a consistent need for individuals to contribute to charitable institutions—including religious, educational, and cultural ones as well as those dedicated to helping the poor or needy. The Jewish community can take pride in its long history of ensuring that people—both Jews and non-Jews—do not starve or lack clothing. Maimonides went so far as to say this: "We have never seen nor heard of an Israelite community that does not have a charity fund" (Maimonides, *Mishneh Torah, Laws of Gifts to the Poor* 9:3). What a given Jewish community could provide depended on its resources, but the historical record presents an estimable model and motivation for our own contemporary efforts. Moreover, Jewish sources give us some guidance in how Jewish social service agencies should distribute their aid.

First, as we saw in Maimonides' famous ladder of the degrees of charity, lending money to people is preferable to giving them support directly—similar to the old adage of teaching a person to fish rather than giving him or her a fish. Investing in a common business with poor people is even better than giving them money for their own enterprises because working with poor people trains them in the skills they need to succeed. It also affords an even greater measure of dignity: after all, the donor thinks enough of the person not only to invest money in his or her future, but also to invest time and effort and, furthermore, to interact with him or her on an ongoing basis. Although Maimonides spells out this hierarchy in greater detail than had been previously done, its roots are in the Talmud.

> Rabbi Abba said in the name of Rabbi Simeon ben Lakish: "He who lends money [to a poor person] is greater than he who gives charity; and he who throws money into a common purpose [to form a partnership with the poor person] is greater than either" (Babylonian Talmud, *Shabbat* 63b).

Second, prevention is better than cure. Specifically, it is better to come to a person's aid when his or her problems are just beginning rather than after he or she becomes destitute.

> "If your kinsman, being in straits, comes under your authority, you shall uphold him" (Leviticus 25:35). Do not allow him to fall into utter poverty. The injunction may be explained by analogy with a load on a donkey: as long as he is standing up, one may grab him [to keep him from falling] and keep him standing upright. Once he has fallen, however, five men cannot make him stand up again (*Sifra, Leviticus,* on Leviticus 25:35 [ed. Weiss, p. 109b]).

Third, the extent to which a person should be eligible for the community's aid should depend, at least in part, on the depth of that person's roots in the community, for that determines the degree of duties the community has toward that person.

> The soup kitchen [provides enough food] for a full day, but the communal fund gives [sufficient food to last] from one week to the next. The soup kitchen [provides food] for anybody, but the communal fund [gives support only] to the poor of that locale. [A poor person] living there for thirty days attains the status of being a resident of the locale for [purposes of receiving assistance] from the communal fund. But [to receive] shelter [he must have lived there] for six months, and to be liable to the town tax [he must have been a resident] for twelve months (Tosefta, *Peah* 4:9).

Presumably, the extent of a person's need would be another factor that the community must take into account, but there was a strong sense that the community must first help its own. What results is concentric circles of care and concern.

> Anyone who gives money to his adult children, mature enough that the parent is no longer obliged to sustain them, in order that the adult males may study Torah and the females may live uprightly [and] so, too, anyone who gives gifts to his needy father and mother may consider these gifts a fulfillment of the duty to give charity. Indeed, he needs to give these relatives priority over others in his charity giving. He should give a similar priority to his relatives over all others. The Torah commands that the needy of his household come first, then the poor of his city, and they, in turn, have priority over the poor of another city ... Rabbi

Saadia (882–942) wrote that a person is required to put his own sustenance first, and is not duty bound to give charity to others until after providing for his own. The Torah says, "And your brother shall live with you" (Leviticus 25:36), a verse that clearly establishes that your life comes first and only then the other person [following the Babylonian Talmud, *Bava Metzia* 62a]. Also remember what the widow of Tzarefat said to the prophet Elijah [1 Kings 17:12]: "And I have done this for me and my son," first for herself and afterward for her son, a comment he [Elijah] approved of since Elijah [first] said [v. 13], "Do it for yourself," and [he said] "and for your son" only afterward. After one has seen to his own sustenance, he may then give priority to the sustenance of his needy parents over that of his adult children, and then he should see to the sustenance of his adult children (Jacob ben Asher (d. 1340), *Arba'ah Turim, Yoreh De'ah,* chapter 251).[1]

Fourth, the community has a duty to ensure that funds collected for charity are distributed honestly and fairly. Toward that end, while two people were entrusted with collecting such monies, three people (the same number that constitutes a court for monetary matters in Jewish law) determined who would receive it:

Our Rabbis taught: The charity fund is collected by two persons [jointly] and distributed by three. It is collected by two because any office conferring authority over the community must be filled by at least two persons. It must be distributed by three, on the analogy of monetary cases [because the people involved have to adjudge the merits of various claimants].

—*Babylonian Talmud,* Bava Batra *8b*

Furthermore, those who distribute the funds must be morally beyond reproach and efficient.

> He [Rabbi Hanina ben Teradyon] said to him [Rabbi Jose b. Kisma]: "I mistook Purim money [i.e., money set aside for distribution among the poor for celebrating Purim but for no other purpose] for ordinary charity money, so I distributed [money of the same amount from my own pocket] to the poor" (Babylonian Talmud, *Avodah Zarah* 17b).

> Only a person who is as trustworthy as Rabbi Hanina ben Teradyon is qualified to administer the communal charity fund. But a ... person who is forgetful should not be nominated as administrator, no matter how upright and moral he may be, for he will forget how much he paid out, and he cannot be trusted to receive donations [either], for it [the donation] may slip his mind ... You cannot satisfy everybody. Sometimes a treasurer of a charity fund gives money to dignified people who are in straits. He should tell only two or three of the leading members of the community because if the matter became public knowledge, it would be a source of deep embarrassment to the recipient ... The treasurer should not pay attention to vile characters who say that they do not trust him. But if the majority of the community expresses displeasure and wants to depose him, he should say to the board of directors, "Since the majority of the members are opposed to me, go ahead and elect someone who is to your liking."
>
> —*Rabbi Yehudah He-Hasid,* Sefer Chasidim *192–193, Avraham Finkel, trans. (Northvale, N.J.: Jason Aronson, 1997), p. 116*

Finally, the Talmud and later Jewish law have an amazing provision: Jews must care for non-Jews as well as Jews. In light of the concentric circles just described, the degree of aid that Jews provided to non-Jews would surely be less than that given to Jews; but the fact that Jewish law requires Jews to help non-Jews at all is truly remarkable, for historically non-Jews were much more likely to maim and kill Jews than to help them.

> In a city with both Jews and idolaters [non-Jews], the collectors of charity collect from Jews and non-Jews for the sake of peace; we support the poor among non-Jews along with the Jewish poor for the sake of peace; [we visit the sick among non-Jews with the sick among Jews;][2] we mourn and bury the non-Jewish dead [assuming that they do not do that themselves] for the sake of peace; and we comfort those mourning non-Jews for the sake of peace (Tosefta, *Gittin* 3:18; see Babylonian Talmud, *Gittin* 61a).

6

Ransoming and Surrendering Captives

Thick and Thin Communities

> All Jews are responsible for each other (Babylonian Talmud, *Shavu'ot* 39a).

> Hillel says: "Do not separate yourself from the community" (Mishnah, *Pirkei Avot* 2:4).

The thick sense of community that is articulated in these sources, where every Jew is responsible for one another and may not separate himself or herself from the community, where one is to see one's fellow Jew as a member of one's extended family, has many implications. As the last chapter indicates, it is this strong communal sense that is one of the rationales for providing for the Jewish poor. It is also a key element in the Talmud's requirement to establish schools to educate everyone's children.

> Rabbi Judah said in the name of Rav: "Rabbi Joshua ben Gamla should be remembered for good, for had it not been

for him the Torah would have been forgotten in Israel. For at first, the boy who had a father was taught Torah by him, while the boy who had no father did not learn. Later, they appointed teachers of boys in Jerusalem, and the boys who had fathers were brought by them [to the teachers] and were taught; those who had no fathers were still not brought. So then they ordered that teachers should be appointed in every district, and they brought to them lads of the age of sixteen or seventeen. And when the teacher was cross with any of the lads, the lad would kick at him and run away. So then Rabbi Joshua ben Gamla ordered that teachers should be appointed in every district and in every city and that the boys should be sent to them at the age of six or seven years" (Babylonian Talmud, *Bava Batra* 21a).

As discussed in chapter 2, this thick sense of community is also the basis for making each of us responsible for rebuking others when they have done something wrong, thus doing one's part to ensure that the community is a just one.

Do not hate your brother in your heart. Reprove your kinsman so that you do not bear a sin with regard to him (Leviticus 19:17).

Whoever is able to protest against the wrongdoings of his family and fails to do so is punished for the family's wrongdoings. Whoever is able to protest against the wrongdoings of his fellow citizens and does not do so is punished for the wrongdoings of the people of his city. Whoever is able to protest against the wrongdoings of the world and does not do so is punished for the wrongdoings of the world (Babylonian Talmud, *Shabbat* 54b).

Along with Abraham (Genesis 18:25), Jeremiah (31:29–30), and Ezekiel (18:20–32), we moderns have moral and theological problems with this. Both they and we question God's apparent lack of fairness in punishing the innocent along with the guilty—and therefore our entire conviction that God is just. Furthermore, because we are heavily influenced by Enlightenment thought, we moderns find it difficult to accept responsibility for the iniquities of others in our community altogether, let alone those who came before us or will come after us. Articulated by thinkers such as John Locke and Claude Montesquieu and incorporated into the United States' founding documents and widespread practice of Americans, the Enlightenment approach to life pictures us as rugged individuals with only those duties to the community that we voluntarily take on, at least tacitly, by continuing to live in the United States after reaching the age of adulthood.

All communities, in this way of thinking, are voluntary, allowing anyone to leave at will. Thus one may join or leave at will a synagogue, a health club, or a volunteer organization. Although it is hard to become an American, if you have American citizenship you can, unless you have committed a felony, renounce that national connection at a moment's notice. Enlightenment communities are thus "thin" in the connections and duties that they create among their members.

In contrast, Jewish texts, such as the ones just quoted, depict us not as members of a thin, voluntary community but rather as part of a thick, organic one. Just as a part of your body cannot decide to leave you, so too all Jews are part of the organism of the Jewish People and cannot sever that organic tie. In this Jewish way of thinking, the texts quoted above make perfect sense: every Jew is responsible for every other Jew because if any part of the body politic of the Jewish People is diseased, the entire body is diseased.

Ransoming Captives: Who Is Saved First?

The duty to ransom Jewish captives is perhaps the most graphic illustration of this thick sense of community. It is as if the body has been dismembered, and it cannot rest until the lost member has been reattached. Jewish law gives priority to the legal requirement to ransom captives over everything else, a vivid illustration and a direct implication of Judaism's thick sense of community.

> Redeeming captives takes precedence over sustaining the poor and clothing them, and there is no commandment more important than redeeming captives. Therefore, for everything commanded for which the community collected money they may change its usage for the sake of redeeming captives. Even if they collected it for the sake of building a synagogue, and even if they bought the wood and stones and designated them for building the synagogue, such that it is forbidden to sell them for another commanded purpose, it is nevertheless permitted to sell them for the sake of redeeming captives. But if they built it already, they should not sell it ... Every moment that one delays redeeming captives where it is possible to do so quickly, one is like a person who sheds blood (*Shulhan Arukh, Yoreh De'ah* 252:1, 3).

Following mishnaic and talmudic sources, the *Shulchan Arukh* (*Yoreh De'ah* 252:8) maintains that the community should redeem a woman before a man because even though both are in danger of torture or even death, the woman is also at risk for being raped by her male captors. On the other hand, if the captors are known to rape men as well, we must redeem men first because the Rabbis, who were all men, thought that as bad as rape of a woman is, rape of a man through forced anal sexual penetration was worse because it did not even follow the form of what in other circumstances is loving, consensual sex. (The Rabbis and—at least until recently—the rest of the Jewish tradition condemned anal penetration of one male by another as an "abomination," following Leviticus 18:22.) This rule, with its exception, indicates that the one who is at greatest risk, and who therefore needs our help most, gets it.

The Talmud also includes a story that establishes the principle of one's primary responsibility to save one's own life.

> Two people are traveling on a journey [far from civilization], and one has a pitcher of water. [They realize that] if both drink [from it], they will [both] die, but if only one drinks, he can reach civilization. Ben Petura taught: "It is better that both should drink and die rather than that one should behold his companion's death," until Rabbi Akiva came and taught: "that your brother may live *with you*" (Leviticus 25:36), [implying that] your life takes precedence over his life [for only if you are alive can your brother live with you].
> —*Babylonian Talmud,* Bava Metzia *62a*

Based on this principle, the *Shulchan Arukh,* again following earlier sources, maintains that one must first seek to redeem oneself, then one's teacher, and then one's parent. The "teacher" referred to here is not one of many teachers that one has in one's life but rather the one mentor with whom one lives and studies for all of one's learning after elementary education. As the Mishnah explains elsewhere regarding whose lost object one should search for first (Mishnah, *Bava Metzia* 2:11 [33a]), one's teacher deserves to take precedence over one's father "because one's father brings one into this world, but one's teacher brings one into the world to come."

However, in redeeming from captivity, one's mother takes precedence over both one's father and one's teacher because of the risk of rape noted above.

> If he, his father, and his teacher are in captivity, he takes precedence over his teacher, and his teacher takes precedence over his father; but his mother takes precedence over all of them (*Shulchan Arukh, Yoreh De'ah* 252:9).

Despite the talmudic principle that saving oneself comes first, because a woman is much more likely than a man to be subjected to rape, a man must ransom his wife before himself (assuming that he lacks the funds to ransom them both).

> If a man and his wife are in captivity, his wife takes precedence over him. The court invades his property to redeem her. Even if he stands and shouts, "Do not redeem her from my property!" we do not listen to him (*Shulchan Arukh, Yoreh De'ah* 252:10).

Finally, a person has a duty to redeem one's children using one's own personal funds. A person who has money to do this may not rely instead on the community as a whole, for children, like oneself, one's wife, and one's teacher, have a special claim on a person. Rabbi Moses Isserles, in his gloss to this passage, indicates that among Ashkenazic (northern European) Jews this duty stretched to other relatives as well, the extent of the duty depending on how close the relative was.

> A father must redeem his son if the father has money but the son does not. Gloss: And the same is true for one relative redeeming another, the closer relative comes first, for all of them may not enrich themselves and thrust the [redemption of] their relatives on the community (*Shulchan Arukh, Yoreh De'ah* 252:12).

Ransoming Captives: Who Pays, and How Much?

This last source indicates that normally a man taken captive must provide the money to ransom himself and his wife. This is made explicit in the following law: "If someone is taken captive and he has property but does not want to redeem himself, we redeem him [with the money that his property will bring] against his will" (*Shulchan Arukh, Yoreh De'ah* 252:11).

When the captive does not have the money to pay for the ransom, however, the community must take on the obligation. Historically, this raised a delicate question: how much should the community spend in ransoming one of its members? On one hand, the community had a clear and overriding duty to free Jewish captives from their captors. On the other hand, Jews were unfortunately often taken captive precisely because kidnappers knew that the Jewish community would come through with the ransom; that is, each Jew had "deep pockets" in the form of communal support. So as much as the Jewish community wanted to redeem its members from captivity, it also wanted to discourage would-be captors from kidnapping other Jews.

As gruesome as this sounds, then, Jewish authorities had to familiarize themselves with the market price of captives and pay accordingly, but no more except in the case of a scholar of the Jewish tradition, for whom the community would pay whatever it took. One complicating factor in this market economy, however, was that the individual could pay as much as needed to free himself, even if that exceeded the current market price and held out the risk of increasing it.

> We do not redeem captives for more than their worth out of considerations of fixing the world, so that the enemies will not dedicate themselves to take other people captive. An

individual, however, may redeem himself for as much as he would like. Similarly, a scholar [*talmid chakham*], or even one who is not yet a scholar but is a bright student and holds the potential of becoming a scholar, we redeem him for much money … (*Shulchan Arukh, Yoreh De'ah* 252:4).

These concerns also affected how much the community was willing to pay for one of its members who had engaged in behaviors that put him at risk of needing to be ransomed. Under such circumstances, Jewish law set a limit to the community's duty:

He who sold himself to a non-Jew or borrowed money from them, and they took him captive for his debt, if it happens once or twice, we redeem him, but the third time we do not redeem him … But if they sought to kill him, we redeem him even if it is after many times (*Shulchan Arukh, Yoreh De'ah* 252:6).

Surrendering a Person to the Enemy: Saving One Person or the Community?

One rabbinic text represents the struggle among these principles more graphically than any other. Not only does it include differing opinions, which themselves are open to differing interpretations, but the story also appears in two different forms. The case poses the opposite problem from what we have been discussing—namely, when may a community *give up* one of its members to an enemy? This was all too often a conundrum that Jewish communities had to face, including many times during the Holocaust, because Jewish community leaders were forced by the Nazis to create lists of who would go to the concentration camps and who would stay in the ghetto.

The first opinion in the first version is this:

Caravans of men are walking down a road, and they are accosted by non-Jews who say to them: "Give us one from among you that we may kill him; otherwise we shall kill you all." Though all may be killed, they may not hand over a single soul of Israel. However, if the demand is for a specified individual like Sheva, son of Bikhri, they should surrender him rather than all be killed (Jerusalem Talmud, *Terumot* 7:20; *Genesis Rabbah* 94:9).

The first clause asserts the ultimate divine value of each human being. The inhabitants of the besieged caravans may not participate in the crime of murder as accessories by singling out any one of them, even though refusing to pick one of their number will mean the death of them all. The second clause asserts, however, that if the enemy singles out a person in the caravan who is liable for the death penalty anyway, as Sheva, son of Bikhri, was in the biblical story of 2 Samuel 20, then the inhabitants should surrender him rather than all be killed. Handing him over may be construed as complicity in the crime, but to a lesser degree, because it was the enemy, and not they, who chose who should die. Moreover, he was independently liable for the death penalty. Even so, handing him over to the enemy, rather than executing him according to legal procedures, is only justified by the need to save everyone else.

In the second section of this source, however, Rabbi Judah maintains that the citizens of the city may save themselves even if the designated person is not liable for the death penalty.

Rabbi Judah said: "When do these words apply [that they may hand over to the enemy only someone who is named and also liable for the death penalty like Sheva ben Bikhri]?[1] When he [the individual in question] is inside [the caravan or the city walls] and they [the enemy] are outside. But if he is inside and they [the enemy] are inside, since he would be slain and they [the other people in the caravan or city dwellers] would be slain, let them surrender him [that is, someone named by the enemy even though that person is not liable for the death penalty] so that not all of them will be slain."

This, then, leads us to interpret the first opinion and Rabbi Judah as we do here, namely, that the first opinion permits handing over only someone who is both designated by the enemy and also liable for the death penalty, while Rabbi Judah says that if the enemy designated someone and the lives of the rest of the city are at stake, the citizens may hand over the designated party, even if he is not liable for the death penalty, in order to save themselves. Under this interpretation, in the next generation, Rabbi Shimon ben Levi (Resh Lakish) in the next clause agrees with the first opinion, and Rabbi Yochanan agrees with Rabbi Judah.[2]

Furthermore, Rabbi Judah disagrees with the first, unnamed opinion, not only regarding who may be turned over but also under what circumstances. Specifically, for Rabbi Judah, if the enemy is still outside the caravan or city walls and therefore there is a chance that all the people in the caravan or the city will be able to outlast the siege and survive, they should not hand over an innocent party, even if the enemy named a specific person. In that situation, Rabbi Judah agrees with the first opinion above. But if the enemy has already broken inside the caravan's perimeter or city walls, such that everyone is in immediate danger of being slain, those being attacked may hand over the named person, even if he or she is not liable for the death penalty. In so doing, they are, of course, indirectly involved in causing the innocent person's death, but Rabbi Judah permits that degree of complicity when the objective situation makes it clear that the people in the caravan or city would otherwise all die and when it is the enemy, and not they, who choose the one to die.

Rabbi Menahem Meiri (1249–1316), an important medieval rabbi, introduces another consideration. He says that if the person designated by the enemy is a *terefah,* that is, one suffering from a terminal illness that doctors presume will kill the person in a year or less (Maimonides, *Mishneh Torah, Laws of the Murderer* 2:8.), he or she may be handed over to the enemy.

> It goes without saying that in the case of a group of travelers, if one of them was a *terefah,* he may be surrendered in order to save the lives of the rest, since the killer of a *terefah* is exempt from the death penalty (Menahem Meiri's commentary to *Sanhedrin* 74a, s.v. *yera'eh li,* p. 271).

Normally, when a rabbinic source records an unnamed opinion and then a named one on the same issue, the former is understood to be the opinion of the majority and therefore the law. As a result, in the source we have been discussing, the law would be according to the first, anonymous opinion and not Rabbi Judah. The Jerusalem Talmud, however, adds two more sections that complicate matters further. The first is this:

> Resh Lakish stated: "[He may be surrendered] only if he is deserving of death as Sheva, son of Bikhri." Rabbi Yochanan said: "Even if he is not deserving of death as Sheva, son of Bikhri, [was]" (Jerusalem Talmud, *Terumot* 47a).

Resh Lakish is ruling in accordance with the unnamed opinion discussed above, and Rabbi Yochanan is ruling in accordance with Rabbi Judah. This is surprising for two reasons. First, it is Rabbi Yochanan who establishes the rule that the law is according to an anonymous Mishnah,[3] and here he is disagreeing with it. Second, Rabbi Yochanan (c. 180–c. 279 C.E.) was the founder of the rabbinical academy in Tiberias and arguably the most important rabbi of his generation, and in his many disagreements with his brother-in-law, Resh Lakish, the opinion of Rabbi Yochanan was generally followed.[4] In other words, if the general rules of authority are followed, there is a shift in one generation in the accepted opinion on this issue such that it is no longer required that the person be culpable to justify giving him or her up to the enemy, as long as the enemy singled him or her out.

The fourth section of this source, however, dispels any sense of an emerging consensus.

> Ulla, son of Qoseb, was wanted by the [non-Jewish] government. He arose and fled to Rabbi Joshua ben Levi at Lydda. They [troops] came, surrounded the city, and said: "If you do not hand him over to us, we will destroy the city." Rabbi Joshua ben Levi went up to him, persuaded him to submit and gave him up [to them]. Now Elijah [the prophet], of blessed memory, had been in the habit of visiting him [Rabbi Joshua], but he [now] ceased visiting him. He [Rabbi Joshua] fasted several times and Elijah appeared and said to him: "Shall I reveal myself to informers [betrayers]?" He [Rabbi Joshua] said: "Have I not carried out a *mishnah* [a rabbinic ruling]?" Said he [Elijah]: "Is this a ruling for the pious *(mishnat hasidim)*?" [Another version: "This should have been done through others and not by yourself."]
>
> —*Jerusalem Talmud,* Terumot *47a*

Since Ulla, son of Qoseb, apparently stood indicted by the government, all of the opinions discussed above would have instructed Rabbi Joshua to do what he did; that is not denied in this last section. He is nevertheless castigated because while ruling that way may fulfill the demands of justice, it is not exemplary. Instead, Elijah claims, he should have been more pious in defending Ulla's life. That course of action, of course, would have endangered all the other inhabitants of Lydda, but this last source seems to demand such a risk; even if it seems quite certain that the troops would kill them all, Rabbi Joshua was obliged to try to save them all, including Ulla. He gave in much too easily.

This position takes human equality to its logical extreme. Later Jewish authorities, presumably on the basis of such a reading of Elijah's words, rule just this way.[5]

Another possible reading of Elijah's first response to Rabbi Joshua understands Elijah to be complaining not about Rabbi Joshua's actions but about his failure to be bothered by the tragedy of the situation. On this reading, it is possible that Elijah is simply demanding that Rabbi Joshua acknowledge that the choice is morally distressing and emotionally heartbreaking and that no matter what one does, there will be rough moral and emotional edges remaining.

The other version of Elijah's response, "This should have been done through others and not by yourself," would lead to yet a different conclusion. Rabbi Joshua's decision was the correct one, according to this reading, and it should be carried out. However, since it appears to lack piety, someone else should have made it. If we then ask who and why, the source is silent. It seems like a classic case of a community leader avoiding the responsibility he or she has and should exercise. We can only guess that if someone else, presumably someone in a position of authority but less well known than Rabbi Joshua, had made the decision, then the community could still retain a sense of its own piety and that of its most visible leaders even while putting into effect what was just and what it had to do.

In my book *Matters of Life and Death: A Jewish Approach to Modern Medical Ethics,* I apply these sources to the issue of access to health care, including who should get it and who should pay for it.[6] Classical Jewish texts apply these sources to another issue that the Jewish community faced, namely, how it should decide which men to give to the ruling power for the army.[7] How would you apply these sources to those questions?

7

Accompanying and Supporting People in Times of Need and Joy

We often think of *tikkun olam* in terms of *practical things* that one person or one group of people does for another. *Tikkun olam* certainly includes such things, as many chapters in this book demonstrate. It also includes supporting people emotionally in their time of need. The most obvious cases occur when people feel diminished—when, for example, they are sick or mourning a loved one. People also need the presence of other people, though, when they want to celebrate a joyous event in their lives, such as a birth or a wedding. This chapter will focus on such kinds of *tikkun olam,* where the fixing involves fulfilling emotional needs at least as much as practical ones.

Healing the Sick in Body and Soul

Jewish sources specify four duties with regard to physical and mental health: To adopt healthful practices and avoid harmful ones; to seek to heal those who are sick; to balance at the same time health care costs with those of other communal needs; and to visit the sick. Some of these apply to society as a whole, and others apply to individuals.

The Duty to Maintain Health

"An ounce of prevention is worth a pound of cure." Before we address our duty to attend to the sick, it is important to note that we have a prior duty to try to avoid illness in the first place. In modern society, people think that they should engage in healthy habits for all kinds of pragmatic reasons. Proper diet, exercise, hygiene, and sleep are, for Americans in particular, ways to feel good, look good, be popular, avoid illness, get a good job, and live a long life. It follows that if I do not want any or all of those things, I have the perfect right to do whatever I want, as long as I do not directly injure others. I may not smoke indoors (at least in certain places) because we now know that secondhand smoke harms others, but I may smoke outdoors. I may not drink and drive, but as long as I do not get behind the wheel of a car, I may get drunk whenever I want. I may eat a half-gallon of ice cream every night of the week even if that will mean that I will weigh five hundred pounds in no time. It is my body, and I may do whatever I want with it.

In stark contrast, the Jewish tradition makes it a duty to take care of our bodies, whether we want to or not. That is, in part, based on the Jewish presumption that God owns our bodies as well as everything else on earth: "Mark, the heavens to their uttermost reaches belong to the Lord your God, the earth and all that is on it!" (Deuteronomy 10:14).

As Owner of our bodies, God can and does insist that we take care of them. It is as if you were renting an apartment: you have fair use of the apartment during your lease, but you may not destroy it or damage it, because it is not yours. Similarly, while suicide is not punished through depriving your heirs of your inheritance or in any other way in any of the fifty states of the United States (although assisted suicide is punishable everywhere but in Oregon), in Jewish law we do not have the right to commit suicide or assist in one.

For your own life-blood I will require a reckoning ... Whoever sheds the blood of man, by man shall his blood be shed; for in His image did God make man (Genesis 9:5–6).

Furthermore, we also lack the right to injure ourselves.

Rabbi Akiva replied: ... "A person is not permitted to injure himself, but if he does so, he is free of liability [to pay the victim the usual five penalties for injuring others, for in the case of self-injury he would be paying himself]."
—*Mishnah*, Bava Kamma *8:6*

In fact, the Rabbis assert this:

Endangering yourself is more strongly prohibited than violating the other prohibitions of the Torah *(sakkanta hamirah m'issurah).*
—*Babylonian Talmud*, Hullin *10a*

We are even duty bound to help others avoid injury or death.

Our Rabbis taught: How do we know that one who sees that someone (literally, "his friend," *haveiro*) is drowning in the river or that a wild animal is dragging him or that highway robbers are attacking him is obligated to save him? Because the Torah says, "Do not stand idly by the blood of your neighbor" (Leviticus 19:16).
—*Babylonian Talmud*, Sanhedrin *73a*

In contrast, only a few states have established a legal duty to rescue; in fact, until the recent adoption of "Good Samaritan" laws in most states, if you tried to help out someone in a jam and injured the person in the process, you could be sued. It is still the case in most states that if you simply do nothing when you see someone in distress, you have violated no laws.

Jews have not only the negative duty to avoid injury but also the positive obligation to preserve their health. This is not for the pragmatic reasons that Americans endorse, such as feeling good, looking good, living a long life, being popular, or getting a good job; Maimonides, as quoted below, says that anyone who takes steps to maintain his or her health for such pragmatic reasons is doing the wrong thing. One should rather engage in proper diet, exercise, hygiene, and sleep to fulfill the responsibility we have to God to preserve God's property and to obey God's commandments without the limitations that illness would impose.

> He who regulates his life in accordance with the laws of hygiene with the sole motive of maintaining a sound and vigorous physique and begetting children to do his work and labor for his benefit is not following the right course. A man should aim to maintain physical health and vigor in order that his soul may be upright, in a condition to know God ... Whoever throughout his life follows this course will be continually serving God, even while engaged in business and even during cohabitation, because his purpose in all that he does will be to satisfy his needs so as to have a sound body with which to serve God (Maimonides, *Mishneh Torah, Laws of Ethics* 3:3).

The Duty to Heal People's Bodies

For the last two thousand years, Judaism has had a virtual love affair with medicine. Many rabbis were also physicians, including some of the most famous ones (e.g., Maimonides). That does not happen as much anymore because even though a rabbinical education takes about the same amount of time as in eras past, a medical education now extends for at least eleven years, and often more. Still, the deep respect for doctors and medicine embedded in the Jewish tradition and the significant contributions of Jews to both clinical practice and medical research continue unabated.

This was not an obvious result of Judaism's origins. The Torah, after all, asserts that illness and health are in God's hands. Thus, one of the ways God rewards us for obeying the commandments is by keeping us safe from illness, and one way God punishes us for disobeying them is by inflicting illness upon us.

> And if you obey these rules and observe them carefully ... the Lord will ward off from you all sickness. He will not bring upon you any of the dreadful diseases of Egypt, about which you know, but will inflict them upon all your enemies (Deuteronomy 7:12, 15).

> But if you do not obey the Lord your God to observe faithfully all His commandments and laws that I enjoin upon you this day, all these curses shall come upon you and take effect ... the Lord will strike you with consumption, fever, and inflammation ... The Lord will strike you with the Egyptian inflammation, with hemorrhoids, boil-scars, and itch, from which you shall never recover. The Lord will strike you with madness, blindness, and dismay ... The Lord will inflict extraordinary plagues upon you and your offspring, strange and lasting plagues, malignant and chronic diseases. He will bring back upon you all the sicknesses of Egypt that you dreaded so, and they shall cling to you. Moreover, the Lord will bring upon you all the other diseases and plagues that are not mentioned in the Book of Teaching, until you are wiped out. You shall be left a scant few, after having been as numerous as the stars in the skies, because you did not heed the command of the Lord your God (Deuteronomy 28:15, 22, 27–28, 59–62).

On the other hand, God is our healer, a theme repeated in many biblical texts by different authors and in different time periods.

God said: "If you will heed the Lord your God diligently, doing what is upright in His sight, giving ear to His commandments and keeping all His laws, then I will not bring upon you any of the diseases that I brought upon the Egyptians, for I the Lord am your healer" (Exodus 15:26).

Come, let us turn back to the Lord:
He attacked, and He can heal us;
He wounded, and He can bind us up (Hosea 6:1).

Bless the Lord, O my soul
and do not forget His bounties.
He forgives all your sins,
heals all your diseases (Psalms 103:2–3).

It is not only we moderns who have theological problems with this association of sin with illness and virtue with health. As early as the Book of Job, written approximately 400 B.C.E., this theology was questioned in memorably poignant terms.

I am blameless—I am distraught;
I am sick of life.
It is all one; therefore I say,
"He destroys the blameless and the guilty."
When suddenly a scourge brings death,
He mocks as the innocent fail (Job 9:21–23; see also 16:12–17).

Still, even if there are voices like those of Job who question the link between sickness and sin, Job and all other biblical and rabbinic sources assert that ultimately illness and health are in God's hands.

How, then, did the Jewish tradition get so involved in medicine? Undoubtedly, Jews were influenced by advances in medicine. Sources in the Bible and Apocrypha see doctors as quacks and, worse, as arrogantly taking over God's prerogatives. Even as late as the time of the Mishnah we find an opinion that states, "The best of physicians should go to hell!" (Mishnah, *Kiddushin* 4:14 [82b]). That is probably a patient's response to the failed promises of doctors to heal, but it may also be a reflection on the fact that doctors' interventions often worsened patients' conditions and sometimes directly caused their deaths. As medicine improved its track record, however, the Rabbis adopted a much more positive attitude toward medicine, and they justified and even mandated the functioning of doctors on the basis of their reading of biblical verses.

Specifically, they maintained that God requires us to heal, basing their assertion on several biblical verses. According to the Talmud, the last words of the following passage give us *permission* to attempt to heal:

> When men quarrel and one strikes the other with stone or fist, and he does not die but has to take to his bed, if he then gets up and walks outdoors on his staff, the assailant shall go unpunished, except that he must pay for his idleness [time lost] and he must surely heal him *(ve-rapo yerapeh).*
> —*Exodus 21:18–19*

> "And he must surely heal him": From this verse we derive the permission [of human beings] to heal (Babylonian Talmud, *Bava Kamma* 85a).

On the basis of "love your neighbor as yourself" (Leviticus 19:18), the Rabbis (*Sanhedrin* 84b and Rashi there, s.v. *ve'ahavta*) conclude that this permission even extends to treatments that require inflicting a wound, for they presume that we would all prefer to suffer from a temporary wound to get well and must therefore have permission to treat other people likewise. This, incidentally, also sets up the basis for judging therapies in terms of the balance of their risks and benefits, for in each case—and especially if the patient is unconscious or mentally incompetent—we must think of what we would want done and do the same out of love for our neighbor. On the basis of an extra letter in the Hebrew text of Deuteronomy 22:2, the Talmud (*Bava Kamma* 81b) declares that the Torah imposes an *obligation* to restore another person's body as well as his or her property and hence to come to the aid of someone in a life-threatening situation. That duty also stems from Leviticus 19:16, which the Talmud (*Sanhedrin* 73a) uses to ground our obligation to do what we personally can to save lives and also to hire those who are more qualified to heal others.

> If you see your fellow's ox or sheep gone astray, do not ignore it; you must take it back to your fellow. If your fellow does not live near you or you do not know who he is, you shall bring it home and it shall remain with you until your fellow claims it; then you shall give it back to him *(ve-hashevato lo).*
>
> —*Deuteronomy 22:1–2*

On what biblical basis can it be derived that it is obligatory to restore the body of a fellow human being [when ill or in danger, just as it is obligatory to restore his or her lost property]? Because the Torah says: "And you shall restore it to him" (Deuteronomy 22:2). ["To him" is superfluous, for to whom else would you return it? The Rabbis, assuming that nothing in the Torah is superfluous, therefore use that extra letter in the Hebrew word indicating "to him" to assert that] the Torah imposes a duty on us to restore lost property to its owner and a person's body to him or her (*avedat gufo,* the loss of one's body) when it is lost through illness or danger. [See Rashi on the *Sanhedrin* passage, s.v. *talmud lomar ve'hashevato lo.*]

—*Babylonian Talmud,* Sanhedrin *73a; see also* Bava Kamma *81b*

Do not stand idly by the blood of your neighbor (Leviticus 19:16).

Our Rabbis taught: How do we know that one who sees that someone [literally, "his friend," *haveiro*] is drowning in the river or that a wild animal is dragging him or that highway robbers are attacking him is obligated to save him? Because the Torah says, "Do not stand idly by the blood of your neighbor."—But is it derived from that verse? Is it not rather derived from "And you shall restore him to himself" (Deuteronomy 22:2)?—From that verse I might think that it is only a personal obligation, but that he is not bound to take the trouble of hiring men [if he himself cannot save the victim]; therefore, this verse [Leviticus 19:16] teaches that he must [also spend his money to hire others, if necessary].

—*Babylonian Talmud,* Sanhedrin *73a*

Furthermore, the duty to strive to heal takes precedence over all but three of the other commandments:

With regard to all transgressions in the Torah except for idolatry, sexual licentiousness, and murder, if enemies say to a person, "Transgress and then you will not be killed," the person must transgress and not be killed. What is the reason? "And you shall live by them [My commandments]" (Leviticus 18:6) [implies] that he not should die by them (Babylonian Talmud, *Sanhedrin* 74a).

Ultimately, Joseph Karo, author of the important sixteenth-century code the *Shulchan Arukh*, says:

The Torah gave permission to the physician to heal; moreover, this is a religious requirement and is included in the category of saving life, and if the physician withholds his services, it is considered as if he were shedding blood (*Shulchan Arukh, Yoreh De'ah* 336:1).

The following midrash is a beautiful rabbinic response to the theological problem mentioned at the beginning of this section. Engaging in medicine is not a violation of God's prerogatives but rather exactly what God would have us do in a divine-human partnership.

It once happened that Rabbi Ishmael and Rabbi Akiva were strolling in the streets of Jerusalem accompanied by another person. They were met by a sick person. He said to them, "My masters, tell me by what means I may be cured." They told him, "Do thus and so until you are cured." The sick man asked them, "And who afflicted me?" They replied, "The Holy One, blessed be He." The sick man responded, "You have entered into a matter that does not pertain to you. God has afflicted, and you seek to cure! Are you not transgressing His will?"

Rabbi Akiva and Rabbi Ishmael asked him, "What is your occupation?" The sick man answered, "I am a tiller of the soil, and here is the sickle in my hand." They asked him, "Who created the vineyard?" "The Holy One, blessed be He," he answered. Rabbi Akiva and Rabbi Ishmael said to him, "You enter into a matter that does not pertain to you! God created the vineyard, and you cut fruits from it."

He said to them, "Do you not see the sickle in my hand? If I did not plow, sow, fertilize, and weed, nothing would sprout."

Rabbi Akiva and Rabbi Ishmael said to him, "Foolish man! … Just as if one does not weed, fertilize, and plow, the trees will not produce fruit, and if fruit is produced but is not watered or fertilized, it will not live but die, so with regard to the body. Drugs and medications are the fertilizer, and the physician is the tiller of the soil" (*Midrash Temurrah* as cited in *Otzar Midrashim,* J. D. Eisenstein, ed. [New York, 1915], 2:580–581).

What happened, then, to the role of God in causing illness and healing? The Jewish tradition sees no contradiction in asserting both that God has ultimate control of these matters and that a Jew must use physicians in seeking to prevent and cure sickness, for it depicts human beings generally, and physicians in particular, as God's agents and partners in the ongoing act of creation and healing.[1] In fact, in *Sanhedrin* 38a, the Rabbis (Pharisees) specifically assert that the Sadducees were wrong in claiming that angels or any being other than humans participate with God in creation. Judaism thus recognizes the ultimate power and authority of God and yet honors human beings enough to give them the role and responsibility to seek to cure. We therefore must pray for healing and also use the services of doctors toward that end. What a remarkable balancing of honor for God and human beings!

Balancing Health Care with Other Communal Needs

As we have seen, the duty to provide health care applies not just to the individual physician; the community is also charged with making it available. On the basis of Leviticus 19:16 ("Nor shall you stand idly by the blood of your fellow"), the Talmud expands our obligation to provide medical aid to include expending financial resources for this purpose. Rabbi Moses ben Nahman (Nahmanides, 1194–1270) explains that this duty derives from the Torah's principle "And you shall love your neighbor as yourself" (Leviticus 19:18).[2]

The community, however, is also responsible for providing other necessities of life and of Jewish living. The Talmud, in fact, specifies ten things that a community must provide its members if it is to be fit for a rabbi to reside there:

> It has been taught: A scholar should not reside in a city where the following ten things are not found: (1) A court of justice which can impose flagellation and monetary penalties; (2) a charity fund, collected by two people and distributed by three [to ensure honesty and wise policies of distribution]; (3) a synagogue; (4) public baths; (5) toilet facilities; (6) a circumciser *(mohel)*; (7) a surgeon; (8) a notary [for writing official documents]; (9) a slaughterer *(shohet)*; and (10) a schoolmaster. Rabbi Akiva is quoted [as including] also several kinds of fruit [in the list] because they are beneficial for eyesight (Babylonian Talmud, *Sanhedrin* 17b).

Note that the list includes several items relevant to health care. Since there was no indoor plumbing then—there wasn't any until the nineteenth or even twentieth century in many places—it was important for purposes of public health to have public baths and toilet facilities. If the latter were not available, raw sewage in the streets would attract disease-bearing flies and rodents, a menace to public health. These facilities were also important, of course, for the general aesthetic quality of the environment. The "surgeon" mentioned in the list was the person who could perform the most important form of curative care known at the time, namely, letting blood. (The surgeon might also try other forms of curative care, but because the medicines available were largely ineffective, the list refers to the strong suit of medicine at the time rather than the more general term *physician* [*rofeh*]). Finally, Rabbi Akiva's addendum concerns one's ability to procure healthy foods in the town, a recognition that our choice of food is important on a preventive basis in assuring health.

The list also includes, however, a number of items not directly related to health care, such as a court of justice, a synagogue, and a schoolmaster. Moreover, because the non-Jewish government of talmudic times provided defense, security, roads and bridges, and other governmental services for the Jewish community, these were not included in the Talmud's list. In a sovereign Jewish state, however, these too would undoubtedly appear in any list of communal needs.

Elsewhere[3] I address the question of how to balance these various needs. In times past, when medicine was much less effective and therefore also much less expensive, the cost of health care was not a major issue for the Jewish community—or, for that matter, for any other community. In our day, as medicine has enabled us to prevent and cure many more conditions, it has in the process become much more expensive. As a result, the cost of health care and how to balance it against other communal needs has become a major social issue worldwide. Although Jewish sources did not know about such costs, the Jewish community, which usually had very limited resources, did face the analogous problem of how to allocate those resources to the ten communal needs listed above, including provisions for the poor and, included in that, redemption of captives. As much as the Jewish tradition valued health care—and, as we have seen, saving lives is at the top of the Jewish agenda—health care nevertheless cannot be the sole service the community provides and must therefore be balanced against the resources expended on other social needs.

Visiting the Sick

The one topic in this area that affects each of us at least as much as doctors on an ongoing basis is visiting the sick. We do not like to visit the sick, especially when they are in hospitals, for all kinds of reasons:

- On the sheer physical level, we do not want to catch a disease from the person we visit or any of the other people in the hospital, whether that fear is warranted or not.
- Sick people remind us of our own vulnerability to illness and even our own mortality, neither of which we like to contemplate. The smells, sights, and sounds of hospitals make those of us not used to such phenomena feel as if we are in a threatening, strange place.
- Engaging with the sick is often depressing for other reasons, because we cannot do with them what we normally like to do together.
- Making the visit is inconvenient. You have to reserve time for your visit, go to an unusual place, pay for parking, and then find the room where the patient is. Worse, once you get there, the patient is likely to be either sleeping or out of the room for tests—and that will surely not encourage you to come back again.
- If the patient is in the room and awake, you then face another problem, namely, what do you say? Visitors and patients both tire of talking about the food and the weather in about ten seconds. You do not want to dwell on the depressing topic of the patient's illness because that is awkward, but if you do not mention it, it becomes "the elephant in the room" that nobody wants to recognize and that everyone dances around. So what do you talk about, and how?

We moderns are by no means the first to feel this way. Our ancestors did not have to go to hospitals to see ill friends or family members, because until very recently in human history, people endured their illnesses at home. On the other hand, the lack of medical knowledge about which diseases were contagious and how must have made our ancestors fear visiting the sick even more than we do. It is precisely because people often have an aversion to visiting the sick that the Jewish tradition made it a mitzvah—not just in the sense of a nice thing to do, but in the original sense of that word as a commanded and obligatory act. Jews are therefore duty bound to visit the sick, whether we want to or not.

There are other reasons the tradition encourages visiting the sick. First, in a source that warrants repeating, the Rabbis assert that in doing so, as with providing for the poor and the bereaved, we imitate God.

> Rabbi Hama, son of Rabbi Hanina, said: "What is the meaning of the verse, 'Follow the Lord your God' (Deuteronomy 13:5)? Is it possible for a mortal to follow God's presence? After all, the Torah says, 'For the Lord your God is a consuming fire' (Deuteronomy 4:24). Rather, the verse means to teach us that we should follow the *attributes* of the Holy One, praised be He. As God clothed the naked, ... you should clothe the naked; the Holy One, blessed be He, visited the sick, as it says, 'The Lord appeared to him by the terebinths of Mamre' (Genesis 18:1) [after the account of Abraham's circumcision], so too you should visit the sick. The Holy One comforted those who mourned ...; you should comfort those who mourn. The Holy One buried the dead ...; you should also bury the dead." (Babylonian Talmud, *Sotah* 14a).

Second, the tradition understood that *illness is isolating.* People are social beings. Although we need some time to be alone, and some of us are more gregarious than others, all of us crave company, at least from time to time. That is why the harshest punishment in prison settings, short of execution and torture, is solitary confinement. Thus it is not surprising that the isolation of illness adds to its ill effects, if not to the illness itself.

Rabbi Abba son of Rabbi Hanina said: "He who visits an invalid takes away a sixtieth of his pain [or, in another version, a sixtieth of his illness] ... "

Rabbi Helbo fell ill. Rabbi Kahana then went [to the house of study] and proclaimed, "Rabbi Helbo is ill." Nobody, however, visited him. Rabbi Kahana rebuked them [the disciples], saying, "Did it ever happen that one of Rabbi Akiva's students fell ill, and the [rest of the] disciples did not visit him?" So Rabbi Akiva himself entered [Rabbi Helbo's house] to visit him, and because they swept and sprinkled the ground before him [that is, cleaned the house and put it in order], Rabbi Helbo recovered. Rabbi Akiva then went forth and lectured: "He who does not visit the sick is like one who sheds blood."

When Rabbi Dimi came [from Palestine], he said: "He who visits the sick causes him to live, while he who does not causes him to die. How does he cause this? ... He who visits the sick prays that he may live ... [while] he who does not visit the sick prays neither that he may live nor die" (Babylonian Talmud, *Nedarim* 39b–40a).

Visiting the sick is an obligation incumbent on everyone. Even the great [those of high social status] visit the small [those of low social status]. And we should visit many times each day, and all who add visits are to be praised as long as they do not burden [the sick person]. And anyone who visits the sick is as if he took away a part of his illness and made things easier for him; anyone who fails to visit the sick is as if he sheds blood (Maimonides, *Mishneh Torah, Laws of Mourning* 14: 4; see also *Shulchan Arukh, Yoreh De'ah* 335).

What, then, should one do while visiting the sick? Here too the tradition has much to tell us. First, sit down (doctors take note!). Why? Because we communicate at least as much through our body language as we do through our words. Visitors who stand while the patient is lying down communicate that they are strong and the patient is weak. That is the last thing you want to convey, for *illness is debilitating.* You surely should not add to the patient's sense of loss of ability that the illness has already inflicted by emphasizing through your standing that you can do more than the patient can. In fact, Maimonides requires that the visitor sit so that his or her head is *below* the level of the patient.

> One who enters a room to visit a sick person [who is lying on the ground with his or her head on a pillow] should not sit on the bed or on a chair or a bench or in an elevated place or above the sick person's head but rather should wrap himself in humility [for, according to the Talmud (*Shabbat* 12b), "the presence of God rests above the head of a sick person"] and sit lower than the sick person's head [presumably prostrating himself or herself] and ask God's mercy for him before leaving (Maimonides, *Mishneh Torah, Laws of Mourning* 14:6). [This, though, applies only when the ill person is lying on the ground so that a visitor who sits will be higher than he or she; but if the patient is lying on a bed, it is permissible to sit on a chair (*Shulchan Arukh, Yoreh De'ah* 335:3).]

Next, what do you talk about? Here, another aspect of illness comes into play: *illness is infantilizing.* In robbing people of what they were able to do before, sickness makes one feel like a child or even, as in the case of incontinence, an infant. Moreover, *illness is boring*; one cannot do what normally occupies one's day and week, and so one seeks anything that will pass the time in an interesting way. To counteract both the sense of diminishment that illness conveys and its boredom, visitors should talk about the same adult topics that they would discuss with the ill person if he or she were not sick, whether that is the family, business, politics, sports, movies, novels, *shul* business, or anything else the people normally talk about. One can even do things to stretch the ill person's mind, because, unless a person suffers from Alzheimer's or another form of dementia, the mind continues to enjoy being stimulated.

The tradition also provides visitors with another suggestion, especially when visiting patients with chronic illnesses where one can benefit from a long-term agenda for conversations—namely, one can help the patient create an ethical will. A product of Jews during the Middle Ages, ethical wills were originally letters that a parent wrote to his or her children, and it can still take that form. Nowadays, though, many instead use an audiotape or a videotape. An ethical will includes the family story; this involves helping the patient recall early memories of childhood, including descriptions and stories of all the relatives, as well as the patient's account of his or her later life. Ethical wills commonly include mention of the person's convictions and moral values (hence the name "ethical will"), his or her suggestions and hopes for the future of the family, and expressions of love. Even if the person's adult children may be tired of hearing the stories, the patient's grandchildren will eagerly want such a record. Patients who know that someone is coming to help them with this project have a real reason to get up in the morning and look forward to the day, because they are clearly doing something meaningful. Because creating such a document or tape can take days or weeks, it helps visitors also to pass the time and even look forward to the visits.[4]

Finally, Jewish law asserts that one has not fulfilled the duty to visit the sick unless one prays with the patient. The prayer need not be long, and it need not use the traditional liturgy—although sometimes people like to use the *Mi-Sheberakh* prayer, the *refa'enu* paragraph in the *Amidah,* or one of the psalms. It can also be whatever comes to mind at the moment or a prayer that the visitor or patient creates after some thought. It can be in Hebrew or in English. The point of insisting on a prayer, though, is to link the patient with God and to enable him or her to express hope—for recovery, if that is possible, or at least for as little pain as possible. The patient may also use the prayer to express hope for other personal things, such as reconciliation with a family member before death. Even visitors and patients who have problems with belief in God or who have not been very religious in their lives should find a way to contemplate and express realistic hopes, to act on them to the extent possible, and to find blessings in each other's company.

Comforting Mourners

If people understand and act on the need to visit the ill, they even more readily recognize that friends and family members who have lost a loved one need to have others surrounding them to help them cope with their loss. That is especially true if the loss is sudden, unexpected, and tragic; but it is also true if the deceased suffered through an illness for a long time, such that death was ultimately a blessing for everyone, including (perhaps especially) the deceased. After all, every death is a loss, and relatives and friends need help in making their peace with it. Even more important, they need others to help them mourn.

Some forms of aid that mourners need are material and easy to recognize. Thus, people are supposed to bring food with them when they visit so that the family does not have to worry about such matters during the first seven days of mourning *(shiva)*. Coordinating who is bringing what and making sure that people are there to set the food out on the table and clean up afterward are essential parts of this duty, and those who perform these tasks are doing a real, concrete service for the mourners. Similarly, helping the family with carpool duty for their children and other mundane but essential tasks is crucial. Finally, showing up for a *minyan* (prayer quorum) during each morning and evening of the *shiva* period and walking mourners around the block after the last morning service of the week to symbolize their reentry into life are clear, physical things that one can and should do.

The harder part of being there for mourners is helping them mourn. Mourning is the process by which relatives and friends separate themselves first physically and then psychologically from the deceased. We separate ourselves physically from the person who has died through the funeral and burial. To make that separation clear, it is customary for everyone attending the interment to shovel three shovelfuls of earth onto the casket once it has been lowered into the ground. The thud the dirt makes as it hits the casket makes it clear to everyone, in a very physical way, that the deceased will no longer be in our physical world.

Separating ourselves physically from the dead, though, only begins the process of separating ourselves psychologically. To do that, everyone who knew him or her—and especially close relatives and friends—must express (literally, "press out of themselves") their memories of the deceased. People do that by talking out their memories, crying as they think of some of them, and laughing as they think of others.

How can you help mourners do that? When I was a child, I was told that you should talk about anything but the deceased in order to get the mourners' minds off their loss. "Talk about baseball," I was told. *That is exactly the wrong advice.* If you do that, the subtext that you are communicating very graphically to the mourners is that you do not want to hear about the deceased, that you either cannot bear the emotional stress or do not want to endure it. Mourners will understand that and will not share their memories with you. They probably will not talk much about baseball either, for that is just not where their heads and hearts are.

What one needs to do is help the mourners mourn—that is, to call up memories of the deceased and express them. How does one do that? There is a very simple way: just ask questions. If it is a spouse that died, ask when the widow or widower first met him or her. If it is a parent that died, ask about the earliest memories that the children have of him or her. In doing so, you communicate that you are willing to listen, and you allow the mourner to talk about the person he or she has just lost.

It is important to ask about *early* memories. Mourners tend to fixate on the last days or hours of the deceased's life because that is when the physical separation took place. Mourning can only bring psychological separation, however, if the whole life of the person is remembered. Moreover, it is an honor to the deceased to remember how he or she lived, for even in heroic deaths, the meaning and value of a person's life comes from its entire expanse, not just the last few days or hours.

Attending to the physical and psychological needs of mourners is clearly a boon to them, but the tradition saw it also as a favor to the deceased. Burying the dead is even more obviously an act of love and care, because the deceased can never pay you back.[5]

And when the time approached for Israel [Jacob] to die, he summoned his son Joseph and said to him: "Do me this favor, place your hand under my thigh as a pledge of your steadfast loyalty (*chesed v'emet,* or, more literally, "Do for me an act of loving-kindness and truth"): please do not bury me in Egypt" (Genesis 47:29). Is there an act of loving-kindness that is a lie such that he has to say "an act of loving-kindness and truth"? ... He said to him: "If you do this for me after my death, it will be an act of kindness and truth" (*Genesis Rabbah* 96:5).

An act of kindness and truth (chesed v'emet). An act of loving-kindness that one does for the dead is an act of loving-kindness of truth (*chesed shel emet,* an authentic act of loving-kindness) because one does not expect to be repaid [since the dead cannot do that].

—*Rashi on Genesis 47:29*

Celebrating Births and Marriages

Burying the dead and comforting mourners by helping them remember the deceased may seem obvious acts of *chesed* and *tikkun olam,* for they respond to people in clear need. The Jewish tradition recognizes however, that people celebrating joyous events in their lives also need companionship.

Why is that so? In part, it is because, as social beings, we want our family and friends to celebrate with us. Their absence diminishes our own joy, and their presence makes it all the more exuberant. In part, though, it is because people celebrating a wedding, a birth, a bar or bat mitzvah, or even a birthday also recognize that something important is going on in their lives, that in some important ways they will be different after the event, and they want their family and friends there to help them through this life passage. They also want help unpacking the meaning of such events, which they feel in their gut but cannot always consciously articulate. As a result of all these factors, people celebrating these events are often quite nervous, partially because they do not want to look bad in front of their family and friends but also because they know that these events will transform them in important ways.

One of the earliest rabbinic texts already recognizes the need for family, friends, and even complete strangers to help a wedding party celebrate, even at the expense of giving up one's study of Torah for a time.

> If two scholars sit and study Torah and before them passes a bridal procession or the bier of a dead man, then if there are enough in the procession, they ought not neglect their study; but if not, let them get up and cheer and hail the bride or accompany the dead.
>
> Once as Rabbi Judah bar Il'ai sat teaching his disciples, a bride passed by. So he took myrtle twigs in his hand and cheered her until the bride passed out of his sight.
>
> Another time as Rabbi Judah bar Il'ai sat teaching his disciples, a bride passed by.
>
> "What was that?" he asked of them. "A bride passing by," they replied. "My sons," he said to them, "get up and attend upon the bride. For thus we find concerning the Holy One, blessed be He, that He attended the bride; as it is said, 'And the Lord built the rib' (Genesis 2:22). If He attended upon a bride, how much more so should we!"
>
> And from where [in the Torah] do we find that the Holy One, blessed be He, attended upon a bride? For it is said, "And the Lord God built [*banah*] the rib." Now, in the sea towns they call plaiting *binyata*. Hence we learn that the Holy One, blessed be He, fixed Eve's hair and outfitted her as a bride and brought her to Adam, as it is said, "And He brought her unto the man" *(ibid.)*. The first time the Holy One, blessed be He, acted as best man for Adam; henceforth one must get a best man for himself (*Avot de-Rabbi Natan*, ch. 4).

Similarly, the meal after the circumcision of a baby boy is called a *se'udat mitzvah*, a meal accompanying a commanded act or, possibly, even a commanded meal, for Rabbi Moses Isserles, who added comments to Joseph Karo's code of Jewish law (the *Shulchan Arukh*) indicating where the practice of northern European (Ashkenazic) Jews differed from Mediterranean (Sephardic) Jews, says that one who refuses to take part in such a meal is almost as if excommunicated by God.[6] Similarly, it has always been customary for the family of a newborn girl to sponsor a *kiddush* on the day she is named in the synagogue and/or, in our time, to include a celebratory meal as part of a completely separate ceremony (a *simchat bat*). These "meals accompanying a commandment" include those that are not technically celebratory, namely, the ones after the circumcision of a newborn boy or the redemption of a firstborn boy from priestly service thirty-one days after his birth (his *pidyon ha-ben*), so that mourning relatives may attend after the initial seven days of mourning (and even during them if the ceremony takes place in one's home).[7] Family and friends need to be there to mark and celebrate the arrival of a new person in the life of the family and the community.

It is fitting to end this chapter, then, with a summary statement by Maimonides:

It is a positive commandment of rabbinic authority to visit the sick, comfort mourners, accompany the dead [to the burial ground], bring the bride under the wedding canopy, to accompany visitors to their destination, and to deal with all the needs of burial, including carrying the casket on one's shoulder, walking before it, saying a eulogy, tearing one's clothing, and burying the dead. Similarly, [it is a duty imposed by the Rabbis] to help the bride and groom rejoice and to provide for all their needs. These acts are forms of loving-kindness that one does with one's body [in contrast to those done with one's money], for which there is no limit [to determine when you have done enough or too much].

Even though all these commandments are rabbinic [in origin and authority], they are in the category of "Love your neighbor as yourself" (Leviticus 19:18): Everything that you would want others to do for you, you must do for your fellow Jew [literally, "for your neighbor in Torah and commandments"] ...

—*Maimonides,* Mishneh Torah, Laws of Mourning *14:1*
(see also Shulchan Arukh, Yoreh De'ah *335)*

Part Three

Tikkun Olam within Families

8

Duties of Spouses to Each Other

Our family relationships are, in many ways, the most important ties to other human beings we have. It therefore should not be a surprise that the Jewish tradition has much to say about how we relate to our spouses, parents, and children. In fact, Jewish law has much more to say about those relationships than secular law does, partly because Jewish law is a *religious* legal system. The Bill of Rights in American law specifically denies jurisdiction of the government to many areas of life. Because God is presumed to know and care about everything in our lives, however, Jewish law asserts competence and jurisdiction to govern our personal relationships as well as our social ones. Furthermore, because people can do bad things to each other in their personal relationships at least as much as in their social ones, Jewish law has a particular agenda of *tikkun olam* in the family as well as in the larger society. In each of the following chapters—one each on our relationships to our spouses, our parents, and our children—I shall first describe how the Jewish tradition understands that relationship and then explore how it pushes us to acts of *tikkun olam* with regard to that relationship.

Marriage as Covenant, Social Structure, and Sacred Event

The Jewish tradition understands marriage to operate on three independent, but interlocking, planes: the contractual, the social, and the sacred. That is, marriage is not exclusively a matter of a contract between the two people or families, and it is not simply a social structure governed by the rules of society or a sacred event with solely religious meaning; it is all three at once. Moreover, each element affects the functioning of the others.

The Covenantal Element of Jewish Marriage

Jewish marriage is, first, a covenant between the parties. Like a contract, a covenant is an agreement between two parties in which each gets something and gives something (lawyers call what each party gets "consideration"). Unlike a contract, though, a covenant is not designed to accomplish a specific task, after which it terminates; rather, those entering a covenant intend to create a long-term relationship. As a result, the terms of a covenant are generally less well spelled out than those of a contract, because it is harder to anticipate what might happen in a long-term relationship than it is in taking on a particular task. Thus, a covenant of marriage in all cultures and legal systems is typically much shorter and much less specific than, for example, a contract to rent an apartment.

Even though a covenant differs in important ways from a contract, it shares one important aspect that affects marriage—namely, the parties can create the covenant or dissolve it at will. Both the man and the woman must agree to be married for the marriage to be valid.[1] As the Rabbis of the Mishnah and Talmud understood the Torah (specifically, Deuteronomy 24:1–3), a man must initiate a divorce but can simply throw the writ of divorce within six feet (four cubits) of the woman to deliver it and effect the divorce.[2] After the enactment of Rabbenu Gershom toward the end of the tenth century, however, the woman as well as the man must agree to a divorce to make it valid.[3] Even in the time of Torah, as far as we can tell, and certainly by the time of the later Mishnah and Talmud, if both members of a couple agree to a divorce, they need not supply a justification for dissolving their marriage to judges or other officials; the covenantal nature of marriage enables them to create and dissolve their marriage at will.

> The School of Shammai says, "A man may not divorce his wife unless he has found something improper in her, as it is said, 'because he finds something obnoxious about her'" (Deuteronomy 24:1). But the School of Hillel says, "Even if she spoiled a dish for him, as it is said, 'because he finds something obnoxious about her.'" Rabbi Akiva says, "Even if he found another more beautiful than she is, as it is said, 'She fails to please him'" (ibid.).[4]
>
> —*Mishnah,* Gittin *9:10*

As late as 1970, all American states except Nevada required that a divorcing couple justify their divorce as a response to adultery, insanity, imprisonment, or some other communally accepted reason for the couple to separate. In contrast, the covenantal nature of Jewish marriage had enabled couples to divorce simply for "irreconcilable differences" almost two thousand years earlier.

Furthermore, the covenantal character of Jewish marriage enables the couple to create special conditions for their marriage, usually regarding the monetary arrangements between them, but sometimes also other matters. The only condition that Jewish law forbids the couple to make with each other is to promise never to engage in conjugal relations, because the Rabbis construed sexual intercourse to be the defining characteristic that distinguishes marriage from other close relationships.[5] After they have produced both a male and a female child to fulfill the Torah's commandment,

"Be fruitful and multiply" (Genesis 1:28),[6] they may mutually decide never to have sex again, but they may not put that decision into their marriage covenant.

Nowadays, couples—especially those where one member brings much more money into the marriage than the other, or where there are children or property from a prior marriage—often create a prenuptial agreement that can be very specific about certain matters. This, however, is a relatively new phenomenon in Anglo-American law. Jewish law provided for such mutually agreed-upon conditions to a marriage from as early as the second-century Mishnah as a manifestation of the covenantal character of Jewish marriage.

The Social Element of Jewish Marriage

Marriage is a social phenomenon in several senses. It is, first, a social occasion, in which family and friends are invited to join in the celebration. Moreover, as we have seen in chapter 7, if there are not enough people present to help the bride and groom rejoice, other members of the community must even interrupt their study of Jewish texts, let alone other activities, to help the wedding couple celebrate. Because marriage affects the entire community, members of the community must be present to mark it and celebrate it.

This communal element of marriage has legal ramifications. According to traditional Jewish law, the seven blessings of the wedding ceremony may only be recited in the presence of a *minyan,* ten adult Jews, which officially marks a Jewish community.[7]

Marriage is also "social" in the sense that society—in our case, Jewish law—establishes conditions that are imposed on every marriage. In recent American law, those conditions have been altered by court decisions and legislation to drop the demand that, for example, the couple be of the same race and, at least in some states, to insist that the couple be a man and a woman. In Belgium, Canada, Holland, Spain, and currently in Massachusetts, marriage may apply to two people of the same gender as well. In other jurisdictions (Vermont, California and Connecticut), legally defined "civil unions" or "domestic partnerships" are possible for couples of the same gender. In all states and countries, laws define and prohibit incestuous unions; most ban polygamous unions; and most, if not all, declare minimum ages for marriage.

In addition to defining who may marry whom, state codes often say something about what is entailed in marriage, although that statement is usually perfunctory. California law is typical: "Husband and wife contract toward each other obligations of mutual respect, fidelity, and support."[8] The California code then ignores the issues of "mutual respect" and "fidelity," the former probably because it cannot find legal ways to define it and the latter because since the 1970s, state laws in all fifty states have recognized the legality of private, consensual sex between adults, regardless of their marital status. The code does spell out some of the elements of its third obligation of marriage, "support," because secular law can and does regulate money and property in marriage as it does in other commercial transactions, although with some differences in deference to the special relationship between the two parties.

Jewish law is much more specific. It establishes a number of "constructive conditions" of marriage—that is, conditions that are built into the very construct of marriage as the Rabbis define it. As a result, whether or not a husband specified these benefits to his wife, they are part of his duties in marriage "as a condition of the court." These include duties to support her from the time of betrothal, whether or not he marries her after the usual waiting period (at that time) of twelve months, and to support her (if he divorces her) or to arrange for his estate to support her (if he predeceases her) until she remarries; to ransom her from captivity; to distribute the property she brought into the marriage only to her male children and not to those of his other wives; to support her female children until they marry; to pay for her medical expenses and her "adornments"; to allow her continued ties to her family and community; to avoid professions that would make him smell bad as well as diseases that would make him unattractive to her; and to offer to have sexual intercourse with her at reasonable intervals, as measured by his way of earning a living. Here are some of the sources in *Mishnah Ketubbot* for some of these obligations of the husband:[9]

> 4:8: If he had not written for her, "If you are taken captive, I will ransom you and I will take you back as my wife," ... he is nevertheless liable because that is a condition enjoined by the Court.
>
> 4:9: If she were taken captive, he must ransom her; and if he said, "Here is her bill of divorce and her marriage settlement, let her redeem herself," he has no such power. If she came to harm, he must heal her. If he said, "Here is her bill of divorce and her marriage settlement, let her cure herself," he is entitled to do so ...
>
> 5:6: If one put his wife under a vow to have no connubial intercourse, the School of Shammai says, "[He may continue to maintain the vow] for two weeks"; but the School of Hillel says, "For one week only." Students may leave their wives at home to study the Torah without their wives' permission for thirty days; laborers for one week. The time for marital duties enjoined in the Law are: for men of independent means every day, for workmen twice weekly, for ass-drivers once a week, for camel-drivers once every thirty days, for sailors once every six months. This is the opinion of R. Eliezer....
>
> 7:4: If one placed a vow upon his wife that she was not to go to her father's house, if he lived with her in the same town and the vow was for one month, he may continue to keep her as his wife, but if for two months, he must divorce her and give her her marriage settlement; but if he lived in another town, and the vow was for one Holy Day, he may continue to keep her as his wife, but if for three he must divorce her and grant her her marriage settlement.

7:5: If one set a vow upon his wife that she was not to go to a house of mourning or to a house of feasting, he must divorce her and grant her her marriage settlement because he closes all doors to her ...

The wife's duties include the household duties that one would expect in the patriarchal society of old. As the following selections from the *Mishnah Ketubbot* indicate, however, they also include being reasonably modest in her social conduct; enabling her husband to obey Jewish law in eating (through proper tithing of the dough and, it is simply assumed, through making their home kosher) and in sexual intercourse (by informing him as to when she is menstruating so that they avoid sexual intercourse then); and doing work of her own, both to help support the family and to avoid boredom, "for idleness leads to lewdness ... and lightmindedness."

5:5: These are the tasks that a wife must carry out for her husband: she must grind corn, bake, and do washing, cook, suckle her child, make his [her husband's] bed for him, and work in wool. If she brought him one bondwoman, she need not grind nor bake nor wash; if two, she does not have to cook, nor give suckle to her child; if three, she is not required to make his bed for him, nor work in wool; if four, she may sit on a raised seat. R. Eliezer says, "Even if she brought him a hundred bondwomen, he can compel her to work in wool, since idleness leads to lewdness." Rabban Simeon ben Gamliel says, "If one places his wife under a vow not to perform any task, he should divorce her and give her her marriage settlement, as idleness leads to lightmindedness." ...
5:7: If a woman is refractory against her husband [in not letting him have sex with her], he may reduce her marriage settlement by seven *denars* every week. Rabbi Judah says, "Seven half-*denars*." How long is the reduction to be

continued? Until it reaches the full amount of her marriage settlement. Rabbi Jose says, "He may continue to diminish it, in case an inheritance may fall to her from some source and he can then claim [the amount beyond her marriage settlement] from her." Similarly, if a man rebels against his wife [by not offering to have sex with her], they [the Rabbis] may add to her marriage settlement three *denars* ...

7:6: And these are the women who are divorced without their marriage settlement: she who transgresses the Law of Moses and [she who transgresses] Jewish custom. And what constitutes "transgressing the Law of Moses"? If she gives him food which has not been tithed, or if she has sexual intercourse with him when she is a menstruant, or if she does not separate the priest's share of the dough, or if she makes a vow and does not fulfill it. And what constitutes "transgressing Jewish custom"? If she goes out with her hair uncovered, or if she spins wool in the marketplace, or if she converses with every man. Abba Saul says, "Also if she curses his parents to his face." Rabbi Tarfon says, "Also if she is a loud-voiced woman." And what constitutes "a loud-voiced woman"? One who speaks in her house such that her neighbors hear her voice ...

Two things should be noted about these lists of responsibilities. First, while the man has a right to sex within marriage just as much as a woman does, he may never force himself upon her.[10] That is, the Rabbis long ago recognized marital rape and prohibited it, a very recent addition to American law. As a result, if a wife refuses to engage in conjugal relations with her husband, his remedy is not rape, but rather reducing the amount that he would have to pay her in a divorce settlement in amounts that extend over the time that she refuses, until he can divorce her without paying her anything and marry someone else.

Second, the Mishnah has a keen understanding of the importance of work in the lives of women as well as men. Although family takes precedence over work in Jewish sources, in sharp contrast to the way many Americans order their priorities, work is also important. The lack of it leads to "lewdness" and "lightmindedness"—whatever those terms mean—and certainly lack of self-esteem, boredom, and possibly even criminal activity. Hence the insistence of the Jewish tradition that we saw in chapter 5 to help the poor find a job, and hence the Mishnah's provisions here that even wealthy women who can carry out their household duties through hired help must have some form of work to do. In our own day, that might include volunteer projects as well as work for pay, and in old age it may mean volunteer work (helping children or adults to learn to read) or babysitting grandchildren; "working in wool" is clearly meant here simply as one example of what a wealthy woman might do. The Mishnah knows full well, though, that it is not healthy for either men or women to remain idle and, conversely, it values work.

Forms of *Tikkun Olam* in Spousal Relations

The Jewish understanding of marriage as simultaneously a covenant, a social occasion, and a sacred event suggests several forms of *tikkun olam* in supporting marriages: Preparing for marriage to give couples the skills to communicate effectively and to handle life's tasks, joys, and sorrows together; periodically setting aside time together to refresh and strengthen their relationship; finding ways to mediate their disputes, either by themselves or with the help of others; and avoiding violence within the family setting.

Preparation for Marriage

Although Judaism does not consider divorce to be a sin, and though sometimes it is the right thing to do for both members of the couple and even for their children (if any), divorce, even under the best of circumstances, is always sad. At the very least, the couple must give up and mourn their dreams of a long, happy life together. They must also deal with the feelings of frustration and self-doubt that often accompany divorce. Some will be "gun-shy" for quite some time in looking for a new partner, not daring to trust their instincts.

Moreover, divorce is hard. There are, first, all the legal issues to take care of in both civil and Jewish law, including the disposition of their property. If the couple has children, they face the often difficult and extremely important issues of custody, education, and financial and emotional support, so that the divorce harms them as little as possible. Often that means that the couple, despite their distaste for each other, must interact with one another for a long time to come. The welfare of their children demands that they learn to do that with civility, all the while supporting the children's respect and love for their former spouse, but that is often much easier said than done.

Because divorce, while not a sin, is nevertheless sad and hard, it is crucial that a couple contemplating marriage engage in some preventive measures to raise the chances that they will stay married. At the initiative of Rabbi Aaron Wise, of blessed memory, and Dr. Sylvia Weishaus, a psychologist, the University of Judaism established a preparation for marriage course in 1975, consisting of ten sessions for groups of ten couples who are about to be married or have just been married. Five sessions are led by a marriage counselor, in which the couples discuss such matters as these: how to handle their parents; how to deal with friends of one partner but not the other; how to balance their careers and children; how to please each other sexually when one partner is not in the mood and one is; and how to have an argument and still come out married. One session is devoted to economic issues, led by a financial counselor, because especially during the first years of marriage arguments often center around money. Finally, four sessions are devoted to creating a Jewish home.

In 2000, on the twenty-fifth anniversary of the program, its directors commissioned a survey of all the couples who had gone through the program. Instead of the current American divorce rate—in the neighborhood of 50 percent of all couples who get married—the divorce rate among those who had taken the program was 8 percent. Given those figures, I will not officiate at a wedding in Los Angeles unless the couple has taken that preparation for marriage course; I think it is actually rabbinic malpractice to perform the ceremony without such preparation.

Couples sometimes object to such a course because they find the very thought of it demeaning. After all, they think, they should know how to handle themselves and interact with each other in marriage by "doing what comes naturally." If they cannot manage their marriage on their own, they think, they must be stupid, clueless, or somehow deficient in this most personal of areas.

The fact, though, is that there are many skills involved in marriage that need to be learned. Some couples do indeed intuit these skills, and some learn them through trial and error over time; but all can benefit immensely from some advice from those who have experience in helping couples understand what is important in a marital relationship and how to handle its inevitable ups and downs. As I tell couples, you spend years preparing for your careers; you can spend ten sessions preparing for your marriage. This is preventive *tikkun olam*.

Booster Shots

Marriage only begins on the wedding day, and it hopefully lasts long after the honeymoon. As life presents its challenges, couples can and often do deepen their relationship as they face them together and manage them. Children, careers, parents, and friends all demand their attention. In the midst of all of this, it is important that the couple not let the rush of their lives blind them to each other. Too many couples find that after the children have grown up and left the house, their own relationship has to be reborn. It is appropriate that the relationship be redefined as new factors play into the couple's lives, but it is important that they retain enough connection to each other through thick and thin so that they can build on their mutual feelings for each other and redirect their relationship as needed.

To retain and even deepen that reservoir of love, couples need to take some time off for each other. If they do not have the money to hire a babysitter, they can exchange babysitting nights with another couple. Then, once every week or two they should go out and do something they enjoy—dinner, a movie, a play, dancing, or whatever. The few hours they spend away from their children will not only contribute to their relationship but will also make them better parents and even better at their jobs. Later, when the children are grown, a weekend away every once in a while, in addition to a vacation together, can ensure that the relationship does not become routine. Many couples also find programs such as Jewish Marriage Encounter helpful. Even though these "booster shots" may seem obvious and even a little silly, they are actually a crucial way to tend to their relationship, fixing and strengthening their personal world in critical ways.

Bringing Peace between Husband and Wife

Sometimes, couples find themselves at odds with each other in ways that they themselves cannot resolve. At such times, it is important that they get help, be it from a rabbi, a social worker (perhaps through the counseling services of Jewish Family Service), a marriage counselor, or a therapist. Men, in particular, find it hard to admit that they need help and often resist discussing their problems with anyone else, even close friends. That is in part because men are socialized in our society to be self-reliant and independent. (This also leads to men consulting doctors about their physical ailments much less than they should and often too late to stop a problem before it becomes serious.)

The fact of the matter is that none of us is God, that we all need help in a variety of areas; it is only wise to reach out for it when we need it. Thus, one version of the Talmud's list of activities that bring immediate benefit and bear fruit for a long time to come includes "bringing peace between a husband and wife."[11]

Domestic Violence

Sometimes problems escalate to the point of one spouse battering the other or abusing the other sexually, verbally, and/or psychologically. Physical abuse is relatively easy to see. Sexual abuse, where the man effectively rapes his wife by insisting on having sex with her against her will, is usually clear to both parties but somewhat less easy for others to identify, especially when the man claims that the sex was consensual, at which point it becomes a case of "he said, she said." Verbal and psychological forms of abuse are yet harder to identify, but no less real. Verbal abuse consists of cases where one spouse continually demeans the other out of anger and spite for no good reason ("You are so stupid," for example), to be distinguished from constructive and loving criticism for a specific act. Psychological abuse occurs when one spouse creates an atmosphere of intimidation and fear.

Domestic violence of all these types does occur in Jewish families of all religious denominations, among avowedly secular Jews, among all ethnic subgroups of Jews (Ashkenazi, Sephardi, Persian), and among all levels of educational and financial status. Worse, sometimes the Jewish religion is invoked as the justification for such abuse.

It is therefore crucial to understand that rabbis in all Jewish denominations have declared the following:

- Spousal abuse violates some of the most basic beliefs and values of the Jewish tradition.
- People subjected to such abuse do not deserve it and must find ways to extricate themselves from such abuse, even if

that means some shame for themselves and their family, for every Jew has a primary duty to God to protect himself or herself and his or her children from harm.

- Members of the Jewish community who witness abuse or its effects have a duty to help its victims find ways to get help, even if that means turning over the abuser to governmental authorities.
- People abusing their spouses or children in any or all of these ways must get help to stop.

In my rabbinic ruling on family violence, approved unanimously by the Conservative Movement's Committee on Jewish Law and Standards and reprinted in an earlier book,[12] I define the various kinds of violence—physical, sexual, and verbal—and discuss Jewish norms governing such abuse of spouses, parents (especially elderly ones), and children. I then argue for prohibiting even those forms of assault that were permitted by the tradition in the past (such as beating one's wife and children). The ruling then successively deals with the responsibilities of victims of abuse, witnesses to it, and batterers.

For those experiencing or witnessing family violence, rabbis and Jewish Family Service can often be of help in finding shelters (Jewish Family Service of Los Angeles, for example, operates two such shelters for battered women and children), and they can also be of help in finding treatment programs for batterers. This is a scourge on the Jewish community that we must acknowledge as real as a first step in stopping it. To help batterers confront why they batter and how to change their behavior, and to protect women (almost always, but some men too) and children from physical, sexual, verbal, and psychological abuse is *tikkun olam* in a sorely needed and most graphic sense.

9

Filial Duties

Tikkun olam also involves regulating the relationships between parents and children such that parents are taken care of in their old age and children are taught the norms and skills of relating to others in their youth. If the former does not happen, society as a whole will bear the burden of aiding seniors who can no longer live independently; if the latter does not happen, children will grow into antisocial and perhaps even criminal adults. So society as a whole has serious stakes in both directions of the parent-child relationship, and hence Jewish sources try to structure that relationship to assure—or at least make it more probable—that these social ends are met.

Beyond these pragmatic goals, proper parent-child relationships go to the very heart of the Jewish vision of what kinds of people we should be. That is, even if the pragmatic needs of parents and children could be met by other children, teachers, or other people in society, the very nature of the parent-child relationship as conceived in the Jewish tradition requires that all parents fulfill parental duties to their children and that all children fulfill filial duties to their parents. It is simply a matter of character, of the kind of person one should be and the kind of society one should help create.

In describing filial and parental duties in this chapter and the next, I speak about *tikkun olam* in two separate senses. First, these Jewish norms seek to establish parent-child relations so that society's practical needs for the care of parents and the raising of children can be met at least in part by the parents and children themselves and not wholly by society. This will "fix" society in the sense of *ordering* it, distributing the responsibility of fulfilling its needs among its members, which will in turn enable society to meet its members' needs more effectively and efficiently than social agencies alone could accomplish. Second, these parental and filial norms will "fix" society in the sense of *improving* it by setting guidelines to inform and foster the character development of its members through educating them to recognize and fulfill their duties as proper parents or children. Thus, society will hopefully be filled with people who not only carry out their minimal duties to their close family but who also go beyond that to treat the members of their family in a noble and virtuous way.

The Two Basic Filial Duties: Honor and Respect

Two of the Torah's commandments establish the foundation for the Jewish concept of parent-child relationships—the duties to honor one's parents and to fear or respect them:

> Honor your father and your mother, that your days may be long upon the land which the Lord your God is giving you (Exodus 20:12).

> You shall fear every man his mother and his father, and you shall keep My Sabbaths: I am the Lord your God (Leviticus 19:3).

In typical rabbinic fashion, the Rabbis immediately try to define what each of these commandments entails and how they differ from each other. As a boy, I always thought that the commandment to honor my parents applied to me and my young friends and that it commanded us to obey our parents. That, however, is not how the Rabbis define it. Instead, they determine that it applies to adult children who have positive duties (that is, things they must do) to care for their elderly parents when they cannot care for themselves. As long as the parents have financial resources, the children may use them to carry out this obligation, but once the parents' money runs out, the children must use their own resources to finance the services required by this commandment.

The duty to respect (or fear) one's parents, on the other hand, involves negative duties to refrain from actions that would reduce the parents psychologically and socially to the level of their children. They may therefore not sit in either parent's chair (assuming that the parent has a special one) or contradict the parent in public. The latter duty, however, does not mean that the child must always agree with the parent or may not challenge the parent in private; this is rather a matter of preserving the honor of the parent in public forums. As the Talmud makes clear, these duties apply to both sons and daughters and to both mothers and fathers, and so "he" and "father" in these sources also refer to "her" and "mother."

Our Rabbis taught: What is "fear" and what is "honor"? "Fear" means that he [the son] must neither stand nor sit in his [the father's] place, nor contradict his words, nor tip the scales against him. "Honor" means that he must give him food and drink, clothe and cover him, lead him in and out. The Scholars propounded: At whose expense? Rav Judah said: The son's. Rabbi Nahman b. Oshaia said: The father's. The Rabbis gave a ruling to Rabbi Jeremiah—others state to Rabbi Jeremiah's son—in accordance with the view that it may be at the father's expense. An objection is raised: The Bible says, "Honor your father and your mother," and it also says, "Honor the Lord with your substance": just as the latter means at personal cost, so the former too. But if you say [that the son provides goods and services to his father] at the father's [expense], how does it affect him [the son] such that it is a duty of his?—Through loss of time (Babylonian Talmud, *Kiddushin* 31b–32a).

The last line of the source above indicates that the Rabbis presumed that adult children would personally carry out these duties of honor. This is made explicit in the following source, which compares the way we should honor our parents with the way we should honor God.

> You are My children, and I am your Father ... It is an honor for children to dwell with their father, and it is an honor for the father to dwell with his children ... Therefore make a house for the Father in which He can dwell with His children (*Exodus Rabbah* 34:3).

As we shall discuss in the next section of this chapter, this raises questions in our day about placing elderly parents in nursing homes.

The connection between the honor of parents and the honor of God is a common theme among the Rabbis. That is, in part, because the Rabbis maintained that along with one's mother and father, God is one of our parents, and so honoring our earthly parents is a way to honor our heavenly Parent as well.

> There are three partners in the production of the human being: the Holy One, blessed be He, the father, and the mother. The father provides the white matter from which are formed the bones, sinews, nails, brain, and the white part of the eye. [The Rabbis probably thought this because semen is white.] The mother provides the red matter from which are formed the skin, flesh, hair, and the pupil of the eye. [The Rabbis probably thought this because menstrual blood is red.] The Holy

One, blessed be He, infuses into him/her breath, soul, features, vision, hearing, speech, power of motion, understanding, and intelligence (Babylonian Talmud, *Niddah* 31a).

The Rabbis say: "Three combine in the making of each person: God, the father, and the mother. If people honor their father and mother, God says, 'I ascribe merit to them as if I dwelled among them and as if they honored Me.'" (Babylonian Talmud, *Kiddushin* 30b)

Philo of Alexandria, a first-century thinker who is arguably the first Jewish philosopher, expands on the connection between honoring parents and honoring God by focusing on the placement of the commandment to honor parents in the Decalogue (the ten commandments). A common rabbinic theme is that the first five of those commandments govern the relationships between God and human beings, and the second group of five regulates the relationships that human beings have with each other. Parents, of course, are human beings, and so the fact that the Torah places the commandment to honor them as the last of the first group of five indicates that it makes parents akin to God. Like God, our parents are responsible not only for our physical existence but also for our moral and theological education. Furthermore, parents function as a bridge from God to the human world and from the human world to God.

After dealing with the seventh day [the fourth of the ten commandments], He gives the Fifth Commandment on the honor due to parents. This commandment He placed on the borderline between the two sets of five: it is the last of the first set, in which the most sacred injunctions, those dealing with God, are given, and it adjoins the second set of five, which contain the duties of human beings to each other. The reason, I think, is this: we see that parents by their nature stand on the borderline between the mortal and the immortal sides of existence—the mortal, because of their kinship with [other] people and with other animals in that their bodies are perishable; the immortal, because the act of generation assimilates them to God, the progenitor of everything ...

Some bolder spirits, glorifying the name of parenthood, say that a father and mother are in fact gods revealed to sight, who copy the Uncreated in His work as the Framer of life ... How can reverence be rendered to the invisible God by those who show irreverence to the gods who are near at hand and seen by the eye?

—*Philo,* Treatise on the Decalogue

As one can see from the Talmud's definitions of "honor" and "fear" of parents, the Jewish tradition here, as usual, translates what looks like matters of feeling and attitude into demands for concrete actions. It never takes lip service to be sufficient. At the same time, it was certainly not blind to the importance of the tenor and feelings with which one fulfills commandments, especially ones as personal as these. Thus, the Talmud includes this remarkable passage, in which the Rabbis make clear that while the proper feelings are not enough, the proper actions are not enough either; one needs to do the right things for one's parents in the context of an attitude of honor and respect.

A man may feed his father on fattened chickens and inherit Hell as his reward, and another may put his father to work in a mill and inherit Paradise.

How is it possible that a man might feed his father fattened chickens and inherit Hell? It once happened that a man used to feed his father fattened chickens. Once his father said to him: "My son, where did you get these?" He answered: "Old man, old man, eat and be silent, just as dogs eat and are silent." In such an instance, he feeds his father fattened chickens, but he inherits Hell.

How is it possible that a man might put his father to work in a mill and inherit Paradise? It once happened that a man was working in a mill. The king decreed millers should be brought to work for him. The son said to his father: "Father, go and work in the mill in my place, (and I will go to work for the king). For it may be (that the workers will be) ill-treated, in which case let me be ill-treated instead of you. And it may be (that the workers will be) beaten, in which case let me be beaten instead of you." In such an instance, he puts his father to work in a mill, but he inherits Paradise (Babylonian Talmud, *Kiddushin* 31a–31b).

Limits on the Filial Duties of Honor and Respect

The filial duties that Jewish law prescribes are extensive and demanding, but they do have limits. Children should not fulfill a parent's command that violates God's laws, undermines the child's welfare, or is unreasonable. Furthermore, although it is certainly desirable that children love their parents, Jewish law does not require that.

God's Commandments

The tie between honoring parents and honoring God has direct implications for determining the hierarchy of our duties to honor our parents and to honor God. For the Rabbis, the order was very clear: because all Jews, including one's parents, are duty bound to obey God, God's commandments take precedence over those of one's parents when they conflict.

Because one might think that one is obliged to obey one's father or mother who desires that one violate a commandment,

the Torah therefore says [immediately following the commandment to fear or revere one's parents in Leviticus 19:3],
"and you shall keep My Sabbaths," [meaning that] you are
all required to honor Me (*Sifra Leviticus, Kedoshim* 1:10).

It was taught: One might think that the honor of father and
mother supersedes the Sabbath, [but that is not so:] the
Torah says, "You shall fear every man his mother and his
father, and you shall keep My Sabbaths; I am the Lord your
God," [meaning] that all of you are obligated to honor Me
(Babylonian Talmud, *Yevamot* 5b).

Clearly, this aspect of Jewish law should not be an excuse for
children to dishonor their parents in a kind of religious "one-
upmanship." If the children decide to become more religiously
involved and observant than their parents, they must do so in a
way that continues to show their parents honor in attitude, word,
and deed. If the children are teenagers, they need to work out with
their parents exactly how the new patterns of observance they want
to adopt can fit into the family structure. Sometimes, for example,
the parents may be convinced to make the home kosher or to
refrain from some of their customary family activities on the
Sabbath and instead do things appropriate to the Sabbath as they
grow in their Judaism along with their children. In other families,
the parents and children have to negotiate a way in which each can
"live and let live" in his or her own, distinct way while living under
the same roof. The critical thing is not the ultimate agreement;
rather, it is that the conversations in which these negotiations take
place remain calm and mutually respectful and that all family members continue to interact with each other in the same manner.

If the children are adults living on their own and the issue is
visits to each other's homes, the situation is somewhat easier, both
because the time spent together is considerably shorter and because

parents presume that college-age and older children will be making their own life decisions about religion and, indeed, everything else. Still, if, say, the children keep kosher and the parents do not, then the parents and children need to work out some modus vivendi to make it possible for them to see one another and socialize together. The situation is even worse on Passover, when Jewish dietary laws are even stricter. If both parents and children keep kosher, or kosher for Passover, but in different ways, it is usually best for each simply to give "full faith and credit" to the other without asking questions. Again, the tone in which these issues are negotiated is usually more important than the specific agreement.

Another increasingly common issue that falls under this category occurs when parents have made it clear that upon their death they want to be cremated. It is bad enough if only one adult child is involved in this decision, because then if the child has the parent buried, he or she must bear the burden of acting against the express wishes of the parent after the parent has died and cannot protest or even argue. On the other hand, if the child acquiesces to the parent's wishes, he or she must suffer the guilt of violating Jewish law. The situation is yet worse when there are two or more children involved, one or more of whom want to bury Mom or Dad according to traditional Jewish rites, despite the parent's instructions to the contrary, and one or more of whom want to carry out the parent's wishes, whether or not they agree with Mom or Dad. Jewish tradition is clear: neither the parent nor the children have the right to violate Jewish law, and so the children should bury, and not cremate, the parent. Putting that decision into practice, however, is often not nearly as simple as that, and the adult children would be well advised to get the help of their rabbi in working this out so that they can have reasonable relationships with each other after this is over.

Such an approach is even more important when the requirements of Jewish law are not clear. This happens often when adult children face the decision of whether to remove life support systems from Mom or Dad when there is no reasonable hope for recovery. Although Jewish law is clear in its prohibition of cremation, rabbis differ on what Jewish law does and does not demand with regard to end-of-life care, especially the status of artificial nutrition and hydration.

On one end of the spectrum, some, but certainly not all, Orthodox rabbis demand that absolutely everything be done to keep a body alive, even if that means the person will never regain consciousness and will have to be on machines forever. On the other end of the spectrum, some Reform rabbis maintain that here, as always, individual family members should seek the advice of their rabbi but in the end should make their decisions however they think is best. In the middle are multiple positions that rabbis of all movements have taken on these issues. Some, for example, see artificial nutrition and hydration as food and liquids and therefore require that they be administered under all circumstances, while others maintain that artificial nutrition and hydration are medicine and therefore may be withheld or withdrawn.

All Jewish authorities would say that patients must be kept as comfortable as possible, for, unlike some forms of Christianity, Judaism does not regard pain as a good. Furthermore, each movement in Judaism has produced its distinctive form of advance directive, so that a person can indicate which medical treatments he or she would choose at the end of life, as framed by the choices open to him or her according to his or her movement's approach to Jewish law. In addition, books on these general issues of medical ethics and, in particular, on how adult children should understand their duty to feed their parents at the end of life have been published from the viewpoints of all movements in Judaism.[1] Adult children would also be well advised to consult with their rabbi in such circumstances to determine exactly what their approach to Judaism requires of them.

In sum, one must take into account that the Jewish tradition demands honor and respect for parents, even while one is not supposed to follow their directions to violate the other commandments.

When Jewish law is clear on a given issue and the parents want the child to do something else, one must find a way to honor parents even if disobeying them in the name of Jewish law, and this may even mean compromising one's standards of observance in the name of such honor. After all, religion should be an instrument for strengthening families, not dividing them. When Jewish law is not clear on a given issue, or when it permits several different options, the parent's wishes should play a stronger role in how the children honor them. In the end, then, Jews must find a way to uphold *both* of these Jewish duties—to abide by Jewish law, on one hand, and to honor parents, on the other, recognizing full well that that may be difficult for some families on at least some issues and that to do this may require us to be more creative and flexible than we might otherwise be.

One's Own Welfare

As we saw in chapter 6, the Talmud establishes a principle that saving one's own life takes precedence over saving anyone else's life, including one's parents or teachers. Does the same hierarchy apply to one's property? On one hand, the Talmud maintains that honoring parents extends to allowing them to squander your property. On the other hand, Rabbenu Yitzhak, one of Rashi's grandchildren and one of the Tosafists (important twelfth-century commentators on the Talmud), maintains that recovering one's own property takes precedence over some acts of honoring one's parents.

> They asked Rabbi Eleazar, "What is the limit for honoring one's father and mother?" He said, "To the point where the parent takes [his or her child's] wallet or money and throws it into the ocean, and his child does not rebuke him" (Babylonian Talmud, *Kiddushin* 32a).

> Rabbenu Yitzhak is of the opinion that one should defer parental honor as well as the return of a lost object to another

in order to recover one's own lost property. For when the Talmud says that parental honor has precedence [over the property of the child], that is only in a case such as permitting one's parent full license with one's money, for that is honor *per se*. However, when it comes to recovering one's lost article, the son need not forgo its recovery on account of his father's honor (Tosafot to Babylonian Talmud, *Kiddushin* 32a).

In other words, if the parent is going to get some benefit from the child's property, even if it is an apparently irrational benefit, the parent has a right to use the child's property. But if the parent is not going to get any benefit from the child's loss of money and simply has to have the patience to wait while the child retrieves his property before doing something to honor the parent, then the child should first retrieve his or her property.

This clearly sets a limit on the degree to which parental honor can take precedence over a child's finances, but it undoubtedly seems to many moderns like much too limited a restriction on the parents. This is at least in part because Enlightenment ideology has convinced us that we as individuals have a right to "life, liberty, and the pursuit of happiness," as Thomas Jefferson proclaimed in the American Declaration of Independence, basing himself on John Locke's contention that each of us has a right to "life, liberty, and property."[2] It may also stem from the fact that technology has made our world change so rapidly that parents no longer know as much about how to navigate the world and thus have lost one of the reasons for honoring and respecting them. Whatever the reason, modern children might set tighter limits on how much honoring their parents may cost them, especially when the issue is not just retrieving a lost object but, for example, spending much of one's property in providing for parents' health care in their old age. Thus what was only broached in a rather tentative mode by Rabbenu Yitzhak in the twelfth century has become an issue with far-reaching ramifications today.

How would you draw the limit now between the child's right to retain his or her money and the parent's right to that money? To what extent does it matter, for example, if the parents paid for the day school and/or college and graduate school tuition for the child long ago? What about all of the parents' expenses in simply providing the child with food, shelter, and clothing during childhood and through the many years of the child's education? Just as the factors warranting the child's control of his or her money have been enhanced in modern times, so too have the factors justifying a greater financial duty to parents grown during our time. Only one thing is certain about all this: drawing sensible and morally sensitive guidelines about this matter, with substantial input from the Jewish tradition's demand of honor and respect for parents, is definitely not easy!

Unreasonable Demands

Jewish sources demand a high degree of tolerance for one's parents and their demands. Interestingly, this is learned from the model of a non-Jew.

Rabbi Eliezer the Great's disciples asked him, "How far does honor of father and mother extend?" He replied, "Go and see what Dama B. Netina [a non-Jew] did. He was president of the city council. One time she came and slapped him in the presence of the whole assembly, and all he said was, 'May that be enough for you, my mother.' Our rabbis say that some of our wise men came to him to buy a precious stone in the place of one that had fallen out, and been lost, from the breastplate of the High Priest ... They agreed to give him a thousand gold pieces for the stone. He went in, and he found his father asleep with his leg stretched out upon the box that contained the jewel. He [Dama] would not disturb him and came back without it. When the wise men perceived this, they thought that he wanted more money, and they offered ten thousand gold pieces. When his father woke up, he went in and brought out the jewel. The wise men offered him the ten thousand pieces, but he replied, 'Far be it from me to make a profit from honoring my father; I will take only the thousand that we had agreed on.' And what reward did God give him? Our Rabbis say that in that very year his cow bore a red calf [which is extremely rare and whose ashes are necessary for a number of the Temple rites], which he sold for more than ten thousand gold pieces" (*Deuteronomy Rabbah, Devarim* 1:15; see also Babylonian Talmud, *Kiddushin* 31a and Jerusalem Talmud, *Peah* 15c).

Nevertheless, traditional sources recognize limits to what parents may demand, although they do not spell out those limits clearly. As you read the following passages, try to generalize a rule that defines when a parental demand is legitimate and the children must satisfy it, if they can, and when a parental demand is illegitimate and so the children have no legal requirement to satisfy it. If you cannot devise such a general rule, this may be like the famous problem the United States Supreme Court had in defining pornography, finally giving up, saying, "We cannot define it, but we know it when we see it!" Perhaps the point at which parental demands are so extensive as to be unreasonable is similarly indefinable in general principle but recognizable in practice.

Rabbi Assi had an aged mother. She said to him, "I want ornaments." So he made them for her. "I want a husband."—"I will look out for you." "I want a husband as handsome as you." Thereupon he left her and went to the Land of Israel. On hearing that she was following him, he went to R. Yochanan and asked him, "May I leave Israel for abroad?" "It is forbidden," he replied. "But what if it is to meet my mother?" "I do not know," said he. He waited a short time and went before him again. "Assi," said he, "you have determined to go. May the Omnipresent bring you back in peace."... In the meanwhile he learned that her coffin was coming. "Had I known," he exclaimed, "I would not have left [Babylonia]" (Babylonian Talmud, *Kiddushin* 31b).

If one's father or mother becomes mentally disturbed, he should try to treat them as their mental state demands, until they are pitied by God. But if he finds that he cannot endure the situation because of their extreme madness, he may leave and go away, appointing others to care for them properly (Maimonides, *Mishneh Torah, Laws of Rebels* 6:10; *Shulchan Arukh, Yoreh De'ah* 240:10).

In our day, these sources have a broader application than they did in the past. It is still true that children may not be psychologically able to care for parents who have Alzheimer's disease or some other form of dementia, but it is now also true that many adult children cannot care for parents who are perfectly sane and even warm and loving. With both the husband and the wife often at work in order to support their family, giving personal care to one's elderly parents, which the tradition sees as the ideal, may not be possible because for long stretches of time neither member of the couple is home to tend to the parents. Furthermore, as much as they might love their children and grandchildren, some elderly people, at least, may prefer to have the companionship of people their own age on a regular basis, thus making living with one's children, even if possible, less than desirable. Because many families now face this situation, assisted living facilities and nursing homes have been developed to care for those who can no longer care for themselves.

Love

Although it is certainly ideal not only to honor and respect one's parents but also to love them, Jewish law does not require love. Perhaps this stems from the tradition's recognition that love of parents cannot be legally demanded, because its very nature requires that it flow naturally out of the personal relationship between parents and children.

> Know that the Torah has placed us under a heavy obligation in regard to the proselyte. For we were commanded to honor and revere our parents, and to obey the prophets, and it is possible for a person to honor and revere and obey those whom s/he does not love. But with regard to the proselyte, there is a command to love him/her with a great, heartfelt love ... much as we are commanded to love God (Maimonides, *Responsa*, #448).

Applying the Tradition's Definition of Filial Duties to Today

The Jewish tradition specifies two primary duties that children have toward their parents—honor and respect. It then delineates what is included in each of these duties, together with their limits. Much of what the Torah and rabbinic tradition say are immediately relevant and instructive for our times. Even though parents and children have been around since the dawn of the human species, one cannot mechanically apply all of what the tradition says to our modern context. Far-flung families, people living to much older ages, and the advent of assisted living facilities and nursing homes—all of which will undoubtedly become even more important factors in our relationships with our parents as time goes on—require that we use sensitivity and judgment in applying the tradition's mandates to our relationships with our parents. Still, the attitudes and values that the tradition articulates in shaping the contours of that relationship are as relevant and important today as they ever were.

10

Parental Duties

As conceived in Jewish sources, the parent-child relationship is a two-way street. Just as children have duties to parents, so too do parents have obligations to their children. Thus, what we hope will be a loving, supportive relationship, where parents and children will be there for each other throughout life both materially and emotionally, is not left to the realm of hope but is made the subject of legal duties.

Interestingly, American law says little about children's duties but does prescribe some parental duties. Specifically, parents are held liable for abandonment and neglect and punished even more severely for abuse of their children. On the other hand, American law does not make adult children responsible for the care or financial support of their elderly parents, let alone prescribe duties of honor and respect in attitude. In contrast, as we have seen, Jewish law insists that adult children do have such duties to their parents.

Judaism's specification of legal duties for both parents and children certainly does not preclude warm, supportive relationships between the two parties; it just ensures that at least some of the practical results of such a relationship in fact take place, whether the family has such emotional ties or not. At a minimum, this serves the practical need of saving society from having to care for the children and parents in these ways. It also, though, serves the moral end of establishing a standard for what Judaism asserts are minimal requirements of character for both parents and children in their relationships with each other.

The Primary Rabbinic Source for Parental Duties

The Rabbis summarize parental duties in the following passage:

> Our Rabbis taught: A man is responsible to circumcise his son, to redeem him [from Temple service if he is the first born, *pidyon ha-ben*], to teach him Torah, to marry him off to a woman, and to teach him a trade, and there are some who say that he must also teach him to swim.
>
> Rabbi Judah says: Anyone who fails to teach his son a trade teaches him to steal (Babylonian Talmud, *Kiddushin* 29a).

The following sections of this chapter will examine four of these duties: circumcision, Jewish education, professional education, and finding a marriage partner. Despite the order of this rabbinic source, the discussion of what is involved in the duty to "teach him Torah" will be followed by a description of the parameters of the duty to "teach him a trade" because both involve forms of education that the parents are obliged to provide.

Daughters

Because this list includes circumcision and redemption from Temple service, both clearly understood to apply only to sons, the immediate question arises as to whether the other duties apply to daughters as well. Except for the parental duty to find a mate for one's child, the general answer is "no." That is, mothers were not bound to the duties enumerated in the source above, and daughters were not the recipients of these acts. Thus women do not teach and are not taught, do not redeem the firstborn and are not redeemed if they are born first.[1]

On one issue, there was real controversy—namely, as to whether a man, while not obligated to teach his daughters Torah, should nevertheless do so. The issue is formed around the law of the woman suspected of adultery *(sotah)* against whom there is no actual evidence but who, according to Numbers 5:11–31, is subjected to a water ordeal to test the truth of the suspicion. (Although by modern standards the law is terribly sexist and flies in the face of Jewish law's strong presumption of innocence until proven guilty in court, and although the Rabbis later tried to circumscribe the law so that it would effectively never be used, the law is still in the Torah, and so the Rabbis discussed it at length; in fact, an entire tractate of the Mishnah and Talmud is devoted to it. The Rabbis were convinced that even if the woman were guilty, the effects of the water would be delayed for as much as three years if she had other merits. Ben Azzai therefore declares that this must be taught to women so they will know they are not in the clear until long after the ordeal—and, by implication, that women should be taught Torah generally. Rabbi Eliezer objects strongly to this, asserting that women should be taught only the laws they need to know to lead a Jewish life but not the nuances and implications of the laws, because women cannot absorb such things and thus teaching them these matters is worthless *(tiflut,* "nonsense," possibly even "an obscenity").

> She had scarcely finished drinking [the water] when [if she is guilty] her face turns green, her eyes protrude, and her veins swell, and it is proclaimed, "Remove her so that the Temple court is not defiled!" If she possesses merit, however, it suspends the effect [of the water]: some merit suspends it for one year, some merit for two, and some for

three. Hence Ben Azzai declared: "A man must teach his daughter Torah so that if she does drink she may know that her [previous] merit suspends the effect." Rabbi Eliezer said: "Whoever teaches his daughter Torah teaches her something worthless [*tiflut*]!" ... Can it enter your mind [that it is actually] worthless? [After all, the Torah can never be worthless. No,] rather, it is as if he is teaching her something worthless. Rav Abbahu said: "What is Rabbi Eliezer's reason? Because it is written, 'I, wisdom, am present in subtlety [*ormah*]' (Proverbs 8:12), that is, when wisdom enters a man, subtlety enters with it [but women cannot absorb such subtlety]" (Babylonian Talmud, *Sotah* 20a, 21b).

A certain lady asked Rabbi Eliezer why the one sin in the case of the golden calf was punished by three deaths. He said to her: "A woman's wisdom is only in her spinning wheel, for it is written, 'And any woman of wise heart, with her hands she wove' (Exodus 35:25)." His son Hyrcanus said to him: "Why did you not give her some proper answer from the Torah? Now you have lost me three hundred *kur* [a dry measure] a year in tithe!" He said to him: "Let the words of the Torah be burned and not be [or, rather than being] given to women!" (Jerusalem Talmud, *Sotah* 3:1 [16a]).

Maimonides decides the law in line with Rabbi Eliezer, although he limits his ban on teaching daughters to the Oral Torah, and Joseph Karo quotes Maimonides verbatim:

Women, slaves, and children are exempt from study of the Torah, but a father is obligated to teach his son Torah, as it says, "And you shall teach them [the commandments] to speak about them" (Deuteronomy 11:19). A woman is not obligated to teach her son, for [only] those obligated to learn are obligated to teach ... A woman who learned Torah acquires a reward, but not like the reward of a man because she is not commanded [to learn Torah], and the reward of anyone who does something not commanded is not the same as that of the one who is commanded and fulfills the commandment, but rather less than that. And even though she gains reward, the Rabbis commanded that a man should not teach his daughter Torah because most women cannot absorb the material but rather turn the teachings of Torah into nonsense according to their limited intelligence. The Rabbis said: "Anyone who teaches his daughter Torah is as if he had taught her worthless material." To what does that refer? To the Oral Torah, but as for the Written Torah, as a matter of course he should not teach her, but if he did teach her, it is not as if he is teaching her worthless material (Maimonides, *Mishneh Torah, Laws of Study of Torah* 1:1, 13; also Joseph Karo, *Shulchan Arukh, Yoreh De'ah* 246:6).

In our own day, however, few Jewish communities, even among the Orthodox, refuse to teach their daughters Torah. Some among the Orthodox restrict women's learning to biblical literature and commentaries, Mishnah, and, especially, the laws they need to know to live as a Jew; some modern Orthodox institutions teach women Talmud and its commentaries as well. In the vast majority of Orthodox institutions, women study in classes exclusively for them. The Conservative, Reconstructionist, and Reform movements, in contrast, have people of both genders study the same curriculum together from childhood through adulthood, and those movements have now extended to women the opportunity to become rabbis. Consequently, the sources that describe the nature and extent of the parental duty to educate sons in Torah, which we shall consider below, are in practice understood by the vast majority of Jews to apply in our day to daughters as well.

There is no indication in the Talmud that a man had to teach his daughter a trade. This is not surprising, because the Talmud presumed that when she reached adulthood she would be married and supported by her husband. Instead, as we saw in chapter 8, the Mishnah speaks of her doing household chores and spinning wool, the products of which the husband had a right to sell.[2] In later centuries, women before or beyond the childbearing years would often help their husbands in the family business, sometimes actually running it.[3]

Since bodies of water posed as much risk to girls as to boys, it is frankly a mystery as to why those in the Talmud who require the father to teach his sons to swim do not specify that he must teach his daughters to swim as well. It may be that the Talmud assumes that women would stay nearer to home and therefore would not encounter the risks that men would, especially those engaged in long-distance trade. Still, this remains puzzling. For that matter, one wonders why it is only "some" who require the father to teach his sons to swim, and, even more, why the later codes do not include this requirement, for, after all, swimming seems to be a skill that everyone needs to know—except, perhaps, those who live or travel nowhere near rivers, lakes, or seas.

The father's duties to his sons, then, as specified in the rabbinic source quoted above, did not apply to his daughters, except, perhaps, for education in Torah. He did, however, have other duties toward his daughters, some of which he did not have toward his sons. Specifically, the Rabbis of the Mishnah and Talmud interpreted the Torah to require a man to support his children to age six. Beyond that age, the Rabbis enacted a requirement on their own authority that a man must support his children until they reached puberty. In the talmudic discussion,[4] Rabbi Meir thought that this moral duty was clearer for sons because they study Torah, but Rabbi Judah thought that it was clearer for daughters in order to prevent their degradation (presumably through rape or prostitution) if they were to go begging. Rabbi Yochanan ben Beroka determined that it was a man's *legal* duty to support his daughters until puberty as one of the conditions of marriage that the Rabbis created and built into the marriage contract *(ketubbah),* whether the husband explicitly agreed or not; however, it was only a moral duty to support one's sons until that time. In the end, as Maimonides summarizes, Jewish law provided that if a man was poor, he could send his sons over age six out begging, but men with the financial means were subjected to public defamation for refusing to support their sons beyond age six or even legally forced to do so as part of the charity they were required to give.[5]

Furthermore, a man who wanted to marry was responsible for providing the bride price on his own (Exodus 22:15). Because many men during the first century B.C.E. did not have the money to pay that, Simeon ben Shetah, head of the Pharisees at the time, transformed that to a lien against his property in the event of his divorcing or predeceasing her.[6] This had the double effect of encouraging marriage and discouraging divorce. Still, ultimately, he was responsible for paying the money; his father's duty to "marry him off" did not include that. On the other hand, a father did have the duty to provide a dowry for his daughter (and if he could not, the community bore that responsibility).

> "Take wives and beget sons and daughters; and take wives for your sons, and give your daughters to husbands, that they may bear sons and daughters ... " (Jeremiah 29:6) ...
> A father must provide for his daughter clothing and adornments and must also give her a dowry so that men will be anxious to woo her and so proceed to marry her. And to what extent [must a father go in providing a dowry for his daughter]? Both Abayae and Rava ruled: Up to a tenth of his

wealth (Babylonian Talmud, *Ketubbot* 52b, similar to Babylonian Talmud, *Kiddushin* 30b).

The Rabbis commanded that a man must give [his daughter] from his assets some small amount so that she can be married with it, and this is called "sustenance" (*parnasah* [also *nedunyah*, dowry]). The general rule is that one who marries off his daughter may not give her less than the clothing the Rabbis have defined as the minimum that must be given to the wife of a poor Israelite man, as we have explained.[7] To what does that ruling apply? To the case where the father is poor, but if he is rich, then it is fitting that he give her [a dowry] in accordance with his wealth (Maimonides, *Mishneh Torah, Laws of Marriage* 20:1).

Our Rabbis taught: If an orphan boy and an orphan girl applied for a marriage grant [from the charity fund], the girl orphan is to be enabled to be married first and the boy orphan afterwards [if the funds permit], because the shame of a woman [in having to beg for the funds] is greater than that of a man.

Our Rabbis taught: If an orphan [boy] applied for assistance to marry, a house must be rented for him, a bed must be prepared for him, and [he must also be supplied with] all [household] objects [required for] his use, and then he is given a wife in marriage, for it is said in Scripture, "Sufficient for whatever he lacks" [literally, "sufficient for his need that is lacking to him"] (Deuteronomy 15:8): "sufficient for his need" refers to the house; "that is lacking" refers to a bed and table; "to him [*lo*]" refers to a wife, for so it is said in Scripture, "I will make a fitting helper for him [*lo*]" (Genesis 2:18).

—*Babylonian Talmud,* Ketubbot *67b*

Circumcision

The Torah establishes the parental duty to circumcise one's sons, beginning with Abraham:

> God further said to Abraham, "As for you, you and your offspring to come throughout the ages shall keep My covenant. Such shall be the covenant between Me and you and your offspring to follow which you shall keep: every male among you shall be circumcised. You shall circumcise the flesh of your foreskin, and that shall be the sign of the covenant between Me and you. And throughout the generations, every male among you shall be circumcised at the age of eight days ... Thus shall My covenant be marked in your flesh as an everlasting pact. And if any male who is uncircumcised fails to circumcise the flesh of his foreskin, that person shall be cut off from his kin; he has broken My covenant" (Genesis 17:9–14).

> Speak to the Israelite people thus: "When a woman at childbirth bears a male ... on the eighth day the flesh of his foreskin shall be circumcised" (Leviticus 12:2–3).

If the child's father is no longer alive or is absent, the mother inherits this responsibility, as we learn from a strange story regarding Zipporah, wife of Moses.

> At a night encampment on the way, the Lord encountered him [probably Gershom, Moses' firstborn son]. So Zipporah took a flint and cut off her son's foreskin and touched his legs with it, saying, "You are truly a bridegroom of blood to me!" And when He let him alone, she added, "A bridegroom of blood because of the circumcision" (Exodus 4:24–26).

If neither parent fulfills this duty, the Talmud determines that the community, represented by its court, then becomes responsible for having the boy circumcised. Finally, if none of these parties fulfills the duty, the man himself, upon reaching the age of majority, is legally responsible for having himself circumcised.

> "To circumcise him." How do we know it [that the father is responsible for circumcising his son]? Because it is written, "And Abraham circumcised his son, Isaac" (Genesis 21:4). And if his father did not circumcise him, the communal court is bound to circumcise him, for it is written, "Every male among you shall be circumcised" (Genesis 17:10). And if the communal court did not circumcise him, he is bound to circumcise himself [or have himself circumcised], for it is written, "And the uncircumcised male who will not circumcise the flesh of his foreskin, that person shall be cut off [from the People Israel]" (Genesis 17:14).
> —*Babylonian Talmud,* Kiddushin *29a*

In our own day, some Jews have questioned the wisdom of circumcising boys. The relevant medical associations have wavered on its medical advisability, recommending it during the last several decades of the twentieth century and now saying that its medical risks and benefits are roughly equivalent, making circumcision medically optional.

The Jewish tradition, however, never advocated circumcision for medical reasons. Its purpose was instead religious. First, by literally inscribing a sign of God's covenant with Israel on a man's flesh, circumcision symbolizes that this covenant between God and the People Israel is immutable. Compare this to sealing a document in contrast to signing it: the seal changes the very surface of the paper, making it virtually impossible to change the document. Along these lines, the scene from the movie *Europa, Europa,* in which a teenage Jewish boy assumed by the Nazis to be one of them tries to undo his circumcision in order to hide his Jewish identity in the communal showers, is an especially poignant demonstration of the immutable quality of the covenant that circumcision intends to symbolize.

Second, because circumcision changes the surface of a male's generative organ, it symbolizes that this covenant is to last from generation to generation. The same symbolism was not needed in removing a girl's clitoris, presumably because from ancient times to the modern era the man was the head of the house, and therefore making men part of the covenant throughout all generations immediately made all the female members of their families part of the covenant as well.

Third, circumcision has implications for *tikkun olam* as well. In graphically tying Jews to the covenant, circumcision symbolizes Jews' commitment to Judaism's moral duties at least as much as to its rites. These include, of course, the duties discussed in this and previous chapters regarding speech, the poor, captives, the sick, and one's parents and children.

In light of all these religious meanings of circumcision, meanings that go to the heart of Jewish identity and continuity, it is not surprising that the Rabbis determined that if an infant boy is healthy, his circumcision must take place on the eighth day, as the Torah commands, even if that means making some exceptions to the Sabbath or High Holy Day rules to enable that to happen.[8] Aside from saving a person's life or health, circumcision is the only commandment that supersedes the Sabbath in this way.

"To Teach Him Torah"

This duty begins with Abraham and is articulated in verses made famous through their use as the first and second paragraphs of the *Shema:*

For I [God] have singled him [Abraham] out, that he may instruct his children and his posterity to keep the way of the Lord by doing what is just and right, in order that the Lord may bring about for Abraham what He has promised him (Genesis 18:19).

Hear, O Israel! The Lord is our God, the Lord alone [or, is one]. You shall love the Lord your God with all your heart and with all your soul and with all your might. Take to heart these instructions with which I charge you this day. Impress them [teach them diligently] upon your children. Recite them when you stay at home and when you are away, when you lie down and when you get up. Bind them as a sign on your hand and let them serve as a symbol on your forehead; inscribe them on the doorposts of your house and on your gates (Deuteronomy 6:4–9, the first paragraph of the *Shema*).

Therefore impress these, My words, upon your very heart; bind them as a sign on your hand and let them serve as a symbol on your forehead, and teach them to your children—reciting them when you stay at home and when you are away, when you lie down and when you get up; and inscribe them on the doorposts on your house and on your gates—to the end that you and your children may endure, in the land that the Lord swore to your fathers to assign to them, as long as there is a heaven over the earth (Deuteronomy 11:18–21, the last part of the second paragraph of the *Shema*).

Furthermore, this duty applies to grandparents as well as to parents:

Take utmost care and watch yourselves scrupulously, so that you do not forget the things that you saw with your own eyes and so that they do not fade from your mind as long as you live. And make them known to your children and to your children's children (Deuteronomy 4:9).

Are grandparents responsible for teaching their grandchildren? ... "And you shall teach your children" (Deuteronomy 11:19), from that I only know that I must teach my children; how do I know that I must also teach my grandchildren? Because the Torah says, "and make them known to your children and to your children's children" (Deuteronomy 4:9).
—*Babylonian Talmud,* Kiddushin *30a*

In our own day, this implies that grandparents have a duty to help their children provide a Jewish education for their grandchildren. That includes providing a Jewish model for their grandchildren, especially if they are the product of an interfaith marriage. For grandparents who have greater financial resources than their adult children as well as fewer economic responsibilities, this duty also includes paying the tuition (or part of it) for their grandchildren's Jewish day school or religious school education, camp, or youth group. Grandparents may feel good about themselves in doing this, but not too good: after all, they are simply fulfilling their Jewish legal duty!

In a manner typical of them, the Rabbis sought to define the scope of the obligation to teach one's children.

To what extent is a man obliged to teach his son Torah? Rav Judah said in Samuel's name: "For example, Zevulun, the son of Dan, whom his grandfather taught Scripture, Mishnah, Talmud, laws, and legends." An objection was raised: "[We have a tradition that] if he [his father] taught him Scripture, he need not teach him Mishnah ..." "[The law, then, is] like Zevulun, son of Dan, yet not altogether so

> ... for whereas there [he was taught] Scripture, Mishnah, Talmud, laws, and legends, here [i.e., as a general rule] Scripture alone [suffices]."
>
> —*Babylonian Talmud,* Kiddushin *30a*

That is, the father must teach his son minimally Scripture, but ideally he should teach him all the things that Zevulun, son of Dan, learned. The obligation to teach one's children and grandchildren begins when the child reaches age five, and the curriculum increases in difficulty as the child grows.

> He [Yehudah ben Tema] used to say: "At five years of age—the study of Bible; at ten—the study of Mishnah; at thirteen—responsibility for the commandments; at fifteen—the study of Talmud; at eighteen—marriage; at twenty—pursuit of a livelihood; at thirty—the peak of one's powers; at forty—the age of understanding; at fifty—the age of giving counsel; at sixty—old age; at seventy—the hoary head [or, white old age]; at eighty—the age of strength [or, rare old age]; at ninety—the bent back; at one hundred—as one dead and out of this world" (Mishnah, *Pirkei Avot* 5:23 [5:24 in some editions])

The Rabbis were keenly aware, however, that the curriculum of teaching Judaism should not consist of text knowledge and skills alone; it must crucially engage in character education as well. That obviously includes teaching children values such as respect for people and property, honesty, responsibility, and the like. It also includes negative demands, such as avoiding assault and battery, stealing, and so on. One graphic example of moral education affects parents and children. Since striking a parent or even cursing a parent are, according to the Torah, capital offenses (Exodus 23:15, 17), the Rabbis instructed parents not to strike their grown children lest their children curse them or strike them back, making the parents, in turn, liable for leading the children to sin ("placing a [moral and legal] stumbling block before the blind").[9] Along these lines, a nineteenth-century moralist applied this to both children and parents.

> If a man cannot honor his parents as they should be honored, then ... it is best that he no longer share his father's board, provided his father agrees to this. It is also best that a man [who gets angry]—if he can—send his children from his table, lest he be guilty of placing a stumbling block before them [by provoking them to speak dishonorably to him and thus violating Leviticus 19:14] ... and thus there shall be peace in your home (Rabbi Eliezer Pappo, *Pele Yo'etz*, Part 1, *Kaph*, pp. 170–172).

Because parents were often not very well educated themselves, the Rabbis were concerned that parents or grandparents might not be able to teach their children, even if they wanted to do so. That would mean that they would not only fail to fulfill a commandment of the Torah, but also deprive their children of their heritage. Therefore, although the duty to educate one's children in Judaism falls primarily on the parents, they may delegate it to a Jewish school. In fact, Jews were among the first to establish schools, dating from the second century.

> He who denies a child religious knowledge robs him of his heritage (Babylonian Talmud, *Sanhedrin* 91b).

> Rabbi Judah said in the name of Rav: "Rabbi Joshua ben Gamla should be remembered for good, for had it not been for him the Torah would have been forgotten in Israel. For at first, the boy who had a father was taught Torah by him,

while the boy who had no father did not learn. Later, they appointed teachers of boys in Jerusalem, and the boys who had fathers were brought by them [to the teachers] and were taught; those who had no fathers were still not brought. So then they ordered that teachers should be appointed in every district, and they brought to them lads of the age of sixteen or seventeen. And when the teacher was cross with any of the lads, the lad would kick at him and run away. So then Rabbi Joshua ben Gamla ordered that teachers should be appointed in every district and in every city and that the boys should be sent to them at the age of six or seven years" (Babylonian Talmud, *Bava Batra* 21a).

Even though parents may delegate the duty to educate their children to a school, the parents still retain ultimate responsibility. They therefore must check periodically that the teachers are effectively doing their job. This led to the common practice for parents to ask their children about what they learned in their Jewish schooling that week and to discuss it further with them around the Shabbat table. It has also led the Conservative Movement, for example, to establish a parent education program, in which the parents are taught what the students are learning so that they can interact with their children on Jewish matters and reinforce what they are learning in school. That way, both generations fulfill Judaism's lifelong duty to study the tradition.

Here are just two of many passages that indicate the importance the Rabbis placed on parents teaching children:

Rabbi Meir said: "When the Israelites came to receive the Torah, God said to them: 'Bring to Me good sureties that you will observe it.' They answered: 'Our ancestors will be our sureties.' God answered: 'Your sureties need sureties themselves, for I have found fault with them.' They answered: 'Our prophets will be our sureties.' God replied: 'I have found fault with them also.' Then the Israelites said: 'Our children will be our sureties.' They proved acceptable, and God gave the Torah to Israel" (*Song of Songs Rabbah*, on Song of Songs 1:4).

The world itself rests upon the breath of the children in the schoolhouse (Babylonian Talmud, *Shabbat* 119b).

"To Teach Him a Trade"

Until recently in Jewish history, very few Jews had a formal education in anything. Parents simply could not afford to let their children stay in school very long, because they were needed to help earn a living. Girls got almost no formal education, and even the one that boys got was short. *Fiddler on the Roof* had it right: in the opening number the boys sing, "At three I started Hebrew school, at ten I learned a trade." And when they learned a trade, it was as an apprentice: their father and possibly their uncles taught them how to do what men in the family had done for generations to earn a living.

Much has changed in the last century. In the United States, in 1910, only 13 percent of the population graduated from high school and only 3 percent from college; in 1999, 83 percent of Americans graduated from high school and 25 percent from college.[10] Because Jews and Judaism treasure education so deeply, and because Jews in the early and mid twentieth century found education to be their path into America's middle and upper classes, Jews have tended to be ahead of the curve, and to this day much higher percentages of Jews complete college and professional schools than is true of the general American population. Specifically, as of 1990, 34.9 percent of Jewish men between ages 25 and 44 completed college and another 38.7 percent had postgraduate education, for a total of 73.6 percent who completed a bachelor's degree or more, in comparison to the general American male population of the same age group, where 13.2 percent finished college and another 11.3 percent had postgraduate education, for a total of 24.5 percent with a bachelor's degree or more. That is, American Jewish men completed college at a rate close to *three times* that of other American men. Similarly, 29.6 percent of Jewish women of that age group completed college and another 37.3 percent had postgraduate education, for a total of 66.9 percent who completed college or more. These figures are in comparison to 10.8 percent and 6.3 percent, respectively, for a total of 17.1 percent of the general American female population.[11] That is, American Jewish women completed college at a rate almost *four times* that of other American women.

On one hand, Jews can rightfully be proud of this, because these numbers illustrate the strong Jewish commitment to education. As more and more jobs require more and more education, Jews spending considerable time and money for college and graduate school are putting themselves in a position to do well economically in the future.

On the other hand, though, our ancestors spent all the money they could on enabling at least their sons to get a Jewish education. In our time, some Jewish families are spending equivalent or greater percentages of their incomes on Jewish day schools, camping, and youth groups, but a frightening percentage are giving their children only a perfunctory Jewish education or none at all. The Conservative Movement, for example, has had increasing difficulty insisting that children study at least six hours per week; synagogue schools in the Reconstructionist and Reform Movements have long demanded two or four hours per week. Not much can be done within that amount of time, especially when the hours are after the "regular" school hours or on weekends. All too many parents give soccer, ballet, piano lessons, and Little League greater priority. Furthermore, the high divorce rate among American Jews often means that children cannot spend part of Sunday in Jewish schooling, as was common in the past, because on Sundays the noncustodial parent has only a few precious hours to spend with his or her child and understandably does not want to give up any of it. Even participation in Jewish informal education (camps, youth groups) has been affected by these factors. The result is that contemporary Jews have completely upended traditional Jewish values of education, with "teaching him a trade" taking ever more time and resources and "teaching him Torah" taking ever fewer.

To put it mildly, this situation does not bode well for the future of Jewish identity or the depth of conviction among Jews. Making Jewish formal and informal education once again a serious priority among American Jews, one that parallels their commitment to general and professional education, is a considerable act of *tikkun olam*. In addition, Jews of all ages and economic resources must do everything possible to enable Jewish parents who do take the Jewish future of their children and of the Jewish People seriously to afford a meaningful form of it for their children. Further, through what they do in their own lives, Jews must resume the traditional responsibility of ensuring that they and the schools they use succeed in imparting not only a knowledge of Judaism's skills, concepts, and values, but also a love of practicing Judaism and being part of the Jewish People. In the end, children will take Judaism seriously only if their parents do as well.

"To Marry Him Off"

The Talmud clearly assumes that parents would arrange the marriage for both their sons and their daughters. That system lasted a very long time; my own grandparents had an arranged marriage. They did not know each other until they stood under the *chuppah* (wedding canopy). Years later, when my mother asked her mother why she had agreed to marry my grandfather, she said, "Because I had heard that he was a kind man, and that was enough for me." From everything I could observe and from everything my mother told me, they had an idyllic marriage—in no small measure, I think, because they had begun with much more realistic assumptions about the nature and aims of marriage than the American ideal of romantic love presents us. (Compare the concept of marriage in the song "Some Enchanted Evening," from the musical *South Pacific,* to "Do You Love Me?" in *Fiddler on the Roof.*) Not all arranged marriages worked out that well, of course, but our current system of dating does no better and probably worse in producing long and happy marriages.

Although the system of arranged marriages generally put the decision of whom to marry in the parents' hands, that was not always the case. Rabbi Solomon ben Abraham Adret ("Rashba," c. 1235–c. 1310, Spain) uses the talmudic principle that divine commands supersede parental ones to permit a man to violate his parents' wishes so that he may marry the woman he loves, even if that means the son would live at some distance from his parents and thus be precluded from providing the range of services prescribed as part of the honor and respect due to parents. This does not apply to a marriage that would violate the norms of Jewish law, such as an incestuous marriage or a marriage to a non-Jew; Rashba is addressing the case where a Jewish man and woman who are eligible to marry each other according to Jewish law want to do so over their parents' objections. The man has the right to do this, according to Rashba, to fulfill the commandment "Be fruitful and multiply," for which marriage is a legal prerequisite.[12] Although some rabbis disagree,[13] ultimately Rabbi Moses Isserles, in his authoritative glosses on the important sixteenth-century code the *Shulchan Arukh*, states, "If a father opposes the marriage of his son to a woman of his son's desire, the son need not accede to the father."[14]

By and large, though, parental matchmaking, sometimes with the assistance of a professional matchmaker, was the mechanism that paired off Jewish couples. That system had the distinct advantage of guaranteeing a marriage for virtually every person, usually in his or her teens. In fact, even though the Mishnah quoted above indicates that eighteen was the appropriate age at which a man shall marry, and presumably sixteen or seventeen for a woman, it was often common for marriages to take place in the early teens, thus ensuring that both members of the couple would satisfy their sexual urges in a legal context.[15] The system of matchmaking took away much of the pressure and uncertainty that our contemporary high school and college students have about whom they will marry. It also assured marriage at a time when both the man and the woman were biologically at the most fertile stages of their lives, thus avoiding some of the infertility problems that current couples face when they get married in their late twenties and do not begin to try to have children until their thirties.

For better or worse, though, the old way is not coming back. That leaves current adult children and their parents with a real problem. High school and college provide a natural environment in which people can meet each other, and for some people graduate school lengthens the time in which school can be the venue for meeting one's mate. Once schooling is over, though, there are fewer good places for people to meet each other.

People in their early and mid-twenties—the first generation to pass through adolescence in a world with e-mail—are using the Internet for this purpose to an extent that older generations find intimidating. This has changed the assumptions of getting to know a potential spouse. Dating once implied "a very long process where you disclose things over time," said Robert Rosenwein, a professor of social psychology at Lehigh University. "The Internet speeds that up considerably. There's a renegotiation of the concept of intimacy." Moreover, even with pictures, which young people usually demand before they will respond to an ad, there is always the problem of leaving out pertinent information, because the ads often represent "the author's aspirations, more than the reality."[16]

Even though the Internet can surely help people meet each other, it is not a panacea. Some people will not find a suitable spouse in the traditional places—at work or the synagogue or parties of mutual friends. Parents must not hesitate, then, to help their children find someone, even if the children first object to any parental interventions. Parents can suggest, for example, that their children attend services or a family wedding or some other activities at the synagogue for the express motive of trying to meet someone; after all, the synagogue is not only a *bet tefillah* (house of prayer) and *bet midrash* (house of study); it is most commonly called a *bet kenesset* (house of meeting—although not usually intended in quite this way!). They can also suggest that their children get involved as volunteers in various Jewish communal activities through the Federation or other groups with young adult divisions.

I know two families—the Salters and the Wagners—who formed the S&W Good Company when their children were approaching their mid-twenties with no marital prospects on the horizon. The parents simply had their children invite all of their friends and their friends' friends to their homes once a month for some kind of program—social, social action, intellectual, or religious (such as a holiday celebration)—and lo and behold, all of them found their spouses that way. The methods other parents use may be different, but the message is the same: parents need not stand idly by if their children are having trouble meeting potential spouses.

The problem in fulfilling this talmudic duty for parents in our own day, though, goes beyond *finding* someone to marry; it also involves young adults' *intention* to marry at a young enough age to have a reasonable chance of having children without difficulty. Because of young Jews' extensive educational programs, which in themselves are expressions of their commitment to the Jewish values of education and professional achievement, they rarely plan to marry before their late twenties. Because of the modern techniques that have been developed to overcome infertility, young adult Jews often simply assume that they can have children into their forties, and so there is no rush to get married and procreate.

This is a false assumption, however, because biologically the optimal age for both men and women to procreate is still twenty-two; infertility problems increase somewhat by age twenty-seven, significantly between then and thirty-five, and even more after thirty-five, when birth defects and Down's syndrome also become more prevalent. Moreover, only about half of the couples who suffer from infertility can ultimately bring home a baby using the assisted reproductive techniques currently available, and some 85 percent of those have a child using the least technologically sophisticated of the methods—artificial insemination with either the husband's or a donor's sperm. The younger the couple is, the greater the chances that assisted reproductive techniques will be effective.

The misconceptions about the power of modern medicine to overcome infertility are so great that in April 2002, *Time* magazine ran a cover article on the pitfalls of waiting too long.[17] It unfortunately did not document the problems for men as well as women. It should have done so, because the problem is just as prevalent in men as they age as it is in women. Forty percent of infertile couples cannot have children because of a problem in the man, 40 percent because of a problem in the woman, 10 percent because of a problem in both, and 10 percent because of unknown reasons. In men, sperm counts and sperm motility go down with age, sperm becomes misshapen, and impotence begins; in women, eggs become less viable, blockages develop in the fallopian tubes, implantation becomes more iffy, and miscarriages increase. These problems impose immense strains on the marriage, for each month the couple faces a final examination, as it were, and if they are infertile they are likely to fail most of those final exams. This causes them to wonder about some deeply personal things. Who am I as a man?

Who am I as a woman? Who are we as a couple? Do we have a future together without the children we dreamed of having? If so, what is our future together supposed to be like? All too many marriages break up over these issues.[18]

Marrying and beginning the process of procreation earlier does not guarantee freedom from reproductive problems, but it certainly increases the likelihood of reproductive success. This suggests several things parents can do in a kind of modern interpolation of their talmudic duty to marry off their children:

- Make sure that your teenage children actively participate in a Jewish youth group and date only Jews. Intermarriage always starts with a date, and the intention to seek someone Jewish to marry gets formed primarily during one's teenage years. Recent research suggests that Jewish camps and youth groups are the most critical factors in producing Jews who ultimately marry Jews.[19]

- Make sure that your children apply to, and ultimately go to, a college with a large number of other Jews. This is in part for educational and religious reasons—they may want to take a Jewish studies course or attend a holiday celebration or service—but also, frankly, for social reasons.

- Clarify to your children that even though college is not a failure if they do not emerge married, it is not too early to look for a mate while in college and to get married and begin to have children while in graduate school. The pressures of graduate school are no greater and usually less than the pressures of the first years in one's job or profession.

- At the same time, recognize that there are many single Jews who would like nothing better than to get married (or remarried) but cannot find a suitable spouse. We who are concerned about both Jews and Judaism must walk a delicate tightrope here. On one hand, we must respect the inherent divine dignity of singles, as we must do for all people, and we must make our institutions as welcoming for them as they are for married couples. On the other hand, as part of our empathy and compassion for single people, we need to take active steps to help them find the mates they seek. Computer dating services such as J-Date have been remarkably effective in this effort, but we dare not rely on them alone. Instead, individual Jews and Jewish institutions must create programs where Jewish singles can meet in a supportive and respectful context.

- Ensure that Jewish venues are available and affordable for day care for young children and that formal and informal Jewish education is affordable as well, which is clearly not the case for many families now.[20] Since charity begins at home, it is important to note that, as quoted earlier, Jewish law imposes the duty to educate children in Torah not only on parents, but also on grandparents.[21] Thus, grandparents, who often have more money than young parents do, have a special duty to contribute to their grandchildren's care and Jewish education.

Even though parents no longer "marry off" their children by choosing a mate for them, parents still have a major role to play in carrying out this talmudic duty. For everyone's sake, may they succeed!

Forward: Envisioning an Ideal World, Shaped by *Tikkun Olam*

What are the goals of *tikkun olam*? We have described some of the specific elements that are critical in shaping a better world as Judaism envisions it, but what does the ideal world look like? That is, what kind of world are we as Jews seeking to create?

Clearly, the Jewish ideal world is characterized by the success of all our efforts to fix the world in the ways described in the previous chapters. Thus, in such a world, on a social level, people will:

- Talk to each other with respect and avoid all forms of defamation and gossip;
- Help others learn how to make a living and aid the poor directly in the meantime;
- Take steps to stop the taking of captives and redeem those who have been kidnapped;
- Provide the means for all people and societies to prevent disease whenever possible, cure them when they occur, attend the sick through visits and physical and emotional support, and engage in research to avoid or cure the maladies we cannot yet treat.

Furthermore, on a personal level, in an ideal world, people will:

- Prepare for marriage so they can learn how to care for each other, deepen and broaden their relationship over the years, and avoid divorce;

- Honor and respect their parents, especially as they age, in the ways that Jewish law prescribes, ideally as an act of love but at least in fulfillment of their duties under Jewish law;
- Care for their children in the ways that Jewish law prescribes, ideally in the context of a close, loving relationship but minimally in response to the parents' duties under Jewish law.

In addition to these elements of a Jewish vision of an ideal world, Jewish sources describe other factors that characterize the world we all should strive to create. There is no one official depiction of the Jewish ideal world; in this matter, as on virtually every other topic, Jewish sources include many voices. That is not to say that Judaism is incoherent in its ideals, though, for many of the factors described in some sources complement those in others. There are differences in emphasis, however, and it is important to understand this pluralism in assessing the most important aspects of Judaism's ideal world.

Two other factors need to be mentioned at the outset. First, Judaism portrays all human efforts as being in partnership with God. Sometimes God is the dominant partner, as in the Exodus from Egypt, but even there Moses, Aaron, Miriam, and, according to rabbinic legend, Nahshon ben Aminadav played crucial roles in enabling the Exodus to happen. At other times, human beings must take the initiative, as in our efforts to form a society devoid of gossip and defamatory speech, for example. Most of the time, *tikkun olam* happens as a result of a partnership between God and us, and this is illustrated in cases of finding cures for illness and then ensuring that all the world's people can take advantage of those cures. Thus, as we consider Jewish visions of the ideal, we should take note of the varying roles played by God and by human beings in enabling the ideal to become more and more real.

Second, Jewish visions of the ideal do not end with the Bible and Talmud. Jews in the Middle Ages and in the modern period added their own depictions as well. As a result, while this chapter will certainly not cover all parts of the Jewish imagination of the ideal world, it will describe at least some of the primary features of the visions we find in Jewish classical literature—the Bible and rabbinic literature (Mishnah, Talmud, Midrash, and later summaries of that material in Maimonides' code).

Children

God's very first blessing of Abraham (when he was still called Abram) is that he may have children, and it is the promise of many offspring that changes his name from Abram to Abraham, "father of many nations":

> Some time later, the word of the Lord came to Abram in a vision. He said: "Fear not, Abram, I am a shield to you; your reward shall be very great." But Abram said, "O Lord, God, what can You give me, seeing that I shall die childless?" ... The word of the Lord came to him in reply: "... None but your very own issue shall be your heir." He took him outside and said, "Look toward heaven and count the stars, if you are able to count them." And He added, "So shall your offspring be" (Genesis 15:1–7).

> When Abram was ninety-nine years old, the Lord appeared to Abram and said to him: "I am El Shaddai. Walk in My ways and be blameless. I will establish My covenant between Me and you, and I will make you exceedingly numerous." Abram threw himself on his face; and God spoke to him further: "As for Me, this is My covenant with you: You shall be the father of a multitude of nations. And

you shall no longer be called Abram, but your name shall be Abraham, for I make you the father of a multitude of nations. I will make you exceedingly fertile, and make nations of you; and kings shall come forth from you. I will maintain My covenant between Me and you, and your offspring to come, as an everlasting covenant throughout the ages, to be God to you and to your offspring to come" (Genesis 17:1–7).

[Moses speaking to the Israelites before they enter the land of Canaan:] The Lord your God has increased your number so that today you are as numerous as the stars in the sky. May the Lord, the God of your ancestors, increase your number a thousandfold, and may He bless you as He has promised (Deuteronomy 1:10–11).

Children are seen as part of the ideal world in many places in the Bible, the blessing and reward for obeying God's commandments. Here are two good examples:

If you obey these rules and observe them faithfully, the Lord your God will maintain faithfully for you the covenant that He made on oath with your fathers: He will favor you and bless you and multiply you; He will bless the issue of your womb and the produce of your soil, your new grain and wine and oil, the calving of your herd and the lambing of your flock, in the land that He swore to your fathers to assign to you. You shall be blessed above all other peoples: there shall be no sterile male or female among you or among your livestock (Deuteronomy 7:12–14).

Happy are all who fear the Lord, who follow His ways ...

Your wife shall be like a fruitful vine within your house; your
children, like olive saplings around your table.
So shall the man who fears the Lord be blessed ...
May you live to see your children's children. May all be well
with Israel!

—*Psalm 128:1, 3, 6*

Unfortunately, although this seems like a wonderful promise
for those who are able to have children, it feels like a harsh curse
for those who cannot. Efforts to help Jews meet, marry, and procreate in their twenties so as to avoid the major factor in infertility
(age) and efforts to assist infertile couples medically are very much
a part of *tikkun olam* so that we can all attain the great blessing of
children. In addition, sensitivity to both the fact that many singles
would love to get married and have children but cannot find a suitable mate and to the fact that many couples would love to have
children but cannot will make our community a much more ideal
one, as we support them emotionally while helping them in practical ways to attain these goals.

The Land of Israel

The other part of God's very first blessing to Abram is the Land of
Israel (Genesis 15:7–21), a blessing repeated, as is the blessing of
children, to Abraham (Genesis 17:8), to Isaac (Genesis 26:2–5), to
Jacob (Genesis 28:13–15), and to the People Israel as a whole
(Deuteronomy 28:1–12). To make this promise real, God will help
"dislodge those peoples [of Canaan] little by little; you will not be
able to put an end to them at once, else the wild beasts would multiply to your hurt" (Deuteronomy 7:22). Eventually, however,
Israel would rule the Land of Israel.

Israel's hold on the land, however, was, from the very first
promise to Abram, dependent on obeying God's will. Thus, as the

Bible and Rabbis present it, it was Israel's failure to obey God that prompted God to allow other nations (Assyria, Babylonia, Rome) to conquer Israel and drive them from the land. Part of the promise of the Land of Israel, then, is a war to reclaim the land from Israel's oppressors. Although the universalists among us—and even those who believe in Jewish nationhood but currently live in harmony and even friendship with non-Jewish neighbors—may flinch at the triumphalism of the biblical and rabbinic passages that promise such victory, the twentieth-century experience of Jews with the Soviets and the Nazis may make these sources more understandable and even palatable. The strife is sometimes symbolized by the term "the wars of Gog and Magog," a theme taken from chapter 38 in the Book of Ezekiel but reinterpreted to mean the wars against the enemies of Israel and/or the wars of the enemies of Israel against each other. Elijah would herald the coming of the Messiah, the one anointed to lead the Israelites in battle against their oppressors.

> "For lo! That day is at hand, burning like an oven. All the arrogant and all the doers of evil shall be straw, and the day that is coming"—said the Lord of Hosts—"shall burn them to ashes and leave them neither stock nor boughs. But for you who revere My Name a sun of victory shall rise to bring healing. You shall go forth and stamp like stall-fed calves, and you shall trample the wicked to pulp, for they shall be dust beneath your feet on the day that I am preparing," said the Lord of Hosts. "Be mindful of the teaching of My servant Moses, whom I charged at Horeb with laws and rules for all Israel. Lo, I will send the prophet Elijah to you before the coming of the awesome, fearful day of the Lord. He shall reconcile parents with children and children with parents, so that, when I come, I do not strike the whole land with utter destruction." (Malachi 3:19–24; see also Zechariah 14:12–15).

"When they [the Israelites] will be in the land of their enemies, I [God] will not reject them, neither will I abhor them,
to destroy them utterly, and to break My covenant with
them, for I am the Lord their God" (Leviticus 26:44): "I will
not reject them" in the days of the Greeks, "neither will I
abhor them" in the days of Nebuchadnezzar [the king who
destroyed the First Temple and took the Jews in chains into
exile in Babylonia], "to destroy them utterly" in the days of
Haman [i.e., Persia], "to break My covenant with them" in
the days of the Romans, "for I am the Lord their God" in the
days of Gog and Magog (Babylonian Talmud, *Megillah* 11a).

To hearten the people in their misery and encourage them to
persevere in the face of the severest hardships, the Rabbis preached
the doctrine that there will be "the travail of the Messiah," that is,
pangs of sufferings will precede and predict the coming of the
Messiah, just as a woman about to give birth experiences labor
pains. In this source, the Rabbis imagine that such travails will
include the exact opposite of everything included in the prophets'
and Rabbis' visions of the promised end-time:

In the generation in which the son of David [the Messiah] will
come, youths will insult their elders, the old will have to
stand up before the young, a daughter will revolt against her
mother, a daughter-in-law against her mother-in-law, the face
of the generation will be like the face of the dog [for impu-
dence], and a son will feel no shame in the face of his father
... Meeting places for study will be turned into brothels, the
learning of the scribes will decay, and sin-fearing people will
be condemned (Babylonian Talmud, *Sanhedrin* 97a).

The ultimate, hoped-for product of these wars is that Jews
will again be able to rule themselves. One source, in fact, asserts

that the only difference between current, historical times and the messianic era is that in the latter Jews will be freed of foreign rule and enjoy political independence.

> There is no difference between this world and the days of the Messiah except the oppression of the heathen kingdoms alone, as it is said, "For the poor shall never cease from the land" (Deuteronomy 15:11).
> —*Babylonian Talmud,* Berakhot *34b*

It is this source that led the Chief Rabbinate of the State of Israel to declare in its prayer for the state that its very existence is "the beginning of the flowering of our redemption," for even though the other factors described in this chapter have yet to come, Jewish political independence in the modern State of Israel foreshadows the advent of the other elements in the Jewish messianic vision.

The Ingathering of the Exiles

As part of the dream of political independence in the Land of Israel, both the Bible and the Rabbis asserted that messianic times would bring about the ingathering of Jewish exiles from all over the world to Israel. It is this part of the ideal world of classical Judaism that motivates some religious forms of Zionism. On the other hand, because God is supposed to bring the Messiah, some forms of Orthodoxy see Israel as an improper rushing of the Messiah by human beings, forcing God's hand, as it were. Those sects—including some living in Israel—see Israel as at best a secular state and at worst a violation of God's prerogatives and will.

> And in that day, a great ram's horn shall be sounded; and the strayed who are in the land of Assyria and the expelled

who are in the land of Egypt shall come and worship the Lord on the holy mount, in Jerusalem (Isaiah 27:13; see also Jeremiah 3:14).

Great will be the day when the exiles of Israel will be reassembled as the day when heaven and earth were created (Babylonian Talmud, *Pesachim* 88a).

In the present world, when the wind blows in the north, it does not blow in the south, and vice versa; but in the Hereafter, with reference to the gathering together of the exiles of Israel, the Holy One, blessed be He, said, "I will bring a northwest wind in the world that will affect both directions," as it is written, "I will say to the north, 'Give up,' and to the south, 'Keep not back'; bring My sons from afar, and My daughters from the ends of the earth" (Isaiah 43:6).

—Midrash Rabbah *to Esther 1:8*

Prosperity

Prosperity is part of the Torah's promises for obeying God's commandments, and the Rabbis imagine even greater prosperity in messianic times.

Blessed shall you be in the city, and blessed shall you be in the country. Blessed shall be the issue of your womb, the produce of your soil, and the offspring of your cattle, the calving of your herd, and the lambing of your flock. Blessed shall be your basket and your kneading bowl ... The Lord will ordain blessings for you upon your barns and upon all your undertakings. He will bless you in the land that the Lord is giving you ... The Lord will open for you His bounteous store, the heavens, to provide rain for your land in season and to bless your undertakings. You will be creditor to many nations, but debtor to none (Deuteronomy 28:3–5, 8, 12).

The world to come [the messianic era] will not be like this world. In this world one has the trouble to harvest the grapes and press them [to get wine], but in the world to come a person will bring a single grape in a wagon or ship, store it in the corner of his house, and draw from it enough wine to fill a large flagon, and its stalk will be used as fuel under the pot. There will not be a grape that will not yield thirty measures of wine ... In the Hereafter the Land of Israel will grow loaves of the finest flour and garments of the finest wool; and the soil will produce wheat, the ears of which will be the size of two kidneys of a large ox (Babylonian Talmud, *Ketubbot* 111b).

Although the image of fully formed loaves growing from the ground is clearly fanciful, it indicates the depth of the Jewish dream for prosperity. This extends from Jewish religious literature to Jewish popular culture. Based on Sholem Aleichem's Yiddish story *Tevye the Milkman*, Jerry Bock and Sheldon Harnick created the hit Broadway musical *Fiddler on the Roof*. In it, Tevye sings that if he were a rich man, he "wouldn't have to work hard," and yet he would have "a big tall house with rooms by the dozen right in the middle of the town, a fine tin roof and real wooden floors below," and he would fill his yard "with chicks and turkeys and geese and ducks" so that his wife would have "a proper double chin, supervising meals to her heart's delight."

Notice that although there are some expressions of asceticism in the Jewish tradition,[1] the vast majority of Jewish sources do not see wealth alone as a sin or even a necessary cause of sin; wealth, like everything else in life, gets its moral character from how we use it. Here again, Tevye, in the introduction to that same song, had it right:

"Dear God, you made many, many poor people. I realize of course, that it's no great shame to be poor—but it's no great honor, either."

Still, wealth imposes a special duty on the rich to use their money to help those less fortunate. All of us must certainly recognize that our world is filled with such people. Millions die each year from starvation and homelessness. The Jewish vision of the ideal world, then, provides yet another reason for working to ensure that no human being goes hungry or naked and that everyone has a roof over his or her head at night.

Health

Often associated with the promise of prosperity is God's pledge to prevent disease, as is evident from the continuation of a passage quoted above. If God does allow people to be stricken with diseases, God personally will heal them.

> You shall be blessed above all other peoples; there shall be no sterile male or female among you or among your flock. The Lord will ward off from you all sickness; He will not bring upon you any of the dreadful diseases of Egypt, about which you know, but will inflict them upon all your enemies (Deuteronomy 7:14–15).

> He [God] said: "If you will heed the Lord your God diligently, doing what is upright in His sight, giving ear to His commandments and keeping all His laws, then I will not bring upon you any of the diseases that I brought upon the Egyptians, for I the Lord am your healer" (Exodus 15:26).

Conversely, the Torah and the Rabbis assert a more troubling thesis, namely, that illness is the result of sin.

If you fail to observe faithfully all the terms of this teaching that are written in this book, to revere this honored and awesome Name, the Lord your God, the Lord will inflict extraordinary plagues upon you and your offspring, strange and lasting diseases, malignant and chronic diseases. He will bring back upon you all the sicknesses of Egypt that you dreaded so, and they shall cling to you. Moreover, the Lord will bring you all the other diseases and plagues that are not mentioned in this book of teaching, until you are wiped out. You shall be left a scant few, after having been as numerous as the stars in the skies, because you did not heed the command of the Lord your God (Deuteronomy 28:58–62).

Rabbi Hiyya bar Abba said: "A sick person does not recover from illness until all his [or her] sins are forgiven, as [the juxtaposition in the following verse shows, for] it is written, 'God forgives all your sins, God heals all your diseases' (Psalms 103:3)."
—*Babylonian Talmud,* Nedarim *41a*

Already in the Bible, though, Job strongly challenges this linkage. Furthermore, the claim that illness is the result of sin did not prevent the Rabbis (including Rabbi Hiyya bar Abba himself on the same talmudic page) from engaging in medicine to try to heal the sick. Indeed, many, many medieval and early modern rabbis were also physicians, involved in both clinical care and research.

This vision of a world free of disease imposes a duty on us to work toward that end as individuals. Some of us will work in health care directly, as doctors, nurses, medical social workers, chaplains, and volunteers. All of us have the duty to visit the sick, however distasteful we may find it, and, as described in chapter 7, the Jewish tradition even provides some advice about how to overcome that discomfort and make your visit effective for both the patient and the visitor.[2]

Furthermore, as citizens of our nation and of the world, this Jewish vision of a world without disease imposes on us the duty to ensure that anyone who needs health care has access to it. Thus we must get actively involved in political and economic efforts to provide clean water, food, and medication to those without them, both in our own country and abroad.

Justice

As indicated in chapter 1, a majority of contemporary Jews responding to polls assert that in their view social justice is the core commitment of the Jewish tradition. Such responses were not, as noted there, far off the mark. The demand for justice is indeed a persistent part of Jewish sources from the Bible to our own day, and it is a significant element in Jewish visions for the future.

This includes both procedural justice and substantive justice. Procedural justice demands that people be treated fairly in court and in society generally, with distinctions drawn among persons only for reasons having to do with their own actions or skills. So, for example, a just society is one in which people are not judged guilty or innocent, or fit for a job, according to the color of their skin or how much money they currently have.

> You shall not subvert the rights of your needy in their disputes. Keep far from a false charge; do not bring death on those who are innocent and in the right, for I will not acquit the wrongdoer. Do not take bribes, for bribes blind the clearsighted and upset the pleas of those who are in the right (Exodus 23:6–8; see also Deuteronomy 16:18–20).

> You shall not render an unfair decision: do not favor the poor or show deference to the rich; judge your kinsmen fairly. Do not deal basely with your countrymen. Do not

profit by the blood of your fellow: I am the Lord[3] (Leviticus 19:15–16; see also Deuteronomy 1:16–17).

Parents shall not be put to death for [the sins of their] children, nor children for [the sins of their] parents; a person shall be put to death only for his own crime (Deuteronomy 24:16).

Maimonides makes some of the Torah's procedural concerns more specific:

1. It is a positive commandment for the judge to judge fairly, as Scripture says, "Judge your neighbor fairly" (Leviticus 19:15). What is fair judgment? It is equalizing the two litigants in every respect. One should not let one litigant speak as long as he wants and tell the other to be brief; and one should not be friendly to one litigant, speaking to him softly, while frowning upon the other and speaking to him harshly.

2. If one of the litigants is richly dressed and the other poorly dressed, the judge must say to the former, "Either dress him like yourself before you come to trial against him, or dress like him such that you are equal; then the two of you may stand in judgment."

3. One litigant should not sit and the other stand, but rather both should stand. If the court wanted to permit both to be seated, it may do so. However, one must not sit on a seat higher than the other; they must be seated side by side ...

11. If the judge sees a point in favor of a litigant and finds that the litigant is trying to say it but he cannot articulate it, or he sees that a litigant is desperately trying to defend himself with a truthful claim but he loses the point due to his fierce anger, or he finds that the litigant is confused because

of an inferior intellect, then he is permitted to assist him a little by giving him a lead on the basis of "Speak up for the dumb" (Proverbs 31:8). But the judge must do this carefully so that he does not play the part of an advocate (Maimonides, *Mishneh Torah, Laws of Courts* 21:1–3, 11).

Although some of this may seem obvious to us now, note that much of it took quite a long time to become adopted in Anglo-American law. The guarantee that parents and children not be held liable for each other's offenses, although articulated in Deuteronomy 24:16, which scholars date to the end of the seventh century B.C.E., was not part of British law until about 1830; until then, descendants would suffer for their ancestors' treason, a process known as "attaint." The Founding Fathers of the United States therefore had to ban that explicitly in Article 3, Section 3 of the United States Constitution in 1789. More pervasively, the kind of fairness envisioned in the Torah and by Maimonides was not common practice in the United States until very recently, for poor people and blacks were commonly treated unfairly just because they were poor or black. It is still the case in the United States, in fact, that blacks are much more likely to be executed for killing whites than whites are for killing blacks. Furthermore, American law does not insist on the formal requirements that Maimonides articulates to make both litigants look alike in social status. Thus, the Jewish vision of an ideal world should prompt us to work toward refining the American sense of procedural justice.

If that is true for the United States, which in our day has a relatively refined sense of procedural justice in comparison to its own past and to many other nations of the past and present, the Jewish vision of procedural justice in the ideal society is even farther from reality in most other countries of the world—in Asia, Africa, South America, and Arab lands. Thus biblical and rabbinic standards of procedural justice still have a lot to teach contemporary humanity.

Substantive, in contrast to procedural, justice demands that society be structured so that people have basic food, clothing, and shelter—and, in our own day, health care and access to transportation. Western concepts of substantive justice are rooted in the Torah. Contrary to Mesopotamian, Egyptian, Persian, Greek, Roman, and most other cultures of the ancient world, the Torah demands that such basic care be supplied not only for citizens but also for strangers.

> You shall not wrong a stranger or oppress him, for you were strangers in the land of Egypt. You shall not ill treat any widow or orphan. If you do mistreat them, I [God] will heed their outcry as soon as they cry out to Me, and My anger shall blaze forth and I will put you to the sword, and your own wives shall become widows and your children orphans. If you lend money to My people, to the poor among you, do not act toward them as a creditor: exact no interest from them. If you take your neighbor's garment in pledge, you must return it to him before the sun sets; it is his only clothing, the sole covering for his skin. In what else shall he sleep? Therefore, if he cries out to Me, I will pay heed, for I am compassionate (Exodus 22:20–26).

> You shall not subvert the rights of the stranger or the fatherless; you shall not take a widow's garment in pawn. Remember that you were a slave in Egypt and the Lord your God redeemed you from there; therefore do I enjoin you to observe this commandment (Deuteronomy 24:17–18).

The biblical prophets are perhaps best known for their scathing criticism of people—Jews as well as other nations—who fail to care for the downtrodden and destitute. The following selection exemplifies what they say about people who fail to live up to this element of the Jewish vision of the ideal society.

Ah, you [House of Joseph, i.e., the northern Israelite king-
dom] who turn justice into wormwood
And hurl righteousness to the ground! ...
They hate the arbiter in the gate,[4]
And detest him whose plea is just.
Assuredly, because you impose a tax on the poor
And exact from him a levy of grain,
You have built houses of hewn stone,
But you shall not live in them;
You have planted delightful vineyards,
But shall not drink their wine.
For I have noted how many are your crimes,
And how countless your sins—
You enemies of the righteous,
You takers of bribes,
You who subvert in the gate the cause of the needy!
Assuredly, at such a time the prudent man keeps silent,
For it is an evil time.
Seek good and not evil that you may live,
And that the Lord, the God of Hosts,
May truly be with you, as you think [He is now].
Hate evil and love good,
And establish justice in the gate;
Perhaps the Lord, the God of Hosts,
Will be gracious to the remnant of Joseph ...
Let justice well up like water,
Righteousness like an unfailing stream (Amos 5:7, 10–15,
24; see also Isaiah 1:16–26).

Amos (in chapters 1 and 2) and Jeremiah (in chapters 46–51)
also castigate other nations for similar moral transgressions—adultery, fraud, and murder—and for failing to care for the downtrodden. Ultimately, though, as we shall see shortly, the prophets look

forward to a time when both procedural and substantive justice will prevail, and the message is clearly that we must work to make that happen as part of our *tikkun olam*.

Knowledge of God's Word

The biblical dream of the ideal world is one in which not only Jews but all peoples would know how to be just and behave accordingly. That is because in the ideal world all peoples would learn the Torah. This makes Judaism the exact opposite of traditions that would keep the convictions of the faith in the hands of a few elite; instead, Jewish sources look forward to a time when everyone knows and obeys the Torah.

> Moses wrote down this teaching and gave it to the priests, sons of Levi, who carried the ark of the Lord's covenant, and to all the elders of Israel. And Moses instructed them as follows: Every seventh year, the year set for remission [of debts], at the Feast of Booths, when all Israel comes to appear before the Lord your God in the place that He will choose [the Temple in Jerusalem], you shall read this teaching aloud in the presence of all Israel. Gather the people— men, women, children, and the strangers in your communities—that they may hear and so learn to revere the Lord your God and to observe faithfully every word of this teaching. Their children too, who have not had the experience [of standing at Sinai], shall hear and learn to revere the Lord your God as long as they live in the land that you are about to cross the Jordan to possess (Deuteronomy 31:9–13).

> The word that Isaiah, son of Amos, prophesied concerning
> Judah and Jerusalem:
> In the days to come,

The mount of the Lord's house
Shall stand firm above the mountains and tower above the
  hills;
And all nations shall gaze on it with joy.
And the many peoples shall go and say:
"Come, let us go up to the mount of the Lord,
To the house of the God of Jacob;
That He may instruct us in His ways,
And that we may walk in His paths."
For instruction shall come forth from Zion,
The word of the Lord from Jerusalem.
Thus He will judge among the nations
And arbitrate for the many peoples,
And they shall beat their swords into plowshares
And their spears into pruning hooks.
Nation shall not take up sword against nation;
They shall never again know war (Isaiah 2:1–4).

Isaiah describes a world in which all people worship Israel's God and follow God's word in the Torah that they learn in Jerusalem. Micah, Isaiah's younger contemporary, records the exact same words in Isaiah's speech just quoted here, but then he adds two lines that change the message radically: all peoples will learn Torah from Jerusalem, but in the end each will worship his or her own god.

But every man shall sit under his grapevine or fig tree
With no one to disturb him.
For it was the Lord of Hosts who spoke.
Though all the peoples will walk
Each in the names of its gods,
We will walk
In the name of the Lord our God
Forever and ever (Micah 4:4–5).

Thus, Isaiah imagines a world in which everyone follows one God and one set of rules. Similarly, in a verse made famous by its inclusion at the end of the *Alenu* prayer that ends every service, the prophet Zechariah proclaims, "And the Lord shall be king over all the earth; in that day there shall be one Lord with one name" (Zechariah 14:9). Micah, on the other hand, conceives of a world in which all people learn from Israel's Torah but act according to their own understanding of what is right in a pluralistic world.

The Rabbis also had difficulty imagining non-Jews adopting the Torah as their standard of behavior. They claimed that in messianic times, Israel would be so exalted that non-Jews would attempt to become Jews but would not be accepted.

> In the Hereafter, the Gentile peoples will come to convert to Judaism, but we will not accept any of them; for there is a rabbinic dictum, "No proselytes are to be accepted in the days of the Messiah" (Babylonian Talmud, *Avodah Zarah* 3b).

This obviously disturbs many of us today who welcome converts with open arms and feel enriched by their passion for, and practice of, Judaism. This source illustrates, however, just how bad the relationships were between Jews and non-Jews in talmudic times and how much the Jews' vision of the future required vindication of Israel after our immense suffering at the hands of non-Jewish rulers. In our time, all these sources summon us to work for a world that may include plural beliefs but also manifests a universal commitment to the values we Jews learn from the Torah—children, education, family, community, care for those less fortunate, both procedural and substantive justice, and, finally, peace.

Peace

Unlike some other traditions, war is not valorized in Judaism. Jewish heroes—with the possible exception of the Maccabees—are not warriors; they are instead people who study and practice the values of the Torah and work toward a better world.

> Hillel says: "Be a disciple of Aaron, loving peace and pursuing peace, loving your fellow creatures and attracting them to [the study and practice of] the Torah" (Mishnah, *Pirkei Avot* 1:12).

Although Judaism is not pacifistic—the Talmud says, "If one comes to kill you, rise up early in the morning to kill him first,"[5] and Jewish law permits defensive wars[6]—it nevertheless urges us to work for peace. Thus, every *Amidah*—the prayer said while standing three times each day; four times on Sabbaths, Rosh Hashanah, and festivals; and five times on Yom Kippur—ends with an entreaty to God for peace. But we may not rest by asking God to bring peace; we must do what we can as well. In fact, based on the verse from Psalms, "Seek peace and pursue it" (Psalms 34:15), the Rabbis declare that the commandment to seek peace is unlike any other in that we do not do it only when the occasion arises but must rather go out of our way to find ways to make peace.

> The law does not order you to run after or pursue the other commandments, but only to fulfill them on the appropriate occasion. But peace you must seek in your own place and pursue it even to another place as well (Jerusalem Talmud, *Peah* 1:1 [4a]).

Finally, the Rabbis maintain that peace is an underlying condition for all other blessings and that God's Name is thus associated with peace.

Great is peace, for all blessings are contained in it ... Great
is peace, for God's Name is peace (*Numbers Rabbah* 11:7).

It is not surprising, then, that both Isaiah's and Micah's visions
of the ideal society include a cessation of war. In a later prophecy,
Isaiah goes yet further, combining many of the elements that we
have seen in Judaism's vision of an ideal society and asserting that
in such a time and place even animals that are normally at war with
each other will be at peace.

> But a shoot shall grow out of the stump of Jesse [David's
>   father],
> A twig shall sprout from his stock.
> The spirit of the Lord will alight upon him:
> A spirit of wisdom and insight,
> A spirit of counsel and valor,
> A spirit of devotion and reverence for the Lord.
> He shall sense the truth by his reverence for the Lord:
> He shall not judge by what his eyes behold,
> Nor decide by what his ears perceive.
> Thus he shall judge the poor with equity
> And decide with justice for the lowly of the land.
> He shall strike down the ruthless with the rod of his mouth
> And slay the wicked with the breath of his lips.
> Justice shall be the girdle of his loins,
> And faithfulness the girdle of his waist.
> The wolf shall dwell with the lamb,
> The leopard lie down with the kid;
> The calf, the beast of prey, and the fatling together,
> With a little boy to herd them.
> The cow and the bear shall graze,
> Their young shall lie down together;
> And the lion, like the ox, shall eat straw.

A babe shall play over a viper's hole,
And an infant pass his hand over an adder's den.
In all of My sacred mountain
Nothing evil or vile shall be done;
For the land shall be filled with devotion to the Lord
As water covers the sea.
In that day,
The stock of Jesse that has remained standing
Shall become a standard to peoples—
Nations shall seek his counsel
And his abode shall be honored.
In that day, my Lord will apply His hand again to redeeming
    the other part of His people from Assyria—as also from
    Egypt, Pathros, Nubia, Elam, Shinar, Hamath, and the
    coastlands.
He will hold up a signal to the nations
And assemble the banished of Israel,
And gather the dispersed of Judah
From the four corners of the earth ...
In that day, you shall say:
"I give thanks to You, O Lord!
Although You were wroth with me,
Your wrath has turned back and You comfort me,
Behold the God who gives me triumph!
I am confident, unafraid,
For Yah the Lord is my strength and might,
And He has been my deliverance" (Isaiah 11:1–12; 12:12:1–2).

Christians, of course, assert that the person Isaiah is describing was Jesus. Jews deny that, because Isaiah was probably talking
about someone near to his time period eight centuries earlier who
would bring these things to pass soon, and because Jesus did not
accomplish all these things; he did not fulfill the job description, as

it were. Christians recognize that too; that is why they believe in the doctrine of the Second Coming, when Jesus would presumably finish the job. Jews just think that he was not the Messiah in the first place—a rabbi, a good teacher and preacher, but not the Messiah.

Our ultimate goal in *tikkun olam*, then, is a world at peace. That, as we have seen, does not just mean cessation of hostilities. It also means a world in which we have the blessings of children, a Jewish state in the Land of Israel to which Jewish exiles can and do come to live, prosperity, health, procedural and substantive justice, recognition of Israel's God and of Torah values as authoritative, and peace. May we all work toward those ends in our lives, not only for the sense of meaning and purpose that such efforts give us but also for the good we thereby do in the world. And with God's help, may we succeed!

Notes

Key for abbreviations in the notes below:

M. = Mishnah, edited by Rabbi Judah Ha-Nasi, c. 200 C.E.

T. = Tosefta, edited by Rabbis Hiyya and Oshaya, c. 200 C.E.

J. = Jerusalem (Palestinian) Talmud, edited c. 400 C.E.

B. = Babylonian Talmud, edited by Ravina and Rav Ashi, c. 500 C.E.

M.T. = The code of Moses ben Maimon (Maimonides), the *Mishneh Torah,* completed in 1177.

S.A. = Joseph Karo's code, the *Shulchan Arukh,* first published in 1563.

Introduction

1. *Los Angeles Times,* April 13, 1988, pp. A1, 14, 15.
2. The study, "American Jews and Their Social Justice Involvement: Evidence from a National Survey," was released in 2000 and used to launch Amos: The National Jewish Partnership for Social Justice. Amos received some initial foundation support and functioned with a board and a small staff until its funding ran out a few years later. See Sidney Schwarz, *Judaism and Justice: Values, Community, and Identity,* forthcoming, p. 216 and chapter 25, n. 10 (p. 224) in the manuscript.
3. *Los Angeles Times,* February 1, 2003, part 2, p. 23.

Chapter 1: The Meaning and Significance of *Tikkun Olam*

1. M. *Gittin* 4:2–7, 9; 5:3; 9:4. M. *Eduyot* 1:13. T. *Ketubbot* 12:1; T. *Gittin* 3:12–13; 6:10; T. *Bava Batra* 6:6. See also B. *Ketubbot* 52b; J. *Pesachim* 14b; and the codes on these passages. Throughout the book I shall use "Rabbis" (with a capital *R*) to refer to the classical Rabbis of the Mishnah, Talmud, and Midrash, while "rabbis" (with a lowercase *r*) will refer to rabbis from medieval and modern times. In adherence to standard English form, though, the adjectival form, "rabbinic," will be spelled with a lowercase *r* even when it refers to the classical rabbis.
2. Reuben Alcalay, *The Complete Hebrew-English Dictionary* (Bridgeport, Conn.: The Prayer Book Press, 1965), p. 2835. Abraham Even-Shoshan, *Dictionary of the Hebrew Language* (Jerusalem: Kiryath Sepher, 1970), 7:2898. I want to thank my good friend, Rabbi and Professor William

Cutter, professor of Hebrew literature at Hebrew Union College in Los Angeles, for calling my attention to this original meaning.

3. M.T. *Laws of Rebels (Mamrim)* 1:2.

4. Maharal of Prague, *Tiferet Yisrael,* chapter 58, pp. 175–176.

5. We shall explore some of the more important aspects of the substantive meaning of the term in chapter 5 below and the Forward; for more on that and for the procedural meaning of the term, see Elliot N. Dorff, *To Do the Right and the Good: A Jewish Approach to Modern Social Ethics* (Philadelphia: Jewish Publication Society, 2002), chapters 5 and 6.

6. See, for example, Umberto Cassuto, *A Commentary on the Book of Exodus* (Jerusalem: Magnes Press [Hebrew University], 1967), pp. 260–264, who points out that if Exodus 21–24 were really a law code, it should have clear rules about normal activities in life, such as completing a business deal and getting married. The fact that those chapters do not address such common things indicates that what we have in those chapters is simply a collection of judicial precedents.

7. The term is also used this way and translated as "rules" in Deuteronomy 4:8 and 14; Ezekiel 20:25; Malachi 3:22.

8. It is possible that the original meaning of this verse is different—namely, that both *tzakkik* and *chasid* are synonyms for faithful, or trustworthy. That would preserve the parallelism common in biblical poetry. The Rabbis, however, understood these words as I have translated them here, and so at least in rabbinic theology, if not in biblical thought, justice and kindness are put in balance.

9. Note that the word *yakar* can mean "rare," as Rabbi Elazar is choosing to interpret it here to make his homiletical point. Its original meaning in this context, however, was probably "precious," as the Jewish Publication Society translation has it (quoted above). It is juxtaposed with verses that glory in God's care for those who keep His covenant. The Rabbis frequently cite verses out of context and mistranslate them for homiletical purposes, which is fine, according to their procedures, as long as a given interpretation does not countermand Jewish law or values but rather reinforces them, for "there are seventy faces to the Torah" (*Numbers Rabbah* 13:15–16).

10. For a description of Jewish demands of procedural justice—that judgments be fair and that rules be followed for making them so—see my book *To Do the Right and the Good* (at n. 5 above), chapter 5 and the Forward in this volume.

Chapter 2: Why Should I Care?

1. See also Genesis 14:19; Exodus 20:11; Leviticus 25:23, 42, 55; Deuteronomy 4:35, 39, 32:6. I discuss the medical implications of this belief in *Matters of Life and Death: A Jewish Approach to Modern Medical Ethics* (Philadelphia: Jewish Publication Society, 1998), especially pp. 15–18. I discuss its implications for social ethics in *To Do the Right and the Good: A Jewish Approach to Modern Social Ethics* (Philadelphia: Jewish Publication Society, 2002), chapter 6, and in chapter 5 of this volume.

2. This appears in the paragraphs after the call to prayer, the *barekhu,* in the lines celebrating creation, the subject of the first blessing of the core of the service. In Jules Harlow, ed., *Siddur Sim Shalom: A Prayerbook for Shabbat, Festivals, and Weekdays* (New York: Rabbinical Assembly and United Synagogue of America, 1985), pp. 96 and 98.

3. T. *Peah* 4:20.

4. *Sifra, Kedoshim* 4:12.

5. Marry a fitting woman: T. *Sotah* 5:6; B. *Kiddushin* 41a. That a man should not have sexual intercourse with his wife during the day lest he see something he finds loathsome: B. *Niddah* 17a. That a child may draw blood from his or her parent in an effort to heal him or her despite the Torah's prohibition of injuring one's parents, carrying the death penalty for doing so (Exodus 21:15): B. *Sanhedrin* 84b. The duty to choose "a beautiful death" for those condemned to die: T. *Sanhedrin* 9:3; B. *Pesachim* 75a; J. *Sotah* 1:5 (6a); J. *Sanhedrin* 6:4 (28a).

6. M.T. *Laws of Ethics (Hilkhot De'ot)* 6:3.

7. M.T. *Laws of Gifts to the Poor* 8:10.

8. M.T. *Laws of Mourning* 14:1.

9. *Sifra, Kedoshim* 3:14 (on Leviticus 19:14); *Sifra, Kedoshim* 7:14 (on Leviticus 19:32, on honoring the elderly); *Sifra, Behar* 4:2 and 6:2 (on Leviticus 25:14 and 25:17, forbidding us from oppressing our neighbor).

10. For a more thorough discussion of these motivations, see Elliot N. Dorff and Arthur Rosett, *A Living Tree: The Roots and Growth of Jewish Law* (Albany: State University of New York Press, 1988), pp. 93–109, and, even more extensively, Elliot N. Dorff, *Mitzvah Means Commandment* (New York: United Synagogue of America, 1989), chapters 1, 3, 4, and 5.

11. See Elie Spitz, "The Jewish Tradition and Capital Punishment," in Elliot N. Dorff and Louis E. Newman, *Contemporary Jewish Ethics and Morality: A Reader* (New York: Oxford University Press, 1995), pp. 344–349.

12. See Genesis 1:26–27; 3:1–7, 22–24.

13. See Genesis 2:18-24; Numbers 12:1-16; Deuteronomy 22:13-19. Note also that *ha-middaber,* "the speaker," is a synonym for human being (in comparison to animals) in medieval Jewish philosophy.

14. Maimonides, *Guide for the Perplexed,* part I, chapter 1.

15. See Deuteronomy 6:5; Leviticus 19:18, 33–34; note that the traditional prayer book juxtaposes the paragraph just before the *Shema,* which speaks of God's love for us, with the first paragraph of the *Shema,* which commands us to love God.

16. Consider the prayer in the traditional, early morning weekday service, *Elohai, neshamah she-notata bi,* "My God, the soul (or life-breath) that you have imparted to me is pure. You created it, You formed it, You breathed it into me; You guard it within me ... " Harlow, *Siddur Sim Shalom* (at n. 2 above), pp. 8–11. Similarly, the Rabbis describe the human being as part divine and part animal, the latter consisting of the material aspects of the human being and the former consisting of that which we share with God; see *Sifrei Deuteronomy,* par. 306; 132a. Or consider this rabbinic statement in *Genesis Rabbah* 8:11: "In four

respects man resembles the creatures above, and in four respects the creatures below. Like the animals he eats and drinks, propagates his species, relieves himself, and dies. Like the ministering angels he stands erect, speaks, possesses intellect, and sees [in front of him and not on the side like an animal]."

17. M. *Sanhedrin* 4:5. The relevant passage is this: "Additionally, [Adam was created alone] to proclaim the greatness of the Holy One, blessed be He: for if a man strikes many coins from one mold, they all resemble one another, but the Supreme King of kings, the Holy One, blessed be He, fashioned every person in the stamp of the first person, and yet none of them looks the same as anyone else. Therefore every single person is obligated to say: 'The world was created for my sake.'"

18. Rabbi Bunam, cited by Martin Buber, *Tales of the Hasidim* (New York: Schocken, 1948), vol. II, pp. 249–250.

19. *Genesis Rabbah* 24:7.

20. J. *Eruvin* 5:1. Barukh Halevi Epstein suggests that this is a scribal error, that because the previous aphorisms in this section of the Talmud refer to welcoming scholars, here too the Talmud meant to say that one who welcomes a scholar is like one who welcomes the divine presence: Barukh Halevi Epstein, *Torah Temimah* (Tel Aviv: Am Olam, 1969), p. 182 (on Exodus 18:12, n. 19). He may well be right contextually, but the version that we have states an important, broader lesson that expresses the divine image in every person, regardless of his or her level of scholarship. Along the same lines, Shammai, who was not known for his friendliness and who in the immediately previous phrase warns us to "say little and do much," nevertheless admonishes, "Greet every person with a cheerful face" (*Pirkei Avot* 1:15), undoubtedly in recognition of the divine image in each of us.

21. For a thorough discussion of this blessing and concept in the Jewish tradition, see Carl Astor, "...*Who Makes People Different*": *Jewish Perspectives on the Disabled* (New York: United Synagogue of America, 1985).

22. *Genesis Rabbah* 24:7.

23. Dorff, *Matters of Life and Death* (at n. 1), pp. 291–299. See also Elijah J. Schochet, *A Responsum of Surrender* (Los Angeles: University of Judaism, 1973).

24. B. *Bava Kamma* 119a.

25. Dorff, *To Do the Right and the Good*, chapter 1 (at n. 1), esp. pp. 16–26.

26. This was certainly the practice of all governments in the pre-Enlightenment world, and the political theories of pre-Enlightenment societies supported that practice. Christianity is one possible exception here, but even that is not clear. On one hand, it focuses on the salvation of the individual, regardless of his or her social affiliation, and that would seem to lend at least some support in thinking of people as individuals rather than as members of groups that they cannot ignore or leave. On the other hand, though, based on a passage in the New Testament (Matthew 22:21) in which Christians are told to "give back to Caesar what belongs to Caesar, and to God what belongs to God," Christians in practice have made a sharp dichotomy between the "city of God" and the

"city of Man," as Augustine put it, reserving individualistic thinking for the city of God and ruling earthly societies in accordance with the corporate theories prevalent before the Enlightenment.

27. See also B. *Rosh Hashanah* 17a; M.T. *Laws of Repentance* 3:4.
28. B. *Shabbat* 54b. Along with Jeremiah (31:29–30) and Ezekiel (18:20–32), this offends our sense of justice, but that is only because we are so used to thinking in individualistic terms.
29. Exodus 20:5–6; Deuteronomy 5:9–10; compare Exodus 34:7.
30. Milton R. Konvitz, *Judaism and the American Idea* (New York: Schocken, 1978, 1980), pp. 143, 150; and see chapter 5 generally. Hillel's words are in B. *Sukkah* 53a.
31. Dorff, *To Do the Right and the Good* (at n. 1), pp. 22–26.
32. Report of a poll conducted by the American Jewish Committee in the *Los Angeles Times*, February 1, 2003, part 2, p. 23.
33. Jacob Neusner, *Tzedakah: Can Jewish Philanthropy Buy Jewish Survival?* (Chappaqua, N.Y.: Rossel Books, 1982), pp. 32, 67ff.
34. B. *Bava Metzia* 59b.

Chapter 3: Religion and Ethics

1. Exodus 34:7; Numbers 14:18.
2. Deuteronomy 24:16.
3. Genesis 18:25ff.
4. Job 9:1–35.
5. Isaiah 5:16.
6. Leviticus 19:18; Deuteronomy 6:8, 16:20.
7. For a more thorough discussion of this, see Elliot N. Dorff, *Matters of Life and Death: A Jewish Approach to Modern Medical Ethics* (Philadelphia: Jewish Publication Society, 1998), appendix, especially pp. 396–400, and chapter 6 in Elliot N. Dorff, *The Unfolding Tradition: Jewish Law from Sinai On* (New York: Aviv Press, 2005). For Orthodox writers who maintain that there is an important role for morality in interpreting and shaping Jewish law, see Eliezer Berkovits, *Not in Heaven: The Nature and Function of Halakha* (New York: Ktav, 1983); David Hartman, *A Living Covenant: The Innovative Spirit in Traditional Judaism* (New York: Free Press, 1985), esp. chapter 5; and Shubert Spero, *Morality, Halakha, and the Jewish Tradition* (New York: Ktav and Yeshiva University Press, 1983). On the other hand, those who deny such a relationship, maintaining instead that divine commands must always supersede human understandings of morality, include David Weiss Halivni, "Can a Religious Law Be Immoral?" in *Perspectives on Jews and Judaism: Essays in Honor of Wolfe Kelman,* ed. Arthur A. Chiel (New York: Rabbinical Assembly, 1978), pp. 165–170, and Yeshayahu Leibowitz, *Judaism, Human Values, and the Jewish State* (Cambridge, Mass.: Harvard University Press, 1992). For a landmark comparative study of Jewish approaches to the relationship between Jewish law and morality, see Louis Newman, "Ethics as Law, Law as Religion: Reflections on the Problem of Law and Ethics in Judaism," in *Contemporary Jewish*

Ethics and Morality: A Reader, ed. Elliot N. Dorff and Louis E. Newman (New York: Oxford University Press, 1995), pp. 79–93.

8. Leo Lieberman, "Bubbie—Tzedakah, Discipline, and Arms Designed for Hugs," in his *Memories of Laughter and Garlic* (Margate, N.J.: Comte Q Publishing, 1999), pp. 28–30.

9. Genesis 19:1–11.

10. Lancelot Addison, *The Present State of the Jews* (London, 1675), quoted in Israel Abrahams, *Jewish Life in the Middle Ages* (New York: Atheneum and Philadelphia: Jewish Publication Society, 1969), p. 307.

11. See Elliot N. Dorff, *Love Your Neighbor and Yourself: A Jewish Approach to Modern Personal Ethics* (Philadelphia: Jewish Publication Society, 2003), chapter 4, for a description of parental and filial duties in classic Jewish sources and in modern times, and see chapters 9 and 10 in this volume.

12. In B. *Ta'anit* 7a this is attributed to Rabbi Hanina; in B. *Makkot* 10a it is attributed to Rabbi Judah Ha-Nasi.

13. See, for example, Emanuel Levinas, *Difficult Freedom: Essays on Judaism,* trans. Sean Hand (Baltimore: Johns Hopkins University Press, 1990), pp. 3–23; and "Revelation in the Jewish Tradition," in *Beyond the Verse: Talmudic Readings and Lectures,* trans. Gary D. Mole (Bloomington: Indiana University Press, 1994), pp. 129–150, reprinted in *Contemporary Jewish Theology: A Reader,* ed. Elliot N. Dorff and Louis E. Newman (New York: Oxford University Press, 1999), pp. 164–178.

14. B. *Pesachim* 50b; B. *Sanhedrin* 105a; B. *Arakhin* 16b; B. *Sotah* 22b, 47a; B. *Horayot* 10b; B. *Nazir* 23b.

15. B. *Sotah* 14a.

16. God is depicted as Israel's marital partner a number of times in the Bible, whether fondly, as in Jeremiah 2:2, or angrily when Israel proves to be an unfaithful lover, as in Hosea, chapter 2.

17. See Dorff, *Love Your Neighbor and Yourself* (at n. 11), pp. 323–337, for a discussion of how Samson Raphael Hirsch, Mordecai Kaplan, and Martin Buber conceive of the relationship between study and morality.

18. *Mekhilta* on Exodus 31:13; B. *Yoma* 85a–b; B. *Sanhedrin* 74a b.

Chapter 4: How We Talk to Each Other

1. The talmudic text actually says, "the youth of the enemies of Israel die." Because the Rabbis could not even utter the words that the youth of Israel should die, they used a euphemism.

2. Moses Hayyim Luzzato, *Mesillat Yesharim: The Path of the Just,* trans. Shraga Zilbershtain (New York: Feldheim, 1987), chapter 11; see also *Mesillat Yesharim: The Path of the Upright,* trans. Mordecai M. Kaplan (Philadelphia: Jewish Publication Society, 1966), pp. 164–169. This is my translation.

3. Joseph Telushkin, *Words That Hurt, Words That Heal: How to Choose Words Wisely and Well* (New York: William Morrow and Company, 1996), pp. 18–21.

4. Stephen Bates, *If No News, Send Rumors: Anecdotes of American Journalism* (New York: Henry Holt, 1989), pp. 142–143.

5. Benedict Carey, "Have You Heard? Gossip Turns Out to Serve a Purpose," *New York Times*, August 16, 2005, Science Section. Although this article helpfully reports on some new research on these matters, it suffers from using the word "gossip" to cover many of the disparate forms of speech that I distinguish in this chapter. Still, the evidence seems clear that what Jewish law would prohibit as *lashon ha-ra* may scientifically have some good effects on individuals and groups.

6. For more on the process of return *(teshuvah)*, see Elliot N. Dorff, *Love Your Neighbor and Yourself: A Jewish Approach to Modern Personal Ethics* (Philadelphia: Jewish Publication Society, 2003), chapter 6. For a discussion of how these norms might apply to one community forgiving another for past or present wrongs (the case discussed is Catholics asking Jews for forgiveness for what the Catholic Church did and failed to do during the Holocaust), see Elliot N. Dorff, *To Do the Right and the Good: A Jewish Approach to Modern Social Ethics* (Philadelphia: Jewish Publication Society, 2002), chapter 8.

7. B. *Pesachim* 22b; B. *Mo'ed Katan* 17a; B. *Bava Metzia* 75b.

8. For more on this, see the chapter on family violence in Dorff, *Love Your Neighbor and Yourself* (at n. 6), chapter 5, esp. pp. 192–200 and p. 300, n. 132.

9. *Genesis Rabbah* 48:18 (God changes Sarah's words); B. *Yevamot* 65a (Joseph's brothers' lie and God's advice to Samuel to lie to Saul).

10. J. David Bleich cites such studies in *Judaism and Healing: Halakhic Perspectives* (New York: Ktav, 1981), pp. 31–32.

11. For more on hospice and the Jewish tradition, see Elliot N. Dorff, *Matters of Life and Death: A Jewish Approach to Modern Medical Ethics* (Philadelphia: Jewish Publication Society, 1998), pp. 218–220 and chapter 8 generally. For more on hope in the process of dying, see Maurice Lamm, *The Power of Hope: The One Essential of Life and Love* (New York: Rawson Associates, 1995), esp. pp. 132–133, and Dorff, *Love Your Neighbor and Yourself* (at n. 6), chapter 7.

12. Examples of "Speak to the Children of Israel": Exodus 25:2; 31:13; Leviticus 1:2; 4:2; 7:23, 29; 12:2; 18:2; 23:2, 10, 24, 34; 25:2; 27:2; Numbers 5:6, 12; 6:2; 9:10; 15:2, 18, 38. The commandment to read the Torah to "men, women, and children and the stranger in your midst" every seven years: Deuteronomy 31:10–13.

13. B. *Menachot* 43b.

Chapter 5: Helping the Poor

1. See also *Sifrei* on Deuteronomy 15:7; *Mishneh Torah, Laws of Gifts to the Poor* 7:13; *Shulchan Arukh, Yoreh De'ah* 251:3.

2. This clause appears in the Babylonian Talmud's version of the Tosefta but not in the printed version of the Tosefta itself.

Chapter 6: Ransoming and Surrendering Captives

1. The reference of Rabbi Judah's question is unclear. If we follow the usual stylistic conventions, where the phrase "where does that apply" comes to narrow a previous ruling to make it more lenient, Rabbi Judah comes to

limit the first opinion mentioned (the *tanna kama*). Specifically, while the first opinion says that if the enemy does not designate a particular person nobody may be handed over, Rabbi Judah would say that this only applies if the enemy is still outside the city walls so that there is still a chance that they would all survive, but if the enemy has already managed to break into the city, someone may be handed over to save the rest since that is the only chance that any of them will be saved.

The problem with interpreting Rabbi Judah this way, however, is that if the enemy had not designated someone, how are the city dwellers to choose whom to hand over? Moreover, Rabbi Judah says that "he" may be handed over if the enemy is inside the city walls, which would seem to indicate that the enemy has designated someone.

2. See Saul Lieberman, *Tosefta Ki-Fshutah, Zera'im* (New York: Jewish Theological Seminary of America, 1955), pp. 420–422 [Hebrew]; Elijah J. Schochet, *A Responsum of Surrender* (Los Angeles: University of Judaism, 1973), pp. 6–7; and David Daube, *Collaboration with Tyranny in Jewish Law* (New York: Oxford University Press, 1965), pp. 31–36.

3. B. *Shabbat* 46a.

4. B. *Yevamot* 36a, according to which the law is always according to Rabbi Yochanan when he argues with Resh Lakish except in three instances, and this is not one of those three. Rabbi Yochanan generally wins the day even though on two occasions (B. *Ketubbot* 54b, 84b), when confronted with the differing ruling by Resh Lakish, Rabbi Yochanan remarked, "What can I do when a rabbi of equal status disagrees with me?" I would like to thank my teacher and colleague at the University of Judaism, Dr. Elieser Slomovic, for discussing these sources with me.

5. Maimonides, *Mishneh Torah, Laws of the Fundamental Principles of the Torah* 5:5. The basis for this ruling is discussed in *Kesef Mishneh* there.

6. Elliot N. Dorff, *Matters of Life and Death: A Jewish Approach to Modern Medical Ethics* (Philadelphia: Jewish Publication Society, 1998), pp. 291–299.

7. See Schochet, *A Responsum of Surrender* (at n. 2), pp. 47–48.

Chapter 7: Accompanying and Supporting People in Times of Need and Joy

1. B. *Shabbat* 10a, 119b. In the first of those passages, the judge who judges justly is called God's partner; in the second, anyone who recites Genesis 2:1–3 (about God resting on the seventh day) on Friday night thereby participates in God's ongoing act of creation.

2. B. *Sanhedrin* 73a (quoted above). Nahmanides, *Kitvei Ha-Ramban,* ed. Bernard Chavel (Jerusalem: Mosad Ha-Rav Kook, 1963 [Hebrew]), vol. 2, p. 43; this passage comes from Nahmanides' *Torat Ha-Adam (The Instruction of Man), Sh'ar Sakkanah (Section on Danger)* on B. *Bava Kamma,* chapter 8, and is cited by Joseph Karo in his commentary to the *Tur,* the *Bet Yosef, Yoreh De'ah* 336. Nahmanides uses similar reasoning in his comments on B. *Sanhedrin* 84b.

3. Elliot N. Dorff, *Matters of Life and Death: A Jewish Approach to Modern Medical Ethics* (Philadelphia: Jewish Publication Society, 1998),

chapter 12; Elliot N. Dorff and Aaron L. Mackler, "Responsibilities for the Provision of Health Care," in *Life and Death Responsibilities in Jewish Biomedical Ethics,* ed. Aaron L. Mackler (New York: Jewish Theological Seminary of America, 2000), pp. 479–505.

4. For more on ethical wills, see Israel Abrahams, *Hebrew Ethical Wills* (Philadelphia: Jewish Publication Society, 1926), 2 vols.; Jack Riemer and Nathaniel Stampfer, *Ethical Wills: A Modern Treasury* (New York: Schocken, 1983); and Jack Riemer and Nathaniel Stampfer, *So That Your Values Live On: Ethical Wills and How to Prepare Them* (Woodstock, Vt.: Jewish Lights Publishing, 1991).

5. An especially helpful book for both mourners and those who visit them is Ron Wolfson, *A Time to Mourn, a Time to Comfort: A Guide to Jewish Bereavement* (New York: Federation of Jewish Men's Clubs and Los Angeles: University of Judaism, 1993; 2nd edition: Woodstock, Vt.: Jewish Lights Publishing, 2005), for it not only explains Jewish mourning laws, rituals, and customs, but it also gives people helpful suggestions as to how to make the experience of death and mourning for a loved one meaningful for all concerned, including some vignettes of people engaged in the mourning practices or visiting mourners. Standard works on this topic from a Conservative perspective are Isaac Klein, *A Guide to Jewish Religious Practice* (New York: Jewish Theological Seminary of America, 1979), chapters 19 and 20; and Isaac Klein, *A Time to Be Born, A Time to Die* (New York: United Synagogue of America, 1976). Two Orthodox works on issues of death and mourning are Maurice Lamm, *The Jewish Way in Death and Mourning* (New York: Jonathan David, 1969); and Abner Weiss, *Death and Bereavement: A Halakhic Guide* (Hoboken, N.J.: Ktav and New York: The Union of Orthodox Jewish Congregations, 1991). A Reconstructionist manual on these matters by Richard Hirsch, "A Reconstructionist Guide to Mourning," is included in their new prayer book, *Tefilot Leveyat Ha'evel: Prayers for a House of Mourning,* ed. David Teutsch (New York: Reconstructionist Foundation, 2003). For a Reform approach to these matters, see Mark Washofsky, *Jewish Living: A Guide to Contemporary Reform Practice* (New York: UAHC Press, 2000), pp. 184–204.

6. *Shulchan Arukh, Yoreh De'ah* 265:12 gloss.

7. *Shulchan Arukh, Yoreh De'ah* 391:2 gloss.

Chapter 8: Duties of Spouses to Each Other

1. During biblical times, the consent of the woman to the marriage was sought, but only in a perfunctory way. Thus Laban and Betuel first tell Abraham's servant, "Here is Rebekah before you; take her and go, and let her be a wife to your master's son" (Genesis 24:51), and only afterward do they seek Rebekah's consent (Genesis 24:57–58). The Talmud makes it clear that, in accord with Deuteronomy 24:1, the man must "take" the woman (and therefore presumably consent to the marriage) but that the marriage is valid only if the woman consents as well: B. *Kiddushin* 2a. The strength of this consent, though, must be understood in the context

of the fact that until recently in Jewish history, it was the woman's father who made the arrangement with the husband, and so her consent was really acquiescence.

2. A man must initiate a divorce: B. *Kiddushin* 5b; M.T. *Laws of Divorce* 1:1, 3. To deliver the writ of divorce and thereby effect their divorce, a man may just throw the writ within four cubits of the woman: M. *Gittin* 8:1; M.T. *Laws of Divorce* 5:1 (and the rest of chapter 5, which deals with the details of applying this principle); see also 1:3.

3. In accord with the decree of Rabbenu Gershom, a divorce is valid only if the woman agrees to it: S.A. *Even Hae'zer* 66:3 gloss, 119:6 gloss. Maimonides (twelfth century) still accepts the validity of a divorce against her will: M.T. *Laws of Divorce* 1:2. For a good summary and discussion of these matters in Jewish law, see Simon Greenberg, "And He Writes Her a Bill of Divorce," in *Conservative Judaism* 24 (1970):75–141; Rachel Biale, *Women and Jewish Law: An Exploration of Women's Issues in Halakhic Sources* (New York: Schocken, 1984), pp. 70–101, esp. pp. 79–84; and Judith Hauptman, *Rereading the Rabbis: A Woman's Voice* (Boulder, Colo.: Westview, 1998), pp. 102–129.

4. B. *Gittin* 90a–90b. The law, especially after the decree of Rabbenu Gershom that the woman must agree to a divorce, follows the House of Hillel and Rabbi Akiva, such that a couple may divorce simply because of what we would call "irreconcilable differences." Nevertheless, because the Talmud says that "the Temple altar cries when a man divorces his first wife," a man is supposed to hesitate to do so. See M.T. *Laws of Divorce* 10:21; S.A. *Even Ha'ezer* 119:3 gloss. If she regularly and intentionally violates Jewish law, however, the man is commanded to divorce her, and no other man should marry her: B. *Gittin* 90b; M.T. *Laws of Divorce* 10:22; S.A. *Even Ha'ezer* 119:4–5.

5. That there can be conditions to a betrothal *(t'nai b'kiddushin)*: M. *Kiddushin* 3:2–6; M.T. *Laws of Marriage*, ch. 6—except for things that are out of his control to effect (M. *Kiddushin* 3:5) and except for conditions that would free him from having sex with her: B. *Kiddushin* 19b; M.T. *Laws of Marriage* 6:9–10. For much more on valid and invalid conditions on a marriage, see Committee on Jewish Law and Standards, "T'nai B'kiddushin," *Proceedings of the Rabbinical Assembly* [1968], 229–41; reprinted in Elliot N. Dorff and Arthur Rosett, *A Living Tree: The Roots and Growth of Jewish Law* (Albany: State University of New York Press, 1988), pp. 529–538.

6. M. *Yevamot* 6:6 (61b). In that Mishnah, the School of Shammai says that one has to have two boys and the School of Hillel says that one must have a boy and a girl. The Talmud understands the School of Shammai's position to be based on the fact that Moses had two sons, Gershom and Eliezer (1 Chronicles 23:15); while the Mishnah already states that the School of Hillel's ruling is based on Genesis 1:27, according to which God created the human being, "male and female God created them." A Tosefta (T. *Yevamot* 8:3), included in the Talmud (B. *Yevamot* 62a), asserts that the School of Shammai actually requires two males and two females,

while the School of Hillel requires one of each gender. Yet another talmudic tradition *(ibid.)*, in the name of Rabbi Nathan, states that the School of Shammai requires a male and a female, while the School of Hillel requires either a male or a female. The Jerusalem Talmud (J. *Yevamot* 6:6 [7c]) records the position of Rabbi Bun (Abun), who calls attention to the context of the School of Hillel's ruling right after the School of Shammai's ruling requiring two boys. Rabbi Bun therefore reads the School of Hillel as agreeing that two boys would suffice to fulfill the obligation, but *"even a boy and a girl"* would, and thus the School of Hillel is offering a leniency over the School of Shammai's requirement of two boys, in line with the School of Hillel's general reputation for such leniencies. Rabbi Bun also notes that if that were not the case, such that the School of Hillel were saying that *only* a boy and a girl would fulfill the obligation, then this ruling should appear in the various lists of the stringencies of the School of Hillel in chapters 4 and 5 of M. *Eduyot,* but it does not. Despite Rabbi Bun's arguments, the codes rule that the obligation is fulfilled only when a man fathers both a boy and a girl: M.T. *Laws of Marriage* 15:4; S.A. *Even Ha'ezer* 1:5. Ironically, in our own day, when modern technology has suddenly provided us with some control over the gender of our children but when the Jewish community simultaneously suffers from a major population deficit, we would affirm that technologically assisted gender selection should *not* take place, that we welcome children into our midst regardless of their gender, that we see any two of them as fulfillment of the commandment to procreate, but that we encourage Jewish couples who can have more than two children to do so.

7. *Minyan* necessary for seven blessings: B. *Ketubbot* 7a; M.T. *Laws of Marriage* 10:5; S.A. *Even Ha'ezer* 34:4.
8. California Civil Code, sect. 5100.
9. The husband's duties mentioned in this paragraph that are not included in the sources quoted here can be found in M. *Ketubbot* 4:7, 10–12; 5:2, 9; 7:3, 5, 9, 10.
10. Man may not force himself on his wife: B. *Eruvin* 100b; *Leviticus Rabbah* 9:6; *Numbers Rabbah* 13:2; M.T. *Laws of Ethics (De'ot)* 5:4; M.T. *Laws of Marriage* 14:15; M.T. *Laws of Forbidden Intercourse* 21:11; S.A. *Orah Hayyim* 240:10; S.A. *Even Ha'ezer* 25:2.
11. B. *Shabbat* 127a.
12. Elliot N. Dorff, *Love Your Neighbor and Yourself: A Jewish Approach to Modern Personal Ethics* (Philadelphia: Jewish Publication Society, 2003), chapter 5.

Chapter 9: Filial Duties

1. See Elliot N. Dorff, *Matters of Life and Death: A Jewish Approach to Modern Medical Ethics* (Philadelphia: Jewish Publication Society, 1998). Other American Conservative rabbis who have written books in this field include, in alphabetical order, David Feldman (*Birth Control in Jewish Law* [New York: New York University Press, 1968; republished by New York: Schocken as *Marital Relations, Abortion, and Birth Control in*

Jewish Law]; *Health and Medicine in the Jewish Tradition* [New York: Crossroad, 1986]) and Aaron Mackler (*Introduction to Jewish and Catholic Bioethics: A Comparative Analysis* [Washington, D.C.: Georgetown University Press, 2003]). Aaron Mackler has also edited the decisions approved by the Conservative Movement's Committee on Jewish Law and Standards up to the year 2000 on issues of bioethics in his book, *Life and Death Responsibilities in Jewish Biomedical Ethics* (New York: Jewish Theological Seminary of America, 2000), including responsa by these and other rabbis. One may also access these rabbinic rulings on the web at www.rabbinicalassembly.org under "Contemporary Halakhah." In addition, David Golinkin and some other members of the Israeli Masorti *Va'ad Ha-Halakhah* (Conservative/Masorti Law Committee) have written responsa on bioethical issues, and they may be found in the collections of the Committee's responsa, published in printed form in Hebrew, with summaries in English, and one can find them on the web as well (but in Hebrew only) at www.schechter.edu.

The books and articles by J. David Bleich (including *Bioethical Dilemmas: A Jewish Perspective* [Hoboken, N.J.: Ktav, 1998] and his volumes titled *Contemporary Halakhic Problems* [Hoboken, N.J.: Ktav, various dates]), Fred Rosner (including *Modern Medicine and Jewish Ethics*, 2nd ed. [Hoboken, N.J.: Ktav, 1991]), and Nisson Shulman (*Jewish Answers to Medical Ethics Questions* [Northvale, N.J.: Jason Aronson, 1998]) are generally good resources for Orthodox positions available in English. Immanuel Jakobovits's *Jewish Medical Ethics* (New York: Bloch, 1959, 1975), which began the field of Jewish medical ethics, is still a good, although somewhat dated, Orthodox perspective as well. Those who read Hebrew might also consult the responsa of Moshe Feinstein and Moshe Tendler and of some of the Israeli Orthodox writers on bioethics, including Abraham Abraham, Simon Glick, Abraham Steinberg, and Eliezer Waldenberg. Some of their writings are now also available in English, as is the Israeli journal of bioethics, *Assia*. Undoubtedly the most comprehensive recent Orthodox treatment of these issues is Abraham Steinberg's *Encyclopedia of Jewish Medical Ethics*, 3 vols., trans. Fred Rosner (New York: Feldheim, 2003).

The many books of Reform responsa by Solomon Freehof (published by the Central Conference of American Rabbis (CCAR) Press contain some responsa on bioethics, but they are by now somewhat dated. More recent Reform responsa on bioethics can be found in the collections *American Reform Responsa* (New York: CCAR, 1985), *New American Reform Responsa* (New York: CCAR, 1987), and *Questions and Reform Jewish Answers: New American Reform Responsa* (New York: CCAR, 1992), all edited by Walter Jacob, and more Reform responsa can be found in the books coedited by Walter Jacob and Moshe Zemer, including *Death and Euthanasia in Jewish Law: Essays and Responsa* (Pittsburgh: Freehof Institute of Progressive Halakhah, 1994).

2. John Locke, *Second Treatise Concerning Civil Government* (1690), chapter 2.

Chapter 10: Parental Duties

1. B. *Kiddushin* 29b.
2. M. *Ketubbot* 5:5.
3. See, for example, Immanuel Etkes, "Marriage and Torah Study among the *Lomdim* in Lithuania in the Nineteenth Century," in *The Jewish Family: Metaphor and Memory,* ed. David Kraemer (New York: Oxford University Press, 1989), pp. 164–169.
4. B. *Ketubbot* 49a–49b.
5. M. *Ketubbot* 4:11; B. *Ketubbot* 49b; M.T. *Laws of Marriage* 12:14–15; 13:6; 19:10, 13.
6. T. *Ketubbot* 12:1; B. *Ketubbot* 82b; J. *Ketubbot* 8:11.
7. B. *Ketubbot* 67b; M.T. *Laws of Marriage* 13:1: "He may not give her less than fifty *zuz* [for her clothing]."
8. Even though some of the laws of the Sabbath must be relaxed to enable the circumciser to do his job on that day, normally a *brit milah* (circumcision and the ceremony that accompanies it to mark it as the child's initiation into the covenant) takes place on the Sabbath: S.A. *Yoreh De'ah* 266:2. One exception to this rule occurs when the child is not healthy enough to be circumcised at that time (e.g., in some cases of jaundice), in which case it is postponed until he is medically ready. Another exception occurs when the child was delivered by cesarean section, such that it is not clear when the child would have been born naturally and therefore when the eighth day after that would be. That uncertainty leads Jewish law to balance these two commandments—Shabbat and circumcision specifically on the eighth day—in the reverse way, so that we do not violate Shabbat to perform the infant's circumcision on the eighth day after the birth but rather postpone his circumcision until the next day.
9. Leviticus 19:14. In addition to its literal reference to the physically blind, the Rabbis interpret it to demand that we not mislead those who lack information or who are intellectually or morally blind by tempting them to do what is improper or a transgression of the law. Thus, one violates this law if one leads another person to violate Jewish law in ritual matters (B. *Pesachim* 22b), personal interactions (B. *Mo'ed Katan* 17a), or commercial matters (B. *Bava Metzia* 75b). It also forbids knowingly giving bad advice (*Sifra, Kedoshim* on Leviticus 19:14). The Talmud specifically forbids a father to hit his grown son, lest the father violate this law: see B. *Kiddushin* 32a.
10. Roger Simon and Angie Cannon, "An Amazing Journey: The Mirror of the Census Reveals the Character of a Nation," *U.S. News and World Report,* August 6, 2001, p. 11–18; the statistics on education are on p. 17.
11. Barry A. Kosmin, Sidney Goldstein, Joseph Waksberg, Nava Lerer, Ariella Keysar, Jeffrey Scheckner, *Highlights of the CJF 1990 National Jewish Population Survey* (New York: Council of Jewish Federations, 1991), pp. 10–11, with comparative figures for the general population listed there from the U.S. Census Report P20 No. 428, Table 1, *Years of School Completed by Persons 15 Years Old and Over by Age, Sex, Race, and Hispanic Origin,* March 1987. The *1990 CJF Survey* breaks this

down by Jewish affiliation; I have cited the figures of those born Jewish and affirming Judaism as their religion.

12. *Responsa Rashba Attributed to Ramban* (Warsaw: 1883), p. 272, cited in Basil Herring, *Jewish Ethics and Halakhah for Our Time* (New York: Ktav, 1984), p. 209. Rashba uses B. *Sotah* 2b, "Forty days prior to the formation of the fetus, a heavenly voice says, 'So-and-so will marry So-and-so,'" to justify his claim that the parents do not have the right to interfere in the natural attraction that God has implanted in this particular man and woman for each other. Rabbi Joseph Colon ("Maharik," 1420–1480) takes the same position on the grounds that the Talmud (B. *Kiddushin* 41a) urges a man to marry a woman to whom he is attracted; see *Responsa Maharik* (Warsaw: 1884), #164:3, pp. 177–178, cited in Herring, *Jewish Ethics,* p. 209.

13. For example, Rabbi Naftali Zvi Judah Berlin ("Netziv," 1817–1893) sees a marriage contrary to parents' wishes as a disgrace to the parents, thus falling under Deuteronomy 27:16, "Cursed be he that dishonors his father and mother"; *Responsa Meshiv Davar 50.* Similarly, Rabbi Abraham Isaiah Karelitz ("Hazon Ish," d. 1953) maintains that the man may marry his beloved only if his parents are not totally opposed; *Novellae of Hazon Ish* to B. *Kiddushin* 30a, p. 287.

14. S.A. *Yoreh De'ah* 240:25 gloss. The age-old practice of arranged marriages among Jews thus assumed that the bride and groom agreed to their parents' choice.

15. B. *Yevamot* 62b: "He who marries off his sons and daughters close to their coming of age [*samukh le-firkan*] is the one of whom it is said, 'And you shall know that your tent is at peace.'" Based on this, a fourteenth-century code of Jewish law, the *Tur*, says, "He who marries early, at age thirteen, is fulfilling the commandment in an exemplary manner" (*Tur, Even Ha'ezer* 1:9). Prior to that, however, one should not marry, according to the *Tur*, because that would be like promiscuity (*zenut*) and wasting of the seed (*hashatat zera*) because the woman could not become pregnant—or so he assumes. Sometimes there were economic reasons for early marriages as well, as the twelfth-century Tosafists make clear: "[The Talmud declares,] 'A man is forbidden to marry off his daughter when she is a minor.' Nevertheless, it is our custom to betroth our daughters even if they are minors because day after day the [oppression of] exile [*galut*] increases, and if a man has the possibility of giving his daughter a dowry now [he betroths her], lest he not have it later on and she will remain an *agunah* forever" (Tosafot to B. *Kiddushin* 41a). On this, see Rachel Biale, *Women and Jewish Law: An Exploration of Women's Issues in Halakhic Sources* (New York: Schocken, 1984), pp. 65–69. Arthur Green reports that the Hasidic master Rabbi Nahman of Bratslav (1772–1811) was married by age fourteen and had two or three children by the time he was eighteen; see Arthur Green, *Tormented Master: A Life of Rabbi Nahman of Bratslav* (University: University of Alabama Press, 1979), pp. 34, 43.

16. All of the quotations in this paragraph are from Warren St. John, "Young, Single and Dating at Hyperspeed," *The New York Times,* April 21, 2002, section 9, pp. 1–2.

17. Nancy Gibbs, "Making Time for a Baby" (although the title on the cover is "Babies vs. Career"), *Time,* April 15, 2002, pp. 48–58. That article is the source of the statistics mentioned in the preceding paragraph, with the sources noted there. Unfortunately, however, it does not discuss male-factor infertility.

18. For somewhat earlier, but more comprehensive, statistics and much more on how the Jewish tradition applies to issues of infertility, see Elliot N. Dorff, *Matters of Life and Death: A Jewish Approach to Modern Medical Ethics* (Philadelphia: Jewish Publication Society, 1998), chapters 3, 4, and 6.

19. Bruce A. Phillips, *Re-Examining Intermarriage: Trends, Textures, Strategies* (Brookline, Mass.: The Susan and David Wilstein Institute of Jewish Policy Studies at Hebrew College and New York: The American Jewish Committee, 1997), p. 77.

20. Gerald Bubis, *The Costs of Jewish Living: Revisiting Jewish Involvements and Barriers* (New York: American Jewish Committee, 2002), p. 17.

21. Grandparents have a duty to educate their grandchildren: B. *Kiddushin* 30a.

Forward: Envisioning an Ideal World, Shaped by *Tikkun Olam*

1. For example, M. *Ethics of the Fathers (Avot)* 6:4 and *Chasedei Ashkenaz*, the German pietists of the fourteenth century.

2. See Elliot N. Dorff, *Matters of Life and Death: A Jewish Approach to Modern Medical Ethics* (Philadelphia: Jewish Publication Society, 1998), pp. 255–264.

3. Some will note that two phrases in this verse are translated differently elsewhere. The Jewish Publication Society translation (*Tanakh: A New Translation of the Hebrew Scriptures According to the Traditional Hebrew Text* [Philadelphia: Jewish Publication Society, 1985], p. 185) includes two notes on these verses. One, on the phrase "Do not deal basely with your countrymen," says: "Others 'go about as a talebearer among'; meaning of Hebrew uncertain." The other, on "Do not profit by the blood of your fellow," reads: "literally, 'stand upon'; meaning of Hebrew phrase uncertain." As described in chapter 7, the Rabbis interpreted the latter phrase to assert a duty to come to the aid of those in need, including those who are sick, drowning, victims of a crime, etc. The Rabbis interpreted the former verse to ban gossip, as described in chapter 4 above. Yet, as the JPS translation indicates, the original meaning of these verses probably had to do with fair judicial procedures.

4. Note that the "gate" of ancient cities was not only the entryway, but also a long corridor where all who entered had to pass and where judges and other government officials, such as tax collectors and notaries, performed their functions.

5. B. *Berakhot* 62b; B. *Yoma* 85b; B. *Sanhedrin* 72a.

6. See Elliot N. Dorff, *To Do the Right and the Good: A Jewish Approach to Modern Social Ethics* (Philadelphia: Jewish Publication Society, 2002), pp. 161–183.

Glossary

Sometimes two pronunciations of words are common. This glossary reflects the way that many Jews actually use these words, not just the technically correct version. When two pronunciations are listed, the first is the way the word is sounded in proper Hebrew, and the second is the way it is sometimes heard in common speech, often under the influence of Yiddish, the folk language of the Jews of northern and eastern Europe. "Kh" is used to represent a guttural sound, similar to the German "ch" (as in "sprach").

Alenu (ah-LAY-nu): A prayer that first appears in the fourteenth century as part of the High Holy Day liturgy but has been used since then to end every worship service throughout the Jewish year.

Amidah (ah-mee-DAH or, commonly, ah-MEE-dah): One of the three commonly used titles for the second of the three central units in the worship service, the first being the *Shema* and Its Blessings and the third being the reading of the Torah. It is composed of a series of blessings, many of which are petitionary (except for the Sabbath and holidays, when the petitions are removed out of deference to the holiness of the day). Also called *ha-tefillah* (*"the* prayer") and *shemoneh esrei* ("eighteen"). *Amidah* means "standing," which refers to the fact that the prayer is said standing up.

Amos: One of the biblical prophets; the book in the Bible containing his speeches. Amos lived in the ninth century B.C.E. in northern Israel.

Arakhin (ah-ra-KHEEN): A book of the **Mishnah, Tosefta,** and **Talmud** that deals primarily with vows of valuation (Leviticus 27:1–8).

avodah zarah (ah-voh-DAH zah-RAH or, commonly, ah-VOH-dah ZAH-rah): Worship of foreign gods, idolatry. Also the name of a tractate of the **Mishnah, Tosefta,** and **Talmud** dealing with the laws governing Jews' interactions with idolatry and idolaters.

Avot (ah-VOTE): Literally, "Fathers." A book of the **Mishnah,** generally printed in editions of the Mishnah and **Talmud** at or toward the end of the fourth order of the Mishnah, *Nezikin.* Undoubtedly the most well-known tractate of the Mishnah, it has also been printed many times as a separate volume with translations and commentaries in both Hebrew and

English, and many prayer books reprint it in full following the afternoon service of the Sabbath because by tradition it is studied until the sun has set and the evening service can be recited. It consists of moral aphorisms about what is important in life and how to live it. See also **Pirkei Avot**.

Avot d'Rabbi Natan (ah-VOTE D'RAB-bi Nah-TAHN): Literally, "the [Ethics of the] Fathers of [i.e., according to, or compiled by] Rabbi Nathan. One of the extracanonical, so-called minor tractates of the Talmud, generally printed at the end of the fourth division of the Talmud *(Nezikin)*. It is a commentary on, and an expansion of, an early version of *Pirkei Avot* ("Ethics of the Fathers"), a tractate of the Mishnah, before that tractate reached the final, edited form in which we have it. It is possible that it is called by the name of Rabbi Nathan because it was organized as a commentary on a version of *Pirkei Avot* that the Babylonian Rabbi Nathan had prepared. Rabbi Nathan was an older contemporary of Rabbi Judah Ha-Nasi, editor of the Mishnah. *Avot d'Rabbi Natan* exists in two markedly different versions, one consisting of forty-one chapters (this is the one published in most printed editions of the Talmud), and the other consisting of forty-eight chapters, published on the basis of manuscripts by Solomon Schechter and designated by him as version B. Neither version includes references to rabbis after the period of the Mishnah, and so, while impossible to date with certainty, scholars think that *Avot D'Rabbi Natan* was written at more or less the same time as the Mishnah, i.e., c. 200 C.E.

Babylonian Talmud: See Talmud.

Bava Batra (BAH-vah BAHT-rah): A tractate of the **Mishnah, Tosefta,** and **Talmud** that deals with a number of topics of Jewish civil law, including the sale of real estate and legal forms.

Bava Kamma (BAH-vah CAHLM-ah): A tractate of the **Mishnah, Tosefta,** and **Talmud** that deals with a number of topics of Jewish criminal law, including, for example, personal injuries and theft.

Bava Metzia (BAH-vah Meh-TZI-ah): A tractate of the **Mishnah, Tosefta,** and **Talmud** that deals with a number of topics of Jewish civil law, including contracts, lost objects, rentals, and other property matters.

berakhah (b'-rah-KHAH); pl. *berakhot* (b'-rah-KHOHT): The Hebrew word for "benediction." *Berakhot* also refers to the very first tractate in the **Mishnah, Tosefta,** and **Talmud**. It deals primarily with Jewish liturgy for each day and for various occasions (e.g., the blessings over various foods).

bet k'nesset (BAIT k'NEH-set): "House of assembly." One of the Hebrew names for a synagogue.

bet midrash (BAIT meed-RASH): "House of study" or "house of interpretation." One of the Hebrew names for a synagogue.

bet tefillah (BAIT teh-fee-LAH): "House of prayer." One of the Hebrew names of a synagogue.

biqqur holim (bee-KOOR kho-LEEM): Visiting the sick, and the commandment to do so.

brit milah (BREET mee-LAH): Literally, "the covenant of circumcision." The circumcision of a Jewish boy on his eighth day of life (or thereafter if health reasons require a postponement), together with prescribed blessings and the naming of the child, to mark his entry into the covenant of Abraham and of Israel. See Genesis 17:10–14; Leviticus 12:3. Commonly referred to as a *bris*, meaning "covenant."

Canaan: The name used in biblical times for what we now call the Land of Israel.

Chasidic (khah-SIH-dihk): Of the doctrine generally traced to an eighteenth-century Polish Jewish mystic and spiritual leader known as the Ba'al Shem Tov (called also the *BeSHT,* an acronym composed of the initials of his name). Followers are called *Chasidim* (khah-see-DEEM or khah-SIH-dim); sing., *Chasid* (khah-SEED or, commonly, KHAH-sihd) from the Hebrew word *chesed* (KHEH-sed), meaning both loving-kindness and piety.

Chesed (KHEH-sed): Literally, "loyalty" (to God and to a fellow human being), with secondary meanings of piety and loving-kindness.

Chumash (khoo-MAHSH or, commonly, KHUH-m'sh): The first part of the Bible, which is read in the synagogue on Mondays, Thursdays, the Sabbath, and holidays. Also called the "Five Books of Moses," or "the Torah," it contains the books *B'reishit* (In the Beginning), *Shemot* (Names), *Vayikra* (And [God] Called), *Bamidbar* (In the Desert), and *Devarim* (Words or Commandments). These names are the first key words mentioned in each book, but they allude to the content of each one. The English names for the five books of the Torah—Genesis, Exodus, Leviticus, Numbers, and Deuteronomy—are based on the titles in the Latin Bible, which were drawn from the Greek translations of the Hebrew names.

covenant: *Brit,* in Hebrew. Refers to the marriage, as it were, between God and the People Israel, beginning with Abraham and lasting to our own day. The terms of the covenant are spelled out in Jewish law, beginning with the revelation at Mount Sinai, described in chapters 19–24 of the biblical Book of Exodus, and continuing in Jewish legal interpretations and decisions throughout the ages, including contemporary rabbinic rulings. The essence of the covenant is the ongoing relationship between God and the Jewish People, a relationship shaped by Jewish law, prayer, religious thought, questioning God, and other forms of spirituality, including acts of *tikkun olam.*

Derekh Eretz Zuta (DEH-rekh Eh-retz ZOO-tah): Literally, the small version of the post-talmudic, so-called minor tractate *Derekh Eretz,* dealing with morals and manners.

Ethics of the Fathers: See *Avot* and *Pirkei Avot.*

Exodus Rabbah: See *Midrash Rabbah.*

Ezekiel: One of the biblical prophets, who prophesied to the Jews whom the Babylonians had taken in chains to Babylonia in 586 B.C.E. about their promised return to Israel. His speeches are contained in a biblical book by his name.

Genesis Rabbah: See *Midrash Rabbah.*

gene'vat da'at (g'NAVE-aht DAH-aht): Literally, "stealing a person's mind," that is, deceiving a person.

ge'ulah (g'-oo-LAH): Redemption.

gittin (GEE-teen): Jewish writs of divorce. Also the name of a tractate in the **Mishnah, Tosefta,** and **Talmud** that deals with Jewish laws of divorce.

Hagigah (khah-GEE-gah): The last tractate of the order *Mo'ed* (literally "seasons" or "festivals") in the **Mishnah, Tosefta,** and **Talmud,** it deals with the laws of sacrifices that were offered during the festivals, as well as with subjects related to festival observance such as the duty of pilgrimage. *Hagigah* means "festival offering."

halakhah (hah-lah-KHAH or, commonly, hah-LAH-khah): The Hebrew word for "Jewish law." Used as an anglicized adjective, *halakhic* (hah-LAH-khic), meaning "legal." From the Hebrew word meaning "to walk" or "to go," so denoting the way in which a person should walk through life.

High Holy Days, or **High Holidays:** Rosh Hashanah (the New Year) and Yom Kippur (the Day of Atonement), ten days later. The period between these two days is known as the Ten Days of Repentance. Set by the Jewish lunar calendar, these sacred days usually fall in September but sometimes as late as early October.

Hosea: One of the biblical prophets who lived in the eighth century B.C.E. in the Northern Kingdom of Israel. "Hosea" also refers to a book in the Bible that contains his speeches. Some scholars think that the book consists of the work of two different men named Hosea, one living in the eighth century B.C.E. (chapters 1–3) and the other living in the seventh century B.C.E. (chapters 4–14).

Hullin (khu-LEEN): A tractate of the **Mishnah, Tosefta,** and **Talmud** dealing with the rules of slaughtering animals for eating (in contrast to sacrifices).

Isaiah: A biblical prophet whose writings are contained in the book by his name. Scholars think that the book actually contains the writings of two different people named Isaiah, one living in the second half of the eighth century B.C.E. and prophesying about events at that time in chapters 1–39 of the book; and the other ("Second Isaiah," or "Isaiah of the Diaspora") living some 150 years later, in the middle of the sixth century B.C.E. and prophesying in chapters 40–66 of the book about the promise that the Jews who had been exiled to Babylonia would return to Israel.

Jeremiah: One of the biblical prophets who prophesied in Judah between 627 and 585 B.C.E. about the imminent destruction of the First Temple due to the Jews' sins. His speeches are contained in a biblical book by his name. He is also assumed to be the author of the biblical Book of Lamentations (*Eikhah* [AY-khah]).

Jerusalem Talmud: See **Talmud.**

Job: A non-Jew who is the protagonist of the biblical Book of Job, which scholars date c. 400 B.C.E. and which raises in stark form the problem of evil, that is, why do the righteous sometimes suffer if there is a just and benign God? The book consists of a folk tale (chapters 1 and 2 and the last ten verses of chapter 42), which has a retributive theology (if you sin, you suffer, but if you are righteous, you will ultimately be rewarded), while the middle section openly challenges that thinking and wrestles mightily with a variety of approaches to understanding unjustified suffering.

Kabbalah (kah-bah-LAH or, commonly, kah-BAH-lah): A general term for Jewish mysticism, but used properly for a specific mystical doctrine that was recorded in the *Zohar* in the thirteenth century, and then was further elaborated, especially in the Land of Israel (in Safed), in the sixteenth century. From a Hebrew word meaning "to receive," or "to welcome," and secondarily, "tradition," implying the receiving of tradition.

ketubbot (keh-too-BOAT): Wedding contracts. *Ketubbot* is also the name of the tractate of the **Mishnah, Tosefta,** and **Talmud** that deals with Jewish marriage law.

kibbud av v'em (kee-BOOD AHV v'AYM): Honoring one's father and mother, and the commandment to do so. See Exodus 20:12.

kiddushin (kee-du-SHEEN): Betrothal (literally, "sanctification," or setting aside one person). Also a tractate of the **Mishnah, Tosefta,** and **Talmud** developing Jewish laws of betrothal.

lashon ha-ra (lah-SHOWN hah-RAH): Literally, "speaking of bad things," i.e., slurs.

Leviticus Rabbah: See *Midrash Rabbah.*

lifnim m'shurat ha-din (leef-NEEM mee'shu-RAT hah-DEEN): Moral duties beyond the letter of the law.

Malachi (ma-LA-khee): One of the biblical prophets; also the biblical book containing his speeches, appearing as the last of the prophetic section of the Bible. Scholars believe that he lived around 450 B.C.E.

Megillah (meh-gee-LAH, or commonly m'GILL-ah): The tractate of the **Mishnah, Tosefta,** and **Talmud** that deals with Purim and the reading of the Book of Esther, which also includes material on the reading of the Torah throughout the year.

Menahot (meh-nah-KHOHT): The second tractate in the order *Kedoshim* (lit. "holy things," or "Temple practices"), in the **Mishnah, Tosefta,** and **Talmud.** The meal offering is called *minchah* (meen-KHAH or, commonly, MIN-khah); pl. *menachot* (meh-nah-KHOHT). The text deals with requirements and details of preparation of meal offerings.

Messiah: Literally, "the anointed one." Originally this term is used to designate those authorized to be a king, prophet, or High Priest. In rabbinic times, it designates the one anointed to lead the Israelites in battle against their oppressors, thus ushering in an ideal time.

Micah: One of the biblical prophets; also the book of the Bible containing his speeches. Micah lived in the latter part of the eighth century B.C.E. and was apparently a student of Isaiah.

midrash (meed-RAHSH or, commonly, MID-rahsh); pl. *midrashim* (mid-rah-SHEEM): From the Hebrew word *darash,* "to seek, search, or demand [meaning from the biblical text]"; also, therefore, a literary genre focused upon the explication of the Bible. By extension, midrash refers to a body of rabbinic literature that offers classical interpretations of the Bible.

Midrash Rabbah (meed-RAHSH rab-BAH or, commonly, MID-rahsh RAB-bah): A work made up of ten different midrashic compilations, one of each on the five books of the Torah (*Genesis Rabbah, Exodus Rabbah, Leviticus Rabbah, Numbers Rabbah, Deuteronomy Rabbah*) and the "Five Scrolls" read in the synagogue during the year (namely, Song of Songs, Ruth, Lamentations, Ecclesiastes, and Esther)—e.g. *Song of Songs Rabbah, Ruth*

Rabbah. These ten independent works were compiled at very different times, most probably between the fifth and thirteenth centuries C.E., and in different locales, and they exhibit a variety of midrashic styles. Unlike the **Mishnah,** they are not a code organized by topic. Instead, their material follows the organization of the different biblical books. *Midrash Rabbah* is the most well known, but not the only anthology of classic midrashic texts.

Midrash Tanhuma (meed-RAHSH Tahn-KHU-mah): A **midrash** on the whole of the Torah, first published in Constantinople in 1522 and frequently republished, containing many sayings and proems attributed to Rabbi Tanhuma, a Palestinian rabbi of the second half of the fourth century C.E. It is divided according to the Palestinian triennial cycle of reading the Torah and contains interpretations of the first verse (and sometimes the first two or three verses) of each Torah reading for a given Sabbath according to that cycle. It exists in two primary forms, based on different manuscripts: the Constantinople version, and the one published by S. Buber in 1885 based on the Oxford manuscript, which differs from the first version greatly in the first half of the work.

minyan (min-YAN). A quorum of ten adult Jews, that is, ten Jews beyond their thirteenth birthday. Orthodox and a few Conservative synagogues insist that they be men, but the vast majority of Conservative synagogues and all Reform and Reconstructionist synagogues include women as well, and women may be counted after their bat mitzvah, which may occur as early as age twelve.

Mi-Sheberakh (MEE-sheh-bay-RAHKH or, commonly, MEE-sheh-BAY-rahkh): Literally, "May He who blessed." A prayer recited in the synagogue, usually between the reading of two of the portions of the Torah assigned for that day, asking God to heal the sick. While it comes in various versions, a common one is this: "May He who blessed our ancestors, Abraham, Isaac, and Jacob, Sarah, Rebecca, Rachel, and Leah, bless and heal_____ [at which point the names of the ill are inserted]. May the Holy One in mercy strengthen him/her/them; may He send him/her/them full recovery speedily to all his/her/their limbs and sinews, a recovery of body and soul, along with all the others (of the Jewish People) who suffer illness. And let us say: Amen."

Mishnah (meesh-NAH or, commonly, MISH-nah): After the compilations of laws in several sections of the Torah (e.g., Exodus 20–24; Leviticus 18–27; Deuteronomy 20–25), the Mishnah is the first written summary of "the Oral Law," that is, the laws and customs communicated through example and speech from generation to generation, from approximately the fifth century B.C.E. to the end of the second century C.E. The Mishnah was compiled by Rabbi Judah, the president of the **Sanhedrin,** in the Land of Israel about the year 200 C.E., based on the earlier work of Rabbi Akiva and his students throughout the second century. The Mishnah is divided into six parts, or orders (*Sedarim* [say-dah-REEM]; sing. *Seder* [SAY-dahr]), organized by topic. It treats a whole range of legal subjects, including civil law (e.g., contracts, landlord-tenant relationships, property ownership, lost objects), criminal law (e.g., personal injuries, the forms of theft and murder), penalties for infringement of the law, court procedures, family law (e.g., marriage, divorce), agricultural law dealing with the land of Israel, laws governing the ancient **Temple**'s sacrifices, and the first written description of the structure of Jewish prayer.

Mishneh Torah (meesh-NAY toh-RAH or, commonly, MISH-nah TOH-rah): The title of Maimonides' Code of Jewish Law, completed in 1177 C.E.

mishpat (meesh-PAT); pl. *mishpatim* (meesh-pah-TEEM): Literally, a legal precedent, and, by extension, rules, justice.

mitzvah (meetz-VAH or, commonly, MITZ-vah); pl. *mitzvot* (meetz-VOTE): A Hebrew word used commonly to mean "good deed," but in the more technical sense, denoting any commandment from God, and therefore, by extension, what God wants us to do. Reciting the *Shema* morning and evening, for instance, is a *mitzvah*, and so is helping the poor.

motzi shem ra (moh-TZEE SHAME RAH): Literally, exporting a bad name, i.e, slander.

nazir (nah-ZEER): Or, Nazarite. A person who vows to refrain from wine and other alcohol, shaving, and even attending the funeral of his close relatives for a period of time (Numbers 6:1–21).

Nedarim (neh-dah-REEM): A book of the **Mishnah, Tosefta,** and **Talmud** dealing with the laws of oaths.

nihum aveilim (nee-KHUM ah-vay-LEEM): Comforting mourners, and the commandment to do so.

nivvul peh (nee-VOOL PEH): Literally, "befouling one's mouth," referring to foul language.

Numbers Rabbah: See *Midrash Rabbah.*

ona'at d'varim (oh-nah-AHT d'vah-REEM): Literally, "oppression done by means of words," or oppressive speech.

Oral Torah: In Hebrew, *Torah she-B'al Peh* (TOH-rah shch-bih-ahl-PEH). The commentaries, interpretations, legal writings, and legends that students and teachers have woven around the Written Torah, or *Torah she-Bikhtav* (TOH-rah sheh-BIKH-tahv), that were thought to have been transmitted out loud rather than in writing.

Palestinian Talmud: See **Talmud.**

Peah (PAY-ah): The second tractate in the order *Zeraim* (literally, "seeds," or "agriculture") in the **Mishnah, Tosefta,** and Jerusalem (Palestinian) **Talmud.** *Peah* refers to the corners of the fields, which one must not harvest but must rather leave for the poor (Leviticus 19:9–10).

Pentateuch: The Greek word for "five-volumed book," referring to the Hebrew Bible because the five parts of the Torah were transcribed on separate scrolls. The Hebrew equivalent is *Hamishah Humshei Torah* (khah-mee-SHAH khoom-SHAY Toe-RAH), or, in abbreviated form, the **Chumash.**

Pesahim (peh-sah-KHEEM): The third tractate of the order *Mo'ed* (literally, "seasons," or "festivals") in the **Mishnah, Tosefta,** and **Talmud.** The word *pesah* (PEH-sahkh) refers literally to the paschal sacrifice, but it is applied more broadly to the Passover festival in general. The tractate deals with the paschal sacrifice, the laws of the festival, the issues of leavened and unleavened bread, and the order and liturgy of the *seder.*

Pesikta de'Rav Kahana (peh-SEEK-tah d'rahv kah-HAH-nah): A homiletic midrash compiled of sermons that was put together in the late fifth to early sixth century in the Land of Israel, offering biblical interpretations and homilies for the holidays and special Sabbaths.

pidyon ha-ben (peed-YONE hah-BEN): Redemption of the firstborn son from Temple service by giving five *shekalim* to a *kohen* (descendant of Aaron). See Numbers 3:44–51.

pidyon she'vuyim (peed-YONE sheh-voo-YEEM): Redemption of captives.

Pirkei Avot (pihr-KAY ah-VOTE): Literally, "Chapters of Our Fathers," but more commonly translated as "Ethics of Our Fathers." It is a tractate of the Mishnah, where it is just called *Avot* and is placed at the end of the fourth of the Mishnah's six parts (orders)—namely, *Nezikin*. Because it consists of discrete pieces of advice about how to live life, it became a popular tractate to study between the afternoon and evening services on Saturday afternoon, and so many prayer books include the entire tractate in both Hebrew and English after the Saturday afternoon service under the title *Pirkei Avot*. It also has been published many times as a separate volume with various medieval and modern commentaries.

Plato (PLAY-toe): One of the earliest and most important philosophers of ancient Greece, 427?–347 B.C.E., his writings appear in dialogue form, and often his teacher, Socrates (SOCK-rah-tees), 469–399 B.C.E., is the major protagonist.

Rabbi: Literally, "teacher," or "master of the tradition." The first people called by that title lived in the first century C.E., and the classical "rabbinic period" lasts from then until the close of the Talmud c. 500 C.E. When one speaks of "the Rabbis," one is referring to the rabbis of that period, the ones whose interpretations, opinions, and actions are described in the **Mishnah, Tosefta, Midrash,** and **Talmud.** The title continues from then to our own day, however, to describe those who are themselves committed to the Jewish tradition in their own lives and have learned the tradition well enough to teach it, having been duly authorized to do so.

refa'enu (reh-fah-AY-nu): Literally, "Heal us." The first word of a paragraph recited as part of the daily *Amidah* three times each week day, in which we ask God to heal us. In translation, it reads: "Heal us, O Lord, and we shall be healed. Help us and save us, for You are our glory. Grant perfect healing for all our afflictions. For You are the faithful and merciful God of healing. Praised are You, Lord, Healer of His People Israel." Before the sentence beginning "For You..." worshippers may ask especially for the healing of specific individuals.

rekhilut (reh-khee-LOOT): Gossip, tale bearing.

Sanhedrin (san-HEHD-rin): The tractate of the **Mishnah** and **Talmud** dealing mainly with legal procedures and the court system. The term is also used for any Jewish court, but especially *"the* Sanhedrin," which was the Supreme Court that existed in Israel from the first century B.C.E. to 361 C.E.

Second Isaiah: Also known as "Deutero-Isaiah." Modern scholarship notes a differentiation between chapters 1–39 and 40–55 of the Book of Isaiah, calling them First and Second Isaiah, respectively. There are historical, linguistic, and conceptual differences that separate the two. See **Isaiah.**

Shabbat (shah-BAHT): The Hebrew word for "Sabbath," from a word meaning "to desist [from work]" and thus "to rest." Also the name of the tractate of the **Mishnah, Tosefta,** and **Talmud** devoted primarily to the laws of the Sabbath.

Shekalim (sheh-kah-LEEM); sing. *shekel* (SHEH-kel): Coins; also, in the plural, the name of a tractate of the **Mishnah, Tosefta,** and Jerusalem **Talmud** that deals with the money Jews were to contribute each year for the building and upkeep of the Temple (Exodus 30:11–16). Also the name of a special Sabbath each year in which this section of the Torah is read in addition to the weekly portion as part of the weeks preparing for the Passover holiday, for in ancient times it was in late winter that Jews contributed the half-*shekel* for this purpose so that the Temple would be ready for Passover.

sheker (SHEH-ker): Lies, that is, deliberately telling someone something that one knows to be false.

Shema (sh'-MAH): The central prayer in the first of the three central units in the worship service, the second being the *Amidah* and the third being the reading of the Torah. The *Shema* comprises three citations from the Bible: Deuteronomy 6:4–9, Deuteronomy 11:13–21, and Numbers 15:37–41. The larger liturgical unit in which it is embedded (called the *Shema* and Its Blessings) contains also a formal call to prayer *(Bar'khu)* and a series of blessings on the theological themes that, together with the *Shema*, constitute a liturgical creed of faith. *Shema*, meaning "to hear," is the first word of the first line of the first biblical citation, "Hear O Israel, Adonai is our God, Adonai is One," which is the paradigmatic statement of Jewish faith, the Jews' absolute commitment to the presence of a single and unique God in time and space.

shemirat ha-guf (sheh-mee-RAAT hah-GOOF): Taking care of one's body. and the commandment to do so.

Shemoneh Esrei (sh'-MOH-neh ES-ray): A Hebrew word meaning "eighteen," and therefore a name given to the second of the two main units in the worship service that once had eighteen benedictions in it for the weekday service (it now has nineteen); known also as the *Amidah*.

shevu'ot (sheh-voo-OAT): Oaths; also a tractate of the **Mishnah, Tosefta,** and **Talmud** dealing primarily with oaths. Not to be confused with Shavu'ot, the Feast of Weeks.

Shir Ha-Shirim Rabbah (SHEER hah-shee-REEM RAB-bah): Or, *Song of Songs Rabbah*. A book of *midrash*, a part of *Midrash Rabbah*, containing rabbinic interpretations and expansions of the biblical book Song of Songs.

Shulhan Arukh (Shool-KHAN ah-ROOKH or, commonly, SHOOL-khan AH-rookh): The "Set Table," the title of the code of Jewish law by Joseph Karo, completed in 1563. Shortly thereafter Moses Isserles added glosses to indicate where the practice of northern and eastern European Jews (Ashkenazim) differed from those of Mediterranean Jews (Sephardim) that Karo had articulated in his code. The code is divided into four parts: *Orah Chayyim* (oh-RAHKH KHAH-yim); *Yoreh De'ah* (YOH-reh DAY-ah); *Even ha-Ezer* (EH-ven hah-AY-zehr); and *Choshen Mishpat* (KHOH-shen mish-PAT).

Sifra (seef-RAH): A midrash on the biblical Book of Leviticus, interpreting and expanding its laws in the order of the verses of Leviticus. Scholars think that it was created in the school of Rabbi Akiva in the second century, but since it is not mentioned in either of the two Talmuds, it was probably edited and written down not earlier than the end of the fourth century in Israel.

Sifre D'varim (Seef-RAY D'vah-REEM): Or, *Sifre Deuteronomy*. A book of *midrash* on the biblical Book of Deuteronomy, including both its legal and nonlegal sections, organized according to the order of Deuteronomy. Scholars think that it was created in the school of Rabbi Akiva in the second century, but since it is not mentioned in either of the two Talmuds, it was probably edited and written down not earlier than the end of the fourth century in Israel.

Sotah (SOH-tah): A book of the **Mishnah, Tosefta,** and **Talmud** that spells out the laws of the woman accused of being adulterous (Numbers 5:11–31).

Sukkah (soo-KAH or, commonly, SOOK-ah); pl. *sukkot* (soo-KOTE): The hut that the Torah commands Jews to construct during the harvest festival that follows the High Holy Days in the Fall (see Leviticus 23:42–43); the book of the **Mishnah, Tosefta,** and **Talmud** that deals with the laws of the Sukkot holiday.

Ta'anit (TAH-ah-NEET): A tractate of the **Mishnah, Tosefta,** and **Talmud** that deals with the laws governing fast days.

Talmud (tahl-MOOD or, commonly, TAHL-m'd): The name given to each of two great compendia of Jewish law and lore compiled from the first to the sixth centuries C.E., and ever since, the literary core of the rabbinic heritage. The *Talmud Yerushalmi* (y'-roo-SHAHL-mee), the "Jerusalem Talmud" or "the Palestinian Talmud," is the earlier one, a product of the Land of Israel generally dated about 400 C.E. The better-known *Talmud Bavli* (BAHV-lee), or "Babylonian Talmud," took shape in Babylonia (present-day Iraq), and is traditionally dated about 550 C.E. When people say "the Talmud" without specifying which one they mean, they are referring to the Babylonian version. The word *Talmud* comes from the Hebrew root meaning to learn and, in a different form, to teach.

TaNaKh: An acronym which is derived from the initial letters of the three divisions of the Hebrew Bible: Torah (the Five Books of Moses), *Nevi'im* (Prophets), and *Ketuvim* (Writings).

Temple, First and Second: In ancient times, a central building for the worship of God in Israel. The first Temple was built by Solomon, and its construction is described in the first Book of Kings. In 586 B.C.E., King Nebuchadnezzar and the Babylonians conquered Judah and destroyed the Temple, sending the Jews into exile in Babylonia. In 538 B.C.E., the Persians conquered the Babylonians, and a small remnant of the Jews returned to Palestine. Urged on by Zechariah and Haggai, they rebuilt the Temple and reinstated the sacrificial cult. The Temple was destroyed again by the Romans in 70 C.E. The building was razed, but the retaining wall of the Temple mount remains to this day as the "Western Wall."

Terumot (teh-roo-MOTE): A book of the **Mishnah, Tosefta,** and Jerusalem Talmud dealing primarily with gifts to the Temple. See **Temple.**

tikkun olam (tee-KOON oh-LAHM): Literally, "repairing the world." Today it is commonly used to characterize Jewish forms of social action.

Torah (TOH-rah): Literally, "instruction," "teaching," or "direction." In its narrowest meaning, Torah refers to the first five books of the Bible, also called the "Five Books of Moses," or the *Chumash* (khoo-MAHSH or, commonly, KHUH-m'sh), which is read in the synagogue on Monday, Thursday, the Sabbath, and holidays. In this sense, "the Torah" is sometimes used to refer to the parchment scroll on which these books are written for public reading in the synagogue. Later, during rabbinic times (approximately the first to the sixth centuries C.E.), the Five Books of Moses are referred to as the Written Torah (*Torah she-bikhtav*), in contrast to the Oral Torah (*Torah sh-b'al peh*), which consists of ongoing interpretations and expansions of the meaning of the Written Torah as well as the customs that evolved over time among the Jewish people and ultimately got written down, in large measure, in the Mishnah, Tosefta, and Talmud (see those entries). The term *Torah* is used also, by extension, to mean all Jewish sacred literature, including books written in the Middle Ages, the modern period, and even contemporary times, and including not only topics of Jewish law but also Jewish literature, thought, history, and ethics. Thus, in this extended meaning, one is "studying Torah" when one is studying these texts as well as classical Jewish literature (the Bible, Mishnah, Talmud, Midrash).

Tosafot (toe-sah-FOTE): Also, Tosafists. Several of the grandchildren of Rashi (1040–1105), the most famous and popular medieval commentator on the Torah and the Talmud. These twelfth and early thirteenth century rabbis, whose comments appear on each page of the standard printed edition of the Talmud, raise and try to answer questions about the Talmud or about Rashi's interpretation of it.

Tosefta (toe-SEF-tah): Literally, "an addition." The Tosefta is an additional compilation to that of the **Mishnah** of the Jewish oral tradition of laws and customs to the end of the second century C.E. It was compiled in the Land of Israel by Rabbis Hiyyah and Oshayah c. 200 C.E. Its authority is secondary to that of the Mishnah.

tractate: The term commonly used for a book of the **Mishnah, Tosefta,** or **Talmud,** so called because each tractate is a treatise on a specific area of Jewish law.

Tzedek (TZEH-dek), *tzedakah* (tzeh-dah-KAH or, commonly, tzeh-DAH-kah): Justice, with a secondary meaning of acts of supporting the poor.

yir'at am v'av (yeer-AHT AIM v'AHV): Respecting (or fearing) one's mother and father, and the commandment to do so. See Leviticus 19:3.

Zechariah: One of the twelve minor prophetic books of the Bible dated from the sixth century B.C.E., though there is disagreement as to dating. Zechariah was one of the three prophets to accompany the Exiles who returned from Babylon to Jerusalem in 538 B.C.E. He prophesied together with Haggai and Malachi, in the second year of the reign of King Darius of Persia.

Suggestions for Further Reading

To make this bibliography as helpful as possible, it is divided into the various aspects of *tikkun olam* that each chapter treats. That means that a given entry may be repeated if it is relevant to the topics of more than one chapter.

Chapters 1 and 2: General Books on Jewish Social Ethics

Agus, Jacob B. *The Vision and the Way: An Interpretation of Jewish Ethics.* New York: Frederick Ungar Publishing Company, 1966.

Berkovits, Eliezer. *Not in Heaven: The Nature and Function of Halakha.* New York: Ktav, 1983.

Borowitz, Eugene. *The Jewish Moral Virtues.* Philadelphia: Jewish Publication Society, 1999.

_____, ed. *Reform Jewish Ethics and the Halakhah: An Experiment in Decision Making.* West Orange, N.J.: Behrman House, Inc., 1988.

Cohen, A. *Everyman's Talmud.* New York: E. P. Dutton & Co., 1949, chs. 3 ("The Doctrine of Man") and 6 ("Social Life").

Dorff, Elliot N. *To Do the Right and the Good: A Jewish Approach to Modern Social Ethics.* Philadelphia: Jewish Publication Society, 2002.

Freedman, Shalom. *Small Acts of Kindness: Striving for Derech Eretz in Everyday Life.* Jerusalem and New York: Urim, 2004.

Freund, Richard A. *Understanding Jewish Ethics.* San Francisco: EMText, 1990.

Jacobs, Louis. *Jewish Personal and Social Ethics.* West Orange, N.J.: Behrman House, 1990.

Kaplan, Mordecai M. *The Future of the American Jew.* New York: Macmillan, 1948 (reprinted by New York: Reconstructionist Press, 1967), esp. ch. 15, "Basic Values in Jewish Religion."

Novak, David. *Jewish Social Ethics.* New York: Oxford University Press, 1992.

Shatz, David, Chaim I. Waxman, and Nathan J. Diament, eds. *Tikkun Olam: Social Responsibility in Jewish Thought and Law.* Northvale, N.J.: Jason Aronson, 1997.

Sherwin, Byron L. *In Partnership with God: Contemporary Jewish Law and Ethics.* Syracuse, N.Y.: Syracuse University Press, 1990.

_____. *Jewish Ethics for the Twenty-First Century: Living in the Image of God.* Syracuse, N.Y.: Syracuse University Press, 2000.

Siegel, Daniel. *1+1=3 and 37 Other Mitzvah Principles to Live By.* Pittsboro, NC: Town House Press, 2000.

_____ *Where Heaven and Earth Touch.* Pittsboro, NC: Town House Press, 1998.

Sidorsky, David, ed. *Essays on Human Rights: Contemporary Issues and Jewish Perspectives.* Philadelphia: Jewish Publication Society, 1979.

Vorspan, Albert, and David Saperstein. *Jewish Dimensions of Social Justice: Tough Moral Choices of Our Time.* New York: Union of American Hebrew Congregations (UAHC) Press, 1998.

Chapter 3: Religion and Ethics

Bleich, J. David. "Halakhah as an Absolute." *Judaism* 29:1 (Winter, 1980), pp. 30–37.

Borowitz, Eugene. *Exploring Jewish Ethics: Papers on Covenant Responsibility.* Detroit: Wayne State University Press, 1990, esp. chs. 15, 24, and 26.

Dorff, Elliot N. *Love Your Neighbor and Yourself: A Jewish Approach to Modern Personal Ethics.* Philadelphia: Jewish Publication Society, 2003, esp. ch. 1 and appendix.

_____ and Louis Newman, eds. *Contemporary Jewish Ethics and Morality: A Reader.* New York: Oxford University Press, 1995, esp. chs. 6–15.

Fox, Marvin, ed. *Modern Jewish Ethics: Theory and Practice.* Columbus: Ohio State University Press, 1975.

_____. *The Philosophical Foundations of Jewish Ethics: Some Initial Reflections.* Cincinnati: University of Cincinnati, 1979.

Gordis, Robert. *The Dynamics of Judaism: A Study in Jewish Law.* Bloomington: Indiana University Press, 1990, esp. chs. 3 and 9.

_____. *Judaic Ethics for a Lawless World.* New York: Jewish Theological Seminary of America, 1986.

Green, Ronald. *Religion and Moral Reason: A New Method for Comparative Study.* New York: Oxford University Press, 1988, esp. pp. 3–23.

Greenberg, Simon. *The Ethical in the Jewish and American Heritage.* New York: Jewish Theological Seminary of America, 1977, esp. ch. 1.

Halivni, David Weiss. "Can a Religious Law Be Immoral?" In *Perspectives on Jews and Judaism: Essays in Honor of Wolfe Kelman,* edited by Arthur Chiel. New York: Rabbinical Assembly, 1978, pp. 165–170.

Hartman, David. *A Living Covenant: The Innovative Spirit in Traditional Judaism.* Woodstock, Vt.: Jewish Lights, 1997, esp. ch. 4.

Kellner, Menachem Marc, ed. *Contemporary Jewish Ethics.* New York: Sanhedrin Press, 1978.

Plaskow, Judith. *Standing Again at Sinai: Judaism from a Feminist Perspective.* San Francisco: Harper and Row, 1990, esp. pp. 60–74.

Sidorsky, David. "The Autonomy of Moral Objectivity." In *Modern Jewish Ethics,* edited by Marvin Fox. Columbus: Ohio State University Press, 1975, pp. 153–173.

Spero, Shubert. *Morality, Halakha, and the Jewish Tradition.* New York: Ktav and Yeshiva University Press, 1983, esp. ch. 6.

Chapter 4: Speech

Dorff, Elliot N. *Matters of Life and Death: A Jewish Approach to Modern Medical Ethics.* Philadelphia: Jewish Publication Society, 1998, esp. pp. 255–264.

Grinald, Ze'ev. *Ta'haras Halashon: A Guide to the Laws of Lashon Hara and Rechilus.* New York and Jerusalem: Feldheim, 1994.

Pliskin, Zelig. *Guard Your Tongue: A Practical Guide to the Laws of Loshon Hora Based on Chofetz Chayim.* Brooklyn, N.Y.: Pliskin, 1975.

Potok, Chaim. *Jewish Ethics: The Ethics of Language.* New York: Leaders Training Fellowship of the Jewish Theological Seminary of America, 1964.

Telushkin, Joseph. *Words That Hurt, Words That Heal: How to Choose Words Wisely and Well.* New York: William Morrow and Company, 1996.

Chapter 5: The Poor

Bonner, Michael, ed. *Poverty and Charity in Middle Eastern Contexts.* Albany: State University of New York Press, 2003.

Cottle, Thomas J. *Hidden Survivors: Portraits of Poor Jews in America.* Englewood Cliffs, N.J.: Prentice-Hall, 1980.

Dorff, Elliot N. *To Do the Right and the Good: A Jewish Approach to Modern Social Ethics.* Philadelphia: Jewish Publication Society, 2002, ch. 6 ("Substantive Justice: A Jewish Approach to Poverty").

Gamaron, Hillel, ed. *Jewish Law Association Studies XIV: The Jerusalem 2002 Conference Volume.* Binghamton, N.Y.: Global Academic Publishers, Binghamton University, 2002.

Hirsch, Richard. *There Shall Be No Poor.* New York: Union of American Hebrew Congregations, Commission on Social Action of Reform Judaism, 1965.

Neusner, Jacob. *Tzedakah: Can Jewish Philanthropy Buy Jewish Survival?* Chappaqua, N.Y.: Rossel Books, 1982.

The Poor Among Us: Jewish Tradition and Social Policy. New York: American Jewish Committee, 1986.

Chapter 6: Captives

Bardach, Janusz. *Surviving Freedom: After the Gulag.* Berkeley: University of California Press, 2003.

Ellenson, David. *After Emancipation: Jewish Religious Responses to Modernity.* Cincinnati: Hebrew Union College Press, 2004, pp. 437–449.

Ioanid, Radu. *The Ransom of the Jews: The Story of the Extraordinary Secret Bargain Between Romania and Israel.* Chicago: Ivan R. Dee, 2005.

Lazin, Frederick. *The Struggle for Soviet Jewry in American Politics: Israel versus the American Jewish Establishment.* Lanham, Md.: Lexington Books, 2005.

Tokayer, Marvin. *The Fugu Plan: The Untold Story of the Japanese and the Jews during World War II.* New York: Paddington Press, 1979.

United States Holocaust Memorial Museum. *Flight and Rescue.* Washington, D.C.: United States Memorial Council, 2000.

Chapter 7: The Sick

Cohen, A. *Everyman's Talmud.* New York: E. P. Dutton & Co., 1949, ch. 8 ("The Physical Life").

Dorff, Elliot N. *Matters of Life and Death: A Jewish Approach to Modern Medical Ethics.* Philadelphia: Jewish Publication Society, 1998.

Mackler, Aaron. *Introduction to Jewish and Catholic Bioethics: A Comparative Analysis.* Washington, D.C.: Georgetown University Press, 2003.

_____, ed. *Life and Death Responsibilities in Jewish Biomedical Ethics.* New York: Jewish Theological Seminary of America, 2000.

Steinberg, Avraham. *Encyclopedia of Jewish Medical Ethics.* Translated by Fred Rosner. 3 vols. Jerusalem and New York: Feldheim Publishers, 2003.

Teutsch, David. *Bioethics: Reinvigorating the Practice of Contemporary Jewish Ethics.* Wyncote, Pa.: Reconstructionist Rabbinical College, 2005.

Chapters 8, 9, and 10: Spouses, Children, and Parents

Biale, Rachel. *Women and Jewish Law: An Exploration of Women's Issues in Halakhic Sources.* New York: Schocken, 1984.

Blidstein, Gerald. *Honor Thy Father and Mother: Filial Responsibility in Jewish Law and Ethics.* New York: Ktav, 1975.

Cohen, A. *Everyman's Talmud.* New York: E. P. Dutton & Co., 1949, ch. 5 ("Domestic Life").

Dorff, Elliot N. *Love Your Neighbor and Yourself: A Jewish Approach to Modern Personal Ethics.* Philadelphia: Jewish Publication Society, 2003, esp. chs. 3 ("Sex and the Family"), 4 ("Parents and Children"), and 5 ("Family Violence").

Graetz, Naomi. *Silence Is Deadly: Judaism Confronts Wifebeating.* Northvale, N.J.: Jason Aronson, 1998.

Hauptman, Judith. *Rereading the Rabbis: A Woman's Voice.* Boulder, Colo.: Westview, 1998.

Isaacs, Leora W. *Jewish Family Matters: A Leader's Guide.* New York: United Synagogue of Conservative Judaism, Commission on Jewish Education, 1994.

Isaacs, Ronald H. *Every Person's Guide to Jewish Sexuality.* Northvale, N.J.: Jason Aronson, 2000.

Kraemer, David, ed. *The Jewish Family: Metaphor and Memory.* New York: Oxford University Press, 1989.

Lev, Rachel. *Shine the Light: Sexual Abuse and Healing in the Jewish Community.* Boston: Northeastern University Press, 2003.

Forward: The Ideal Society

Artson, Bradley Shavit. *Love Peace and Pursue Peace: A Jewish Response to War and Nuclear Annihilation.* New York: United Synagogue of America, Commission on Jewish Education, 1988.

Cohen, A. *Everyman's Talmud.* New York: E. P. Dutton & Co., 1949, chs. 7 ("The Moral Life") and 11 ("The Hereafter").

Dorff, Elliot N. *Love Your Neighbor and Yourself: A Jewish Approach to Modern Personal Ethics.* Philadelphia: Jewish Publication Society, 2003, ch. 7 ("Hope and Destiny").

Gillman, Neil. *The Death of Death: Resurrection and Immortality in Jewish Thought.* Woodstock, Vt.: Jewish Lights, 2000.

Siegel, Daniel. *Heroes and Miracle Workers.* Pittsboro, NC: Town House Press, 1998.

Spitz, Elie Kaplan. *Does the Soul Survive? A Jewish Journey to Belief in Afterlife, Past Lives and Living with Purpose.* Woodstock, Vt.: Jewish Lights, 2001.

Index

Enlightenment ideology, 33, 133, 196
Environmental activism, 12–13
Estate planning, 121
Ethical wills, 161
Ethics. *See* Morality
Ethics of the Fathers (Pirkei Avot), 19, 30, 61, 98, 100, 119, 123, 131, 214, 246
Ethnic identity, 38
Euthyphro (Plato), 52
Evil, 10–11, 58, 241–243
Exiles, ingathering of, 233–234
Exodus from Egypt, 55, 227
Ezekiel, Prophet, 133, 231

Family; *See also* Community: duties of spouses, 171–184; duties to children, 201–225; duties to parents, 185–200; God visiting the sins of parents, 35–36
Fear of God, 27–28; *See also* Respect
Fein, Leonard, 1
Fiddler on the Roof, 217, 220, 235–236
Foul language, 71–74
Fraud and deception, 75, 109, 242

Gender: duties toward daughters, 202–207; same-gender marriages, 174–175
Gershom, Rabbenu, 172
God, 1; *See also* Commandments; essence of, 19–20; health of body and, 145–147, 154; honoring parents and, 188; ideal world and, 243–245; insulted by obscenities, 72; in Kabbalah, 10; modeling ourselves after, 45–50, 62–63, 104; the poor and, 111–114; refusal to help others and, 18; sovereignty of, 8, 23–26, 111–113
Golden calf, 28, 47
Goodness, ethics and, 51–53, 61
Gossip, 76–79, 226
Government: aid to poor, 125; Libertarian view, 21–22

Grandparents' duties, 212–213
Gratitude, words of, 100–103
Guilt, helping the poor and, 109

Halakhah, 7
Ha-Nasi, Rabbi Judah, 61
Hanina, Rabbi, 61
Harnick, Sheldon, 235
Hasidic tradition, 31, 60–61, 119
Health, 145–147, 236–238
Hezekiah (biblical king), 94
Holiness, aspirations to, 42–44, 66, 117–118
Holocaust, 58, 138
Honesty: in medical ethics, 97–98; in speech, 76, 84
Honoring parents, 59, 61, 186–200, 227
Hope, speech and, 93–98
Hosea, Prophet, 16–17, 18, 46, 149
Hospice care, 96–98
Huldah, Prophet, 50
Human beings; *See also* Will (human): divine image in, 29–33; environmental activism and, 12–13; ethics and, 54–58; expressing thanks to, 102; partnership with God, 227–228
Humility, 31, 75–76, 102

Illness. *See* Sickness
Individuality: in American system of thought, 33–34; community and, 36
Infertility, 223, 230
Intermarriage, 224
Internet, 221
Isaiah, Prophet, 19–20, 43, 53, 72–74, 94–95, 233–234, 242–245, 247
Islam, 64
Isolation, illness and, 158–159
Israel: covenant with, 62; Land of, 230–233
Isserles, Rabbi Moses, 136, 167, 220

Jakobovits, Rabbi Immanuel, 96–97
Jefferson, Thomas, 196

Shelters for victims of domestic violence, 184
Shema, 63, 211–212
Shetah, Simeon ben, 207
Shevu'ot, 35
Shiva, 163
Shulchan Arukh, 95–96, 134–136, 137–138, 153, 204–205, 220
Sickness, 90, 144–161, 236–238; *See also* Visiting the sick
Siddur, 101
Simchat bat, 167
Sin: atonement of, 18; in parent-child relationships, 35–36, 214–215, 239–240; prophecies and, 241–243; related to speech, 69–91; retribution for, 47–50; sickness and, 89–90, 148–150, 236–237
Sinai, 28, 34, 39, 55, 113, 243
Sipple, Oliver, 80
Slander, 70, 79–85
Slavery, 25–26, 55, 112–113
Slurs, 79–85
Social action, 7–10, 13, 20, 37, 61, 222
Social equality, 1–2
Socialism, 22
Society: ideal, 226–249; parent-child relationships and, 185–186; variety of views toward, 21–22
Socrates, 52
Sodom and Gomorrah, 48, 52
Solomon, King, 80–81
Sovereignty of God, 8, 23–26, 111–113
Speech, 69–106, 226; as mark of divine image, 30; talking about religious observance, 192; visiting the sick, 157–158, 160–161
Stealing, lies and, 75
Stories: in ethical wills, 161; value of, 55–58
Strangers, care for, 42, 241
Study of Torah, 64, 105, 122, 176
Suffering, 49–50; oppressive speech and, 89; for righteousness, 51

Suicide, prohibition against, 145–146
Swimming, duty to teach, 202, 206
Synagogue, 133, 146, 167, 218, 222

Ta'anit, 119
Tact, 92
Talmudic teachings, 7, 14–18; on aiding the poor, 116, 118–121, 126, 128; on aiding the sick, 154–156, 159, 237; on circumcision, 210; on community, 34; on education, 131–132, 203, 212–214, 217; on health and healing, 146–147, 150–152; Land of Israel, 232–233; on Leviticus 19:18, 26–27; love for strangers, 42; on marriage and divorce, 172–173, 189, 219–220; morality of speech, 69–72, 86–87, 89–91, 95, 98, 102–104; on parent-child relationships, 187–188, 190–192, 199, 202–203; on procreation, 189; on ransoming captives, 141–142; responsibility to save one's life, 135; on return of exiles, 234; on saving one's property, 195; on speech, 91–92; story of Abraham and Isaac, 47; thanksgiving in, 101
Teachers and teaching: ransoming, 135–136; of Torah, 202–208, 211–217
Technology, 196, 221
Tefillin, 46
Telushkin, Rabbi Joseph, 79
Ten commandments, 47–48, 189
Teshuvah (return), 66, 87–88
Thanksgiving, 100–103
Therapy, for marital issues, 182–184
Thought, as mark of divine image, 30
Torah and Torah teachings: acts of kindness *(chesed),* 17–20; on aid to the poor, 25–28, 111–112, 128; circumcision in, 209–211; covenant in, 41; on

divine image in human beings, 30, 82–83; duties to daughter, 202–207; on health, 148–149; on honoring parents, 186, 188; in ideal world, 243–244; on justice, 238–239; in Kabbalah, 9–10; Maharal of Prague's view, 10–12; moral requirements in, 53–54, 61, 65; on ownership, 23–26; promise to Abraham, 228–229; on prosperity, 234–235; on responsibility, 34; social equality and, 2; on speaking with others, 70–74, 77, 83, 84–85; study of, 105, 122–123, 176; teaching of, 59, 211–217; words of, 99–100

Printed in the USA
CPSIA information can be obtained
at www.ICGtesting.com
JSHW012021140824
68134JS00033B/2803